HOW WORSHIP BECAME MUSIC

HOW WORSHIP BECAME MUSIC

A Historical Sourcebook

EDITED BY JONATHAN OTTAWAY, ADAM PEREZ,
AND LESTER RUTH

Nashville

HOW WORSHIP BECAME MUSIC:
A HISTORICAL SOURCEBOOK

Copyright © 2026 by Abingdon Press

All rights reserved.

No part of this work may be reproduced or transmitted in any form or by any means, electronic or mechanical, including photocopying and recording, or by any information storage or retrieval system, except as may be expressly permitted by the 1976 Copyright Act, the 1998 Digital Millennium Copyright Act, or in writing from the publisher. Requests for permission should be addressed to Permissions, Abingdon Press, 810 12th Avenue South, Nashville, TN 37203-4704, or emailed to permissions@abingdonpress.com.

Library of Congress Control Number: 2026932788
ISBN: 9781791040758

Scripture quotations unless noted otherwise are from the Common English Bible. Copyright © 2011 by the Common English Bible. All rights reserved. Used by permission. www.CommonEnglishBible.com.

Scripture quotations marked KJV are taken from The Authorized (King James) Version. Rights in the Authorized Version in the United Kingdom are vested in the Crown. Reproduced by permission of the Crown's patentee, Cambridge University Press.

Cover description: The cover features a beige background with the title *How Worship Became Music* in large blue text on the right, and in smaller text the subtitle *A Historical Sourcebook* and the editors' names, Jonathan Ottaway, Adam Perez, and Lester Ruth. On the left, a vertical strip of historical photographs depicts worship scenes across different eras, tinted in yellow, green, red, and blue.

MANUFACTURED IN THE UNITED STATES OF AMERICA

CONTENTS

vii	Acknowledgments
xi	Introduction: When You Say "Worship," Do You Mean "Music"?
1	1. Popular: Using Contemporary Music in Worship; Part 1: From Finney to the First Experiments in Contemporary Worship
31	2. Popular: Using Contemporary Music in Worship; Part 2: The Jesus People and Beyond
63	3. Power: Creating Divine Encounters Through Music
95	4. Flow: Structuring Times of Musical Worship
121	5. Professionals: Musicians as Leaders of Worship
145	6. Excellence: Doing Worship Music Well
175	Conclusion: History as Formation for Worship Renewal
179	Appendix A: Chronological List of Sources

ACKNOWLEDGMENTS

We wish to thank the following people who have supported this project and helped us bring it to fruition.

We are deeply grateful to the Calvin Institute for Christian Worship for their funding of this project and their unwavering support throughout its development. Their willingness to support a wide array of scholarship on Christian worship practices is a gift to the church.

A number of colleagues provided invaluable feedback on early drafts of this material. Jeremy Perigo and Joshua Waggener offered thorough and wise review of the entire manuscript, honing the final work considerably. Participants in the Contemporary Worship Reading Group provided helpful feedback and encouragement on early chapter drafts, while members of the Contemporary and Alternative Worship seminar group of the North American Academy of Liturgy have been important dialogue partners over the years and have encouraged us in this project.

We wish to thank Connie Stella and the team at Abingdon Press for their vision in bringing this project to publication.

Finally, we reserve a special word of gratitude for Elizabeth Chandler at Duke Divinity School, who has been infinitely patient in helping us through the lengthy and complex process of managing this grant and acquiring the many permissions we needed to obtain to make this book a reality.

We gratefully acknowledge the following permissions that have been granted to reproduce the following quotations.

How to Start a New Service by Charles Arn, copyright© 1997. Used by permission of Baker Books, a division of Baker Publishing Group.

The Ministry of Worship and Praise by James Beall, copyright© n.d. Used by permission.

―――― *Acknowledgments* ――――

Song of the Lord by David K. Blomgren, copyright© 1978. Used by permission.

Let Us Praise by Judson Cornwall, copyright© 1973. Used by permission.

Let Us Worship by Judson Cornwall, copyright© 1983. Used by permission.

Worship: The Pattern of Things in Heaven by Joseph L. Garlington, copyright© 1997. Used by permission of Nori Media Group.

Hot Tips for Worship Leaders by Brent Helming, copyright© 2000. Used by permission of Vineyard USA.

Music Ministry by Mike and Vivien Hibbert, copyright© 1982. Used by permission of author.

The Worship Pastor: A Call to Ministry for Worship Leaders and Teams by Zac Hicks, copyright© 2016. Used by permission of HarperCollins Christian Publishing. www.harpercollinschristian.com

Jubilate II by Donald P. Hustad, copyright© 1993 and trans. © 2018. Used by permission of Hope Publishing Company. www.hopepublishing.com

Learning to Worship as a Way of Life by Graham Kendrick, copyright© 1984. Used by permission of Make Way Music. www.grahamkendrick.co.uk

Unto Perfection: The Truth about the Present Restoration Revival by Reg Layzell, copyright© 1979. Used by permission.

The Purpose and Power of Praise & Worship by Myles Munroe, copyright© 2000. Used by permission of Nori Media Group.

How to Lead Worship Without Being a Rock Star: An 8 Week Study by Dan Wilt, copyright© 2013. Used by permission of author.

Rick Warren, "New Churches For a New Generation: Church Planting to Reach Baby Boomers: A Case Study: The Saddleback Valley Community Church" (D.Min. thesis, Fuller Theological Seminary, 1993). Used by permission of author.

Richard K. Avery, "The Church Is Alive and Singing," *Presbyterian Life* (October 15, 1971): 9–10. Used by permission of the Presbyterian Historical Society.

Paul Baloche, "Revealing the Divine," *Worship Leader* 18, no. 1 (January/February 2009), 10. Used by permission of *Worship Leader Magazine*.

Tom Brooks, "Spontaneity in Worship," *Worship Times* (Summer 1986), 4. Used by permission of *Worship Leader Magazine*.

Donald C. Cicchetti, "Is It Time for a Media Pastor: Combining Technology and Ministry," *Worship Leader* (Summer 2000), 20–21. Used by permission of *Worship Leader Magazine*.

John Gillies, "What's So Sacred About Music," *The Church Musician* (May 1974), 50–51. Used by permission of the Southern Baptist Historical Library and Archives, Nashville, Tennessee.

Joannah Glaeser, "The Use of Chord Progressions in Spontaneous Worship," *Symposium* 85: 8th Annual International Symposium (August 1985). Used by permission.

Wayne Graham, "Production Values for Staging Church Dramas," *Worship Leader* (Summer 2000), 8. Used by permission of *Worship Leader Magazine*.

[Barry Griffing], "Catechism Corner," *Music Notes* 2, no. 4 (1980), 4. Used by permission.

J. Harker, "Music of the Message: Music In Present-Day Evangelism," *The Ministry* 12, no. 9 (September 1939), 13. Used by permission of *Ministry Magazine*.

Mack Moore, "Current Trends in Youth Musicals," *The Church Musician* (July 1974), 54. Used by permission of the Southern Baptist Historical Library and Archives, Nashville, Tennessee.

"The Pastor Wears Tennis Shoes," *Circuit Rider* 18, 10 (December 1994/January 1995): 14. Used by permission of United Methodist Publishing House.

Charles E. Pierson, "Right and Wrong Ways of Introducing Contemporary Music," *The Church Musician* (September 1973), 19-22. Used by permission of the Southern Baptist Historical Library and Archives, Nashville, Tennessee.

"The Praise Band," *Worship Times*, July/August 1989, 2. Used by permission of *Worship Leader Magazine*.

Robb Redman, "Expanding Your Worship Worldview: Education and Training for Worship Leaders," *Worship Leader* (May/June 2000), 19. Used by permission of *Worship Leader Magazine*.

1982 Christian Life Magazine. Article entitled "Zip to 3,000 in 5 Years." Written by John Wimber. All rights reserved. Used by permission.

John Wimber, "Worship: Intimacy With God," Worship Conference (1989). Used by permission of Vineyard USA.

Paige Blair, "What Is a U2 Eucharist (or U2charist)?" Used by permission of author.

Mike Herron, "The Song of the Lord" Teaching Notes. Used by permission of author.

INTRODUCTION
WHEN YOU SAY "WORSHIP," DO YOU MEAN "MUSIC"?

What picture comes to mind when you hear the word "worship"? For many, it is an image of people with their hands raised in front of a platform of musicians leading pop- and rock-styled songs to God. Depending on the when and where of your viewpoint, you might call this "Praise & Worship," "Contemporary Worship," or just plain, old "worship."

While Contemporary Praise & Worship[1] happens in different contexts and church traditions, there is a family resemblance to this music-making that makes the phenomenon uniquely identifiable.[2] It often has a shared repertoire of songs, with a loose set of recognizable musical traits. These specific musical practices also contribute toward and take place within a wider worship service that enacts a specific understanding about how Christian worship should be practiced and what that worship means.

To understand this family resemblance, consider the most prominent images of Contemporary Praise & Worship that you might find on a simple Google search.[3] Musicians are front and center. Often there is a row of singers holding microphones in one hand while their other hand is raised

---

1. For the purposes of this book, we will use a fusion of the two most-used terms, "Contemporary" and "Praise & Worship," following Lester Ruth and Lim Swee Hong's *A History of Contemporary Praise & Worship: Understanding the Ideas that Reshaped the Protestant Church* (Grand Rapids: Baker Academic, 2021).

2. Sarah Kathleen Johnson and Anneli Loepp Thiessen, "Contemporary Worship Music as an Ecumenical Liturgical Movement," *Worship* 97 (2023): 205–6.

3. We are indebted to Monique Ingalls for her observation about the popular imagistic understanding of Contemporary Praise & Worship: Monique Ingalls, *Singing the Congregation: How Contemporary Worship Music Forms Evangelical Community* (New York: Oxford University Press, 2018), 17–18.

in a gesture of abandonment or wholehearted commitment. Alongside the singers, guitars are the most visible instrument. The acoustic guitar tends to imply a role of leadership within the worship team. It provides the musical foundation around which other musicians are oriented. These other instrumentalists—keyboard players, electric guitarists, drummers, bass guitarists—are situated further back, demonstrating their supporting role.

This snapshot of the platform, however, doesn't exhaust the musical dimensions of the "family resemblance" for the churches practicing Contemporary Praise & Worship. For example, the musicians are leading a worship set: an extended time of singing where songs tend to progress in a recognizable—sometimes predictable—order. The set often begins with faster and louder songs of praise and thanksgiving that gives way to slower songs to express a more emotionally intimate connection to their Savior. Different churches and networks often have their own take on how to best implement that progression of songs.

It has become increasingly common for worship leaders to follow the structure, instrumentation, and inflection of a popular recording of that song. Many worship leaders also aspire to emulate the production quality of those recordings and the churches and artists that create them. Accordingly, practitioners of Contemporary Praise & Worship often use (or aspire to use) state-of-the-art audio and video technology.

Another critical component of the image of Contemporary Praise & Worship is the inclusion of worshipers in the congregation with their hands upraised and their eyes closed. Both leaders and congregants alike are engaged in the worship of God through the act of singing. The expectation is for all worshipers to participate in singing with all their mind, soul, body, and strength. As worshipers abandon themselves to singing the praise of God, they expect to encounter the imminent presence of God.

If we expand our view globally, we might find some variation in this composite image of Contemporary Praise & Worship since some of the aesthetic values expressed in North America will not be universal. For instance, the predisposition towards leading worship in heavily darkened rooms (like a movie theater) is not universal. However, much of what we have described remains true in contexts across the globe: western instruments, the centrality of musical worship leaders, embodied participation, experiential encounter, and the expectation of an extended time of congregational singing. Say the word "worship" and, for countless numbers of Christians around the world, this is the picture of music that comes to mind.

But how did this come to be? How did "worship" become synonymous with "music"? This development—a much more recent phenomenon than many worship leaders might guess—is the story that this book narrates.

A Historical Snapshot of Music in Worship from the Nineteenth Century

If we look at a snapshot of a typical worship service in America, say, two hundred years ago, the connection between worship and music looks surprisingly different. The practices of congregational music-making that seem normal today would have seemed decidedly strange to Christians at the start of the 1800s. To understand how much has taken place in the last two hundred years, it will be helpful to provide a sketch of musical worship in that period.

Many, if not all, churches at the time had a set structure for their worship (even if loosely adhered to). Congregational song did not receive its own separate block of time. These Christians had no concept of a "worship set" as we now know it.[4] Instead, spoken elements of the service (especially prayers) were the main building blocks of the service. Songs were interspersed between these spoken elements, functioning like the connective sinews for the worship service.

The amount of singing in worship could be surprisingly sparse—perhaps one song at the beginning and one song at the end of the service. Indeed, some Christians at the time were worried that too much singing could make the service overly formal, detracting from the practice of true religion! As one example of this, the 1784 *Methodist Book of Discipline* advised that their churches should sing no more than five or six verses of

---

4. The "song service" in some Black and African American church traditions does date back to at least this time and could include multiple songs sung in sequence along with an interspersed prayer or Scripture reading.

song at a time out of this concern with formality. Moreover, the *Discipline* also encouraged the minister to routinely interrupt the singing to check that the congregation understood and believed the content of the words.

However, sparsity of congregational song did not mean that it was not highly valued. While there would not be much singing, it remained a non-negotiable element of all types of worship services, whether private, family, or public worship. Christian worship needed song.[5] This was not, as if often the case in today's worship, because singing is viewed as a time of encounter with God. Rather, church leaders understood singing as a Christian duty. In the same way that being baptized or receiving the Lord's Supper was an institution and practice that was required of the church, congregational song was also routinely viewed as a "holy ordinance of Christ" such that Christians are obligated to sing in all worship services.[6]

We can see the importance of singing to early American worship by the growing popularity of hymnals at the dawn of the 1800s. Often these hymnals were pocket-sized (especially so with text-only hymnals that omitted music[7]) with the expectation that faithful Christians would carry them around for private worship and bring them out at larger gatherings. Throughout the eighteenth century, many new collections of hymns had been produced by now-famous hymn-writers like Charles Wesley and Isaac Watts. The general enthusiasm for hymnals continued unabated into the nineteenth century. Indeed, with the widespread availability of new hymnals, and the development of new forms of devotional song such as the "spiritual song" (that became popular in the Great Awakening), church leaders did not have to encourage their members to buy hymnals,

---

5. Karen Westerfield Tucker, *American Methodist Worship* (New York: Oxford University Press, 2001), 156.

6. See, for example, Philadelphia Baptist Association, *A Confession of Faith: Adopted by the Elders and Messengers of the Baptist Churches in Pennsylvania, New Jersey, and the Adjacent States, Met in Philadelphia, October 12, 1742; with Two Additional Articles, and the Baptist Catechism* (Philadelphia: Anderson & Meehan, 1818), 57.

7. Collections of hymn tunes were often published in their own stand-alone volume. Hymn texts did not typically have a dedicated hymn tune and might routinely be sung with a wide number of tunes that matched the same meter.

but rather felt that they had to discourage them from buying hymnals that they had not endorsed.[8]

A further indication of the importance of Christian song in this period is seen in the great effort that many churches were making to raise the standard of singing and musicality among their members. In the second half of the 1700s, singing schools had become a popular institution in many regions, especially New England. They were popular not only because people enjoyed learning how to sing better, but the schools served an important cultural and social role as a place where young people could meet and interact in a controlled setting.[9]

Despite the importance of congregational singing, perhaps the key difference was (as has already been mentioned) that Christians did not, as a rule, expect to experience the presence of God in their singing. Even among the early "shouting Methodists" (as they were often called) who especially prized vigorous congregational singing, worshipers did not expect to encounter God during times of singing. Read the accounts of Methodists in 1800 and you will see that while worshipers appreciated the singing, they usually met God in the preaching of the Bible, the testimonies of Christian experience, the intense praying, the administration of the Lord's Supper, or the depth of love they experienced through their fellowship.[10]

What were congregational songs in this period like though? In terms of the words and content of their songs, many American congregations sang lyrics using a type of poetry that followed set meters and rhyme schemes. (Meter refers to the number of syllables per line of poetry and the pattern of emphasis and de-emphasis in those syllables. Several lines would be organized into a stanza, sometimes called a "verse.") While worshipers today can often distinguish between "contemporary" songs and "traditional" hymns

---

8. For instance, the Methodist Episcopal hymnal of 1821 "earnestly" urged members that "if you have any respect for the authority of the Conference, or of us, or any regard for the prosperity of the Church of which you are members and friends . . . purchase no Hymn-Books but what are signed with the names of your bishops." *A Collection of Hymns for the Use of the Methodist Episcopal Church* (New York: N. Bangs and T. Mason, 1821), v.

9. For more on singing schools, see David W. Music, "The Singing School, The Oxford Movement, and The Church Choir in America," *The Choral Journal* 48, no. 12 (2008): 32–39.

10. See Lester Ruth, *A Little Heaven Below: Worship at Early Methodist Quarterly Meetings* (Nashville: Abingdon Press, 2000).

by the style of the lyrics, new songs of the 1800s could not have been distinguished simply by their lyric meter and rhyming patterns.

In fact, whether a song or hymn was thought of as "contemporary" or "traditional" was unconnected to the style of the words. The difference came down to its lyrical content—whether it was a metrical setting of the Psalms in a Psalter (this had been the "traditional" fare for congregational singing in Reformed and Anglican settings since the Protestant Reformation), later Psalm paraphrases by authors like Isaac Watts, or a newly composed (i.e., contemporary) text that could have either a lot or a little connection to a specific Scripture passage (think Charles Wesley's hymn, "Christ the Lord Is Risen Today"). This latter form of hymn had only begun to be sung among English-speaking Protestants in the early 1700s and only really caught on later in the century, especially in some upstart groups like Methodists and Baptists.

In a similar fashion, because songs followed the conventional poetic patterns of the day, the songs of this period would have been sung straight through with no repetition or cycling back. Indeed, at least with newer hymns, the last stanza served as a kind of climax to the narrative trajectory within the song. This is because many of the new hymns described the evangelical salvation experience in narrative form, reaching a clear climactic point at the end of the hymn (when the subject experienced assurance of their forgiveness). It would have seemed strange to then return and re-sing an earlier part! (It would be like returning to the middle chapter of a story after reaching its satisfying conclusion.)

At the time, a new and novel practice of adding a refrain (chorus) onto a hymn was just starting to emerge in churches under the leadership of Richard Allen, the founder of the African Methodist Episcopal (AME) Church. Unlike modern choruses through which serve as the repeated and focal unifying point of a song, in this early stage of innovation, Allen's practice was to add a "wandering chorus" onto the end of the hymn.[11] Called "wandering choruses," because the choruses would "wander" from one hymn to another (i.e., one chorus could be appended onto numerous

---

11. Melva Wilson Costen, *In Spirit and in Truth: The Music of African American Worship* (Louisville: Westminster John Knox Press, 2004), 54.

hymns at the discernment of the song leader), this new practice only further solidified the narrative structure of the strophic hymn. The narrative of salvation was appended by a final acclamation of praise!

What of the actual music though? At the turn of the nineteenth century, denominations were locked in ongoing debates about what kind of music was truly appropriate for Christian worship.

The rise of musical skill through the singing schools in the early eighteenth century led to the eventual establishment of choirs, especially in larger churches. The initial impulse for many of these choirs was to bolster congregational singing by gathering the most skilled musicians in one part of the church. In some cases, choirs were brought together to better lead the practice of "lining out" a hymn.[12] (In the practice of lining out, the song leader would sing out one line of the song at a time, which the congregation would then repeat together. This was a particularly helpful practice in churches where Christians either did not have hymnals or could not read them.)

However, by the turn of the nineteenth century, some denominations were recognizing that the development of choirs who could read music, sing in parts, and handle more complicated arrangements was detracting from the congregation's participation. Some denominations who were worried about this trend officially discouraged their churches from developing choirs or installing organs. Of course, for upstart churches that lacked permanent buildings, this was no great sacrifice. Yet, in New England's Congregationalist, Baptist, Presbyterian, and Episcopal contexts, the choral programs continued to develop beyond the aid of congregational singing and into anthems and service music.

At the same time, the rise of new musical styles such as the use of "fugue tunes" was starting to become an issue in Christian worship. Even though these fugue tunes were not deemed inherently inappropriate, the concern was that new form of music was popular with the youth but hindered the participation of older congregants who struggled to follow

---

12. Arthur B. Ellis, *History of the First Church in Boston, 1630–1880* (Boston: Hall and Whiting, 1881), 204–5.

the new music.[13] This concern mirrors many expressed in each generation, especially those in the 1990s and beyond with the adoption of Contemporary Praise & Worship music into the church's worship today.[14]

One final point of contrast will help us understand the great transformation that has taken place over the last two hundred years. The place and role of music in congregational worship at the turn of 1800 was often reflected in the architecture of worship spaces. Whereas many churches today assume that there will be an elevated platform where vocalists and instrumentalists will be prominently situated, in 1800 this was not the case. The focal point of the building tended to be the pulpit, reflecting the importance of the preached word. The center would have been occupied by a communion table. The importance of these pieces of furniture reflected what the central activities of Christian worship at the time were.

Our Approach

The purpose of this book is to help worship leaders make sense of how today's musical worship seems so different from two hundred years ago. In this book, we chronicle the numerous developments, both subtle and drastic, that have overhauled how many Christians understand the purpose, meaning, and function of musical worship.

This book is a historical sourcebook—a collection of quotes and materials gathered from the people and publications that shaped Contemporary Praise & Worship. In this book, you will encounter the writings and teachings of individual leaders as they explain, argue for, justify, and encourage others to change the church's music practices. Our objective is to immerse you in the story as it happened. You will read important thinkers, pastors, and musicians express their own convictions for themselves. Some of the cast of characters from whom we have excerpted quotes may be familiar to you. Others will be totally new. This does not mean that their significance is less. In our experience, sometimes the most influential

---

13. Westerfield Tucker, *American Methodist Worship*, 160–61.

14. See for instance, Melanie Ross, *Evangelical Worship: An American Mosaic* (Oxford University Press, 2021), 11–38.

Introduction

voices in the development of Contemporary Praise & Worship are not the most well-known. The most familiar voices have sometimes simply popularized ideas that they received from background figures, now forgotten.

Hearing these voices will help you see that the musical practices of Contemporary Praise & Worship—and the ideas that underpin those practices—did not emerge out of nowhere. Much of the groundwork was laid over a long period of time and across multiple, diverse contexts. This book narrates both the roots and the recent developments, highlighting both the musical changes and the ideas that motivated these changes.

Why a Sourcebook?

Many of the key theological developments of church history are often articulated in key texts that have been well-preserved, indexed, and made accessible for scholars today. Not so for Contemporary Praise & Worship. Many of the most important ideas that have shaped Contemporary Praise & Worship were circulated in more transient forms such as sermons, pamphlets, magazine articles, conferences, or books published by now-defunct presses. In short, many of the documents relevant to this history are hard to access. There were no great treatises on Contemporary Praise & Worship carried out by the theological giants of the twentieth century and debated in the major theological schools of the era. Instead, this history took place in the pews and on the stages of many unremarkable, everyday churches. And yet, this history is just as—if not more—significant for the shape of the Christian faith and practice today than many of the theological debates that occupy weightier books. Our aim in this sourcebook is to make these hard-to-access resources available to the reader and student of worship and point you to the sources by which you might further your study.

A sourcebook offers us the chance to immerse the reader in a historical narrative that gives color and texture to the different conversations that took place. Upon a close reading, these sources provide a description of worship that says much more than our summaries of them ever could. For example, it is one thing to hear that Mainline Protestants were concerned over whether their worship was connecting with their congregation while

Pentecostals remained hesitant about new music (see chapters 1 and 2). It is another to read the words of a respected Methodist professor call Sunday worship the dullest hour of the week while a Pentecostal preacher wonders whether the use of "satanic rock music" in worship grieves the hearts of the four-and-twenty elders around God's heavenly throne! We hope that engaging these disparate sources on their own terms makes the history more interesting to read.

Additionally, we believe that engaging with the sources themselves offers an additional outcome: it helps to remind us that the family of traits that comprises the Contemporary Praise & Worship we know today was not inevitable. It can be tempting to look back at history from our vantage point and see a straight line leading directly to the present. The sources in this book will expose you to the wide variety of conversations present across the church.

Because the range of sources that you will hear from in this book is broad and diverse (intentionally so!), not all of the voices you will hear agree with one another. Indeed, many of the voices you will hear will occasionally make mutually opposing claims about the proper worship of the church. Your aim as a reader should not be to try and harmonize this collection of discordant opinions and teachings. Neither should your aim be to adjudicate who is right and who is wrong. For ourselves as editors, we do not present these voices because we endorse or reject these teachings. Instead, we believe that hearing these historical voices should help us to understand the events and ideas that have led to the present practice of worship. These voices are part of swirling currents and cross-currents of theology and practice that have influenced what we do today.

Understanding the Range of Our Sources in This Book

In preparing you to engage the historical narrative that you will encounter in this book and the broad range of voices you will hear from, it will be helpful to imagine Contemporary Praise & Worship as a river—specifically, the Mississippi River as it flows past New Orleans. At this point in its development, the Mississippi is about half a mile wide—a massive and impressive thing! How did the Mississippi get to be so big? It is the effect of multiple tributary rivers that have fed into it throughout its long journey, swelling its volume to gargantuan proportions. And so it is with Contemporary Praise & Worship. It has become a dominant form of worship for the world's evangelicals, Pentecostals, and charismatics. By some estimates, practitioners number nearly half a billion Christians around the world or more. The broad reach and size of this worship tradition, like our river metaphor, is dependent upon many contributing sources. Multiple traditions, theologies, people, places, and practices have all acted as tributaries that have fed the massive phenomenon we now know (although some tributaries make a more noticeable contribution than others.)

What voices should you expect to encounter in this book and what did they contribute?

Already by the early 1800s, numerous streams were beginning to flow that would eventually gush into Contemporary Praise & Worship. A wide variety of evangelical traditions (think of folks like the Baptists) and Mainline Christians who had an evangelical piety (e.g., early Methodists or the nineteenth-century Presbyterian evangelist Charles Finney) were early tributaries to Contemporary Praise & Worship. Indeed, some of these sources are the oldest in this book. These Christians contributed a pragmatic mentality, an emotional piety that stressed the importance of a direct spiritual experience of God's presence, and a strong orientation towards evangelism. These would become bedrock assumptions in American Christianity that would support the river's flow. Black and African American churches in the nineteenth century also nurtured the spiritual fervor and the holistic, embodied worship that would spill into early Pentecostalism. They also contributed to the formation of new song forms that became early forerunners of Contemporary Praise & Worship songs.

These evangelical tributaries continued to develop and grow into the twentieth century. In this book, you will hear their voices—especially since the 1960s when the phrase "Contemporary Worship" was first surging. In this book, you will see that, by-and-large, these evangelicals became some of the most important proponents of a pragmatic approach to worship that sought to make the church attractive (especially to young people). Making worship services hospitable and accessible to newcomers (especially by incorporating popular music) was a significant commitment of these pragmatists, albeit not the only one.

Another critical tributary to Contemporary Praise & Worship comes from the Latter Rain movement. This movement started as a Pentecostal revival in Canada in the late 1940s, but its influence gradually filtered out through a variety of churches, schools, conferences, magazines, and books. These folks will contribute many important developments, including the now all-pervasive emphasis connecting praising God with experiencing God's presence.

However, there are also many Pentecostal voices beyond the Latter Rain who contributed to the development of music in Contemporary Praise & Worship. Their impact became noticeable in the 1960s, steadily increased through the 1970s and 1980s, and became the dominant source of influence from the 1990s forward. The contributors include many of the names and faces we now readily associate with this way of worship. An outlier among these other Pentecostals would be the folks involved in the Jesus People movement of the 1960s and 1970s, particularly as they were involved in the churches known as Calvary Chapel or Vineyard Fellowship. As direct contributors to the shaping of music in Contemporary Praise & Worship—especially in their use of rock- and pop-based forms of music-making—their influence on music was most direct in the 1970s through the 1990s. (These church networks continue to operate into the present day.)

In the last forty years, other tributaries have fed into the system, swelling the river to its current size. The Church Growth movement that first took shape in the 1970s is one of these. In the late 1980s–early 1990s, it began to seriously consider the church's Sunday worship service as one of the chief sites for evangelism and outreach. Closely connected but still distinct are the megachurches (both charismatic and non-charismatic) that rose to prominence in the early 1990s. These churches often presented themselves as models for successful church ministry to whom many other church leaders turned to for guidance and inspiration.

The sources in this book represent a variety of people scattered across many times and places. Hopefully, this brief overview of the major contributors to the river of Contemporary Praise & Worship will help you identify some of the discrete traditions and networks that are important to this story. Each of those has its own context and history that is worth exploring on its own (and only a small fraction of it has been explored in the current secondary literature). Admittedly, there are many more figures and churches of local or regional importance that we have not been able to include. We hope these sources can direct you on your path of additional study.

The Organization of the Book

This book addresses five topics that are fundamental to the ethos of Contemporary Praise & Worship as it is practiced in diverse (but recognizable) contexts today. Chapters 1 and 2 address how the styles of popular music became the predominant tool for Contemporary Praise & Worship. (This is such a large and important topic that we have divided it into two parts.) Chapter 3 explores the expectation that worshipers will experience the presence of God through the time of musical worship. Chapter 4 traces the rationale for, and approaches to, creating a structured block of songs that begins a service—the worship "set." Chapter 5 considers the leadership of worship: Why have musicians come to take such a prominent role in worship as priestly figures who lead the congregation into the presence of God? In the final chapter, we look at the value placed on excellence in the performance of Contemporary Praise & Worship, especially in the way it looks and sounds.

In each chapter, we tell the story of how each aspect of Contemporary Praise & Worship has developed in a generally chronological frame. Because there is a great diversity of voices in the story, we have grouped sources from like-minded church networks or streams, resulting in some back and forth across time and space. We also provide an overview of how these sources fit into the larger historical development of Contemporary Praise & Worship. At the end of the chapters, we have provided discussion questions meant to provoke your own reflection on how this history intersects with your own experience of and leadership in worship.

By organizing the book around these individual topics, we hope to show that the practice of Contemporary Praise & Worship as we know it today is not one, single development. Instead, it is a collection or mosaic of features that have fused together in recent years. For instance, it was not inevitable that Contemporary Praise & Worship should both feature popular musical styles and be led by musicians called "worship leaders." Those are two distinctive elements with their own historical trajectories and theological foundations. While many today accept both elements as a package, they have not always been so.

The structure of the book also reveals not only the diversity of the underlying motivations that have led to the adoption of Contemporary Praise & Worship, but also the diversity of its implementation in different traditions. Accordingly, while two churches may both sing the same songs in the same style, they may do so for different reasons and to different ends. Additionally, some churches have adopted some or most of the features we describe here but not all of them. For instance, some Mainline Protestants have incorporated popular music and worship sets into their services but would be hesitant to emphasize music's capacity to facilitate an experience of God's presence. For these churches, the sacraments of Baptism and the Eucharist alone retain that function. Addressing these topics separately shows how churches may have incorporated certain features of this worship tradition but not others.

Yet some of these features are difficult to uncouple from others because they share overlapping concerns and rationales or arose in tandem with them. For instance, many evangelicals used popular music in worship for the same reason that they believe worship should be done excellently: because of the importance of music to the church's evangelism. In the minds of many evangelical leaders, neither *poorly performed popular music nor excellently performed hymnody* would help them to effectively proclaim the message of the gospel. Yet the larger point remains: Contemporary Praise & Worship was founded by the coming together of diverse historical and theological strands.

One last thing to note: by surveying the significant changes in the church's relationship with music over the last two hundred years, we are not assuming that these developments are all right or all wrong. As worship scholars and practitioners whose spiritual journeys have been shaped by Contemporary Praise & Worship, our predisposition is to present the sources in both a sympathetic *and* analytic way. Our goal is to describe but not judge the history that has shaped today's worship.

At the same time, just because we endeavor to tell this history in a balanced way, it does not mean that we believe that Contemporary Praise & Worship is not in need of renewal. Instead, we believe that understanding its history and development is a prerequisite for evaluating its worship practices. Unfortunately, much of this history has not yet been made available to those who have been some of its most vocal critics. It is from history that we learn the key values and beliefs that have shaped our worship today. The vantage point that history offers is a better position from which to discuss the future of worship.

We hope—and trust—this sourcebook will be a helpful tool in seeking guidance for that future.

CHAPTER 1

POPULAR: USING CONTEMPORARY MUSIC IN WORSHIP

Part 1: From Finney to the First Experiments in Contemporary Worship

Throughout the history of the church, Christians have wrestled with the question of what music is appropriate for Christian worship. From as early as the time of Augustine, theologians and pastors have pondered whether music is something that can enhance Christian worship or whether it is safer to leave it out because of its potential emotional power. Even where church traditions have embraced the role of music in worship, there has often been a wide stylistic gulf between the music used in worship (for instance, Gregorian chant) and the music that was commonly heard and sung outside the church. This is true even among the great Protestant heroes like Martin Luther and Charles Wesley who are often credited with restoring congregational singing to the church. (Note that the widely held belief that Luther [or Wesley] used music that he had heard in a tavern for his hymns is not historically supported.[1])

For the first time in Christian history, there is a widespread, ecumenical consensus that popular music is not only allowed in the church's worship but should be the primary—in many cases, the only—musical expression! What changed and how did we get here? In the first part of this

---

1. Paul S. Jones, *Singing and Making Music: Issues in Church Music Today* (Phillipsburg, NJ: P & R Publishing, 2006) 171–78.

two-part chapter, you will see numerous historical strands developing out of which Contemporary Praise & Worship would evolve.

From the early nineteenth century, American evangelicals increasingly accepted an argument that they needed to pursue the church's vocation of evangelism by embracing the most effective means possible. The Presbyterian evangelist Charles Finney was not the first spokesperson of this view but he became its most recognizable advocate. He encouraged churches to embrace whatever means (or, in his words, "measures") necessary to gain the audience's attention. Churches needed to be pragmatic, creative, and evangelistically oriented. Throughout the nineteenth and into the twentieth century, doing the things that "work" has remained a deeply influential mindset.

From the turn of the twentieth century on, many of these pragmatically oriented evangelicals became concerned about a new target whom they desperately wanted to reach: the youth. New organizations like Young Life and Youth for Christ were founded to reach this critical new social demographic. It is in this context that the legacy of Finney's "new measures" mentality started to include a more systematic reflection on the church's music. Churches began to adopt popular music—music that would speak the language of young people—to communicate the Christian gospel in ways that young people would find meaningful and attractive.

In the 1960s, Mainline and Catholic churches were also starting to experiment with what they called "Contemporary Worship" aimed at making the church's worship meaningful and accessible to a new generation. Incorporating popular music was an important component that comprised a much wider experiment with new forms of music and technology to counter the challenge of the new television age.

While pragmatism was the dominant reason why many churches began to experiment with popular music, a significant minority report existed in the worship of African American and Pentecostal churches. These traditions were, by and large, less motivated by the pragmatism that had energized so many others, especially white, euro-American contexts. Many were also highly skeptical of the idea that musical styles deemed worldly could be appropriate for Christian worship. Yet, their worship emphasized worship as a whole-body response to God. Such a response called for music you could dance to. As we will see in part 2, these traditions remained concerned about the use of popular music late into the twentieth century. They eventually adopted the use of the guitar but did so in tandem with other orchestral instruments, organs, and choral anthems.

New Measures: The Foundations of a Pragmatic Approach to the Church's Worship

In the young American republic, a new mindset began to shape how Christian leaders thought about the church and worship. It focused on numerical growth as an important indicator of church health. This had a spill-over effect on the worship of the church as ministers increasingly evaluated how well worship "worked" to produce new converts or attract people to church services.[2] This was a key foundation for the adoption of popular music in Contemporary Praise & Worship as well as many of its other facets; especially, why music is emphasized as powerful or why excellence of musical worship is deemed so important.

In his lectures on revival, Finney communicated a fundamental concern to use whatever measures that they might to get people into churches to hear the gospel. The church's message was urgent, he felt, but many people were not necessarily interested or concerned unless ministers could grab their attention. Although Finney was not necessarily talking about music here, his lectures established the logic of constantly seeking out new measures to gain an audience for the Christian gospel.

---

2. For a broad historical overview of this pragmatic stream of worship, see James F. White, *Protestant Worship: Traditions in Transition* (Louisville: John Knox Press, 1989), 171–91. White's framing of American revivalist or evangelical worship as a "Frontier Tradition" has been the site of ongoing historical debate. Figures like Melanie Ross have contested this label as a framework through which to see this history. See Melanie C. Ross, "New Frontiers in American Evangelical Worship," *Studia Liturgica* 51, no. 2 (2021): 159–72, https://doi.org/10.1177/00393207211028728; Melanie C. Ross, *Evangelical versus Liturgical?: Defying a Dichotomy* (Grand Rapids: William B. Eerdmans, 2014), 10–31.

Source: Charles G. Finney, *Lectures on Revivals of Religion* (New York: Leavitt, Lord & Co., 1835), 167–68.

Ministers ought to know what measures are best calculated to aid in accomplishing the great end of their office, the salvation of souls. Some measures are plainly necessary. By measures I mean what things should be done to get the attention of the people, and bring them to listen to the truth. Building houses for worship, and visiting from house to house, are all "measures," the object of which is to get the attention of people to the gospel. Much wisdom is requisite to devise and carry forward all the various measures that are adapted to favor the success of the gospel. . . .

Now what shall be done? What measures shall we take? Says one, "Be sure and have nothing that is new." Strange! The object of our measures is to gain attention, and you must have something new. As sure as the effect of a measure becomes stereotyped, it ceases to gain attention, and then you must try something new. You need not make innovations in everything. But whenever the state of things is such that anything more is needed, it must be something new, otherwise it will fail. A minister should never introduce innovations that are not called for. If he does, they will embarrass him. He cannot alter the gospel; that remains the same. But new measures are necessary from time to time, to awaken attention, and bring the gospel to bear upon the public mind.

Catherine Booth was one of the most significant disciples of Finney's pragmatism in the latter nineteenth century. Commonly called "the Mother of the Salvation Army," Booth was at the forefront of that highly significant evangelistic ministry. Her teaching re-emphasized many of the same hallmarks as Finney's earlier lectures, especially the unchangeableness of the Christian gospel but the criticality of changing its presentation. In this quotation, Booth references 1 Corinthians 9:22b—"I am made all things to all men, that I might by all means save some" (KJV)—a critically important biblical text among later evangelistic pragmatists.

Source: Catherine Mumford Booth, *Papers on Practical Religion* (London: Partridge, 1879), 140–41.

Let us keep the message [of the gospel] itself unadulterated and the order of it undisturbed; but in our modes of bringing it to bear on men, we are left free as the air and sunlight.

Adaptation, expediency, is our only law. I may convey it in any kind of language so that it carries the true meaning to the mind of the hearer—words are nothing, only as they convey ideas.... [We must] adapt ourselves and our measures to the social and spiritual condition of those whom we seek to benefit. It is here, I conceive, that our churches have fallen into such grievous mistakes with reference to the propagation of the Gospel in our own times. We have stood to our stereotyped forms, refusing to come down from the routine of our forefathers, although this routine has ceased to be attractive to the people, nay, in many instances, the very thing that drives them away.

The most thoughtful writers on education tell us that the first essential in a teacher of youth is to be able to interest his pupils. True. This is equally true of the people—if you would benefit and bless them, you must interest them. You must clothe the truth in such garb and convey it by such mediums as will arouse their attention and interest their minds. In short, we must come down to them. Whatever has caused it, it is a fact, that the masses of the people have come to associate ideas of stiffness, formality, and uninteresting routine with our church and chapel worship, and if we are to be co-workers with God for them, we must move out of our jog-trot places and become all things to them in order to win them.

At the beginning of the twentieth century, Finney's and Booth's advocacy of new measures was still wildly influential. Churches were continuing to reflect (in many diverse ways) on what new ways they could find to gain an audience for the gospel. This source offers one example of this. Among other attempts to encourage people to worship (such as the inauguration of an annual "Go To Church" Sunday), this source makes an impassioned argument for the use of a new technology—mass publicity. For this author, advertisements not only were consistent with the ministry of Christ but also reflected the heritage of the great Protestant leaders of the past.

Source: Christian Fichthorne Reisner, *Church Publicity; the Modern Way to Compel Them to Come In* (New York, Cincinnati: The Methodist Book Concern, 1913), 18–19.

Jesus made the masses hear him. He did things that attracted attention. He did not do them to demonstrate his own power. He employed them as a method of gathering folks to whom he could preach the gospel. He used a boat as a pulpit and he employed a whip to drive out the thieves from the temple, and so set the people to talking about him. Paul sang in prison and preached in the prisoner's box. He appealed to Caesar when his funds ran out, so that he could be sent down to Rome and preach there, and while there went about the streets, chained to a soldier, preaching to people. He went to the seaside, where the people gathered, to deliver his message. He wrote letters with his own hand. Some think the "thorn in the flesh" was a crippled sight, for in one instance he says, "See how large a letter I have written" (meaning large letters).

Luther did not hide his candle under a bushel when he nailed up his ninety-five Theses and again and again publicly condemned the organized corrupt Roman Church and proclaimed the truth as he saw it in the ears of all the world.

John Wesley was a superb publicist. He preached on his father's tombstone, went into the midst of howling mobs, where thousands were gathered, and proclaimed the truth, hired an old foundry and turned it into a church, peddled books on medicine, and published his sermons to be scattered broadcast at cost.

General Booth was driven out of three Methodist denominations because he was determined to have people know that he had a saving gospel. He spoke to a mere handful until he went through the streets carrying a Publicists placard declaring that a converted drunkard, a reclaimed gambler, and a saved outcast woman would tell how the Lord's power cleansed and made new people of them. That drew the crowd.

As some churches embraced mass media technologies like newspapers and radio in the twentieth century to reach any audience, Christian leaders were increasingly concerned specifically with youth. Accelerating in the period between the First and Second World Wars, evangelicals became increasingly convinced that the youth were a chronically unreached demographic in the American church whose souls were at risk in an increasingly secularized world. This newspaper advertisement, published on the weekend prior to Easter Sunday, was one of the earlier efforts to try and speak the language of young people and to persuade them that worship (including its music) was relevant to their lives. It was notable at the time for its intentionally edgy and provocative attempt to gain an audience, attracting commentary from a wide range of publications like Literary Digest, *the* Milwaukee Journal, *the* Detroit Free Press, *and*

Omaha World-Herald. *It is a precursor to the more fully fledged attention to youth that we'll see in sources below.*

Source: Full-page advertisement in *The Kansas City Star*, Saturday, April 3, 1926.

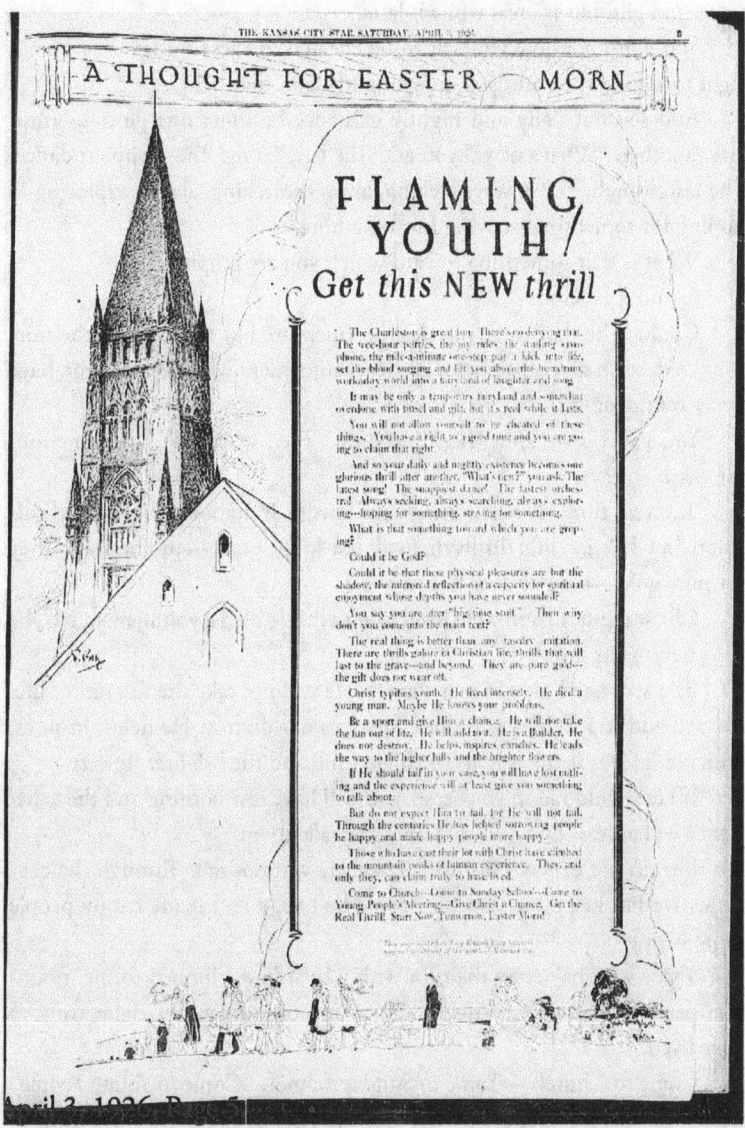

FLAMING YOUTH! Get this NEW thrill

The Charleston is great fun. There's no denying that. The wee-hour parties, the joy rides, the wailing saxophone, the mile-a-minute one-step put a kick into life, set the blood surging and lift you above the humdrum, workaday world into a fairyland of laughter and song.

It may be only a temporary fairyland and somewhat overdone with tinsel and gilt, but it's real while it lasts.

You will not allow yourself to be cheated of these things. You have a right to a good time and you are going to claim that right.

And so your daily and nightly existence becomes one glorious thrill after another. "What's new?" you ask. The latest song! The snappiest dance! The fastest orchestra! Always seeking, always searching, always exploring—hoping for something, striving for something.

What is that something toward which you are groping?

Could it be God?

Could it be that these physical pleasures are but the shadow, the mirrored reflection of a capacity for spiritual enjoyment whose depths you have never sounded?

You say you are after "big time stuff." Then why don't you come into the main tent?

The real thing is better than any tawdry imitation. There are thrills galore in Christian life, thrills that will last to the grave—and beyond. They are pure gold—the gilt does not wear off.

Christ typifies youth. He lived intensely. He died a young man. Maybe He knows your problems.

Be a sport and give Him a chance. He will not take the fun out of life. He will add to it. He is a Builder. He does not destroy. He helps, inspires, enriches. He leads the way to the higher hill and the brighter flowers.

If He should fail in your case, you will have lost nothing and the experience will at least give you something to talk about.

But do not expect Him to fail, for He will not fail. Through the centuries He has helped sorrowing people be happy and made happy people more happy.

Those who have cast their lot with Christ have climbed to the mountain peaks of human experience. They, and only they, can claim truly to have lived.

Come to Church—Come to Sunday School—Come to Young People's Meeting—Give Christ a Chance. Get the Real Thrill! Start Now, Tomorrow, Easter Morn!

Not only were churches trying to find new and innovative ways to reach outside the church to young people. They were also becoming conscious that the resources they developed for people in the church needed to speak the language of youth. Print hymnals remained the norm for most Protestant congregations through the 1980s and many Christian publishers attempted to appeal to youth through hymnal resources like this one from the 1930s, as well as many other denominational hymnal supplements.

Source: H. Augustine Smith, *The New Hymnal for American Youth* (New York and London: The Century Company, 1930).

This is not just another hymnal,— it is a hymnal which has been prepared with painstaking labor, to meet the need of youth for expression through music, in an age when method must keep pace with content; and when training in the art of worship has become a recognized part of the program for the religious education of youth.

This hymnal emerges from a background of practical idealism. . . . Special effort has been made to select those hymns and hymn tunes which will meet the needs of the younger adolescent group, and to relate worship to everyday life.

We, the Music Makers, present this hymnal to the youth of America, with the hope that through its use they may give expression to an ever higher and more vital feeling of desire to find God, and to make his purposes known in a world of persons and things.

Praising with Cymbals, Harps, and Lyres: Music in African American and Pentecostal Churches in the Early Twentieth Century

While white evangelicals were gradually beginning to consider liturgical adaptation to attract more people—particularly youth—other traditions in the early twentieth century had already made significant steps towards the incorporation of popular music into worship, albeit not for the same pragmatic reasons. Forms of musical worship that would later become mainstream were already being practiced among Black and African American and early Pentecostal churches. The range of music in these traditions could be surprising. Organs and choirs could be deployed alongside modern instruments not found in historically white churches. These churches relied on beloved texts like Psalm 150 to argue that the Bible envisioned musical worship in much more fulsome ways than had been common in other traditions. Moreover, these traditions emphasized the embodied and celebratory nature of Christian worship, welcoming musical styles and instruments that fostered greater physical and emotional expression.

Reflecting a common sensibility among many early white Pentecostals, this source demonstrates the sheer variety of musical instruments that might be heard in Pentecostal worship. In the broader scope of the "mainstreaming" of Christian musical worship, Pentecostals and African Americans were some of the earliest proponents of seeing all forms of instrumentation as allowable for worship, especially drums (though not without opposition even from within those same contexts).

Source: A. J. Tomlinson, ed., "Vigilance and Strength: Now Is the Time for Vigorous Actions and Close Fellowship and Harmony," *Church of God Evangel* 8, 5 (February 3, 1917), 1.

When we sing we should sing with life and the love of God floating out on the atmosphere from full and loving hearts. The musical instruments that are used should sound forth the praises of God. There is scarcely any musical instrument that can be rejected. While we use organs and pianos probably the most, others can be used just as well for the glory of God.

A few years ago many were prejudiced against the use the brass bands and stringed instruments, but God has so wonderfully honored the use of nearly all kinds of musical instruments until in more recent years our people have decided that the musical instruments belong to the Lord and his service, the same as houses and lands, trains and autos, money in the mail service. The devil uses the mails, trains, autos, and musical instruments, but we do not have to deprive ourselves of the use of them for God's service just because the devil uses them. . . .

Music and dancing indicates life and vigilance and strength, and calls for vigorous action on the part of all of God's children.

Reflecting on her childhood in the African American Baptist church during the 1920s, Mahalia Jackson recalled how it was common to use a variety of instruments in worship. For these traditions, new instrumentation was often adopted out of necessity and not for pragmatic reasons, as they lacked the funds for the organs, pianos, and choirs that more established churches could afford. Despite these financial limitations, the richness of the church's musical life became the wellspring for what would later evolve into secular popular music. While white churches often drew inspiration from popular music for their worship, in many Black church contexts, worship music fed innovations in broader popular music in later decades.

Source: Mahalia Jackson and Evan Mcleod Wylie, *Movin' On Up* (New York: Hawthorn Books, 1966), 32–33; 62–63.

Those people had no choir and no organ. They used the drum, the cymbal, the tambourine, and the steel triangle. Everybody in there sang and they clapped and stomped their feet and sang with their whole bodies. They had a beat, a powerful beat, a rhythm we held on to from slavery days, and their music was so strong and expressive it used to bring the tears to my eyes.

I believe the blues and jazz and even the rock and roll stuff got their beat from the Sanctified Church. We Baptists sang sweet, and we had the long and short meter on beautiful songs like "Amazing Grace, How Sweet It Sounds," but when those Holiness people tore into "I'm So Glad Jesus Lifted Me Up!" they came out with real jubilation. . . .

A lot of folks don't know that gospel songs have not been handed down like spirituals. Most gospel songs have been composed and written by Negro musicians like Professor Dorsey. . . .

When he began to write gospel music he still had a happy beat in his songs. They're sung by thousands of people like myself who believe religion is a joy.

There are still some Negro churches that don't have gospel singers or choirs and only sing the old hymns and anthems, but among Baptists and the Methodists and the Sanctified church people you will always hear gospel music.

Writing from Aimee Semple McPherson's church in Los Angeles, Angelus Temple, this source highlights the crucial role that a wide variety of musical styles played in the worship life of early Pentecostals. It also announces the establishment of a new music conservatory to preserve the rich musical tradition of this congregation. Like later Pentecostals, this source emphasizes that their embrace of diverse instrumentation faithfully reflects biblical teachings. However, the final sentence draws a key distinction between the sanctified nature of Pentecostal music and the "jazzy" worldly songs that these same instruments often accompanied. In part 2 of this chapter, we will see this distinction continue to define Pentecostal views about worship music.

Source: R. H. Morrison, "The Foursquare Conservatory of Music," *Foursquare Crusader* (February 6, 1929), 12.

As far back as we read in the Bible we find evidence of music. The people clapped their hands as they sang, the handclapping making a pleasing accompaniment to the song. Later we find the oboe, flute and trumpet in use, not like the flute and trumpet of today, but a crude form of brass or reed instrument. Then followed the stringed instruments. A marvelous discovery was made in Chaldea a few years ago. A harp which was used 30 centuries before the Christian era was unearthed, and it is believed that harps and musical instruments superior to those in use today were made and played upon by skilled musicians of that age. . . .

Angelus Temple has been called the church of the singing heart and rightly so. From early morning before midnight and sometimes the whole night through there goes up from the altars of Angelus Temple a song of praise and worship, like incense burning and ever rising-upward thru the portals of glory. Music has found its rightful place inside the great portals of the temple and instruments that once played the jazzy giddy songs of the world are now playing the melodious praises of God.

"Good Music Can Sell Anything": Evangelizing the Youth through Popular Music

In the mid-twentieth century, the pragmatic mindset began to increasingly focus on leveraging music. Many church and para-church leaders realized that the youth had different musical tastes from older generations, motivating them to advocate for incorporating popular styles of music in worship to attract them. Targeting specific demographics (including youth) became a prominent feature of church growth strategies in American evangelical contexts in the mid- to late-twentieth century, even as each generation of youth expressed different aesthetic preferences.

One of the most important youth evangelism programs of the twentieth century was the para-church ministry Youth for Christ, synonymous with the early preaching ministry of Billy Graham. Their concern for the apparent "delinquency"[3] of young people inspired their evangelistic fervor. Building on the important role that music had played in evangelistic ministries in the late nineteenth century, Youth for Christ aimed to used popular music to attract young people to evangelistic events where they would hear the Christian gospel.[4]

> **Source:** Torrey Maynard Johnson and Robert Cook, *Reaching Youth for Christ* (Chicago: Moody Press, 1944), 33–34.
>
> God has been working among young people, wherever He could find a man who would listen!
> Methods are strikingly similar. Over all, the list would be something like this:
>
> A co-operative approach
> Testimonies from two or three born-again Christians
> A radio broadcast in connection with the service
> Good music—the best available
> A definite gospel invitation.
>
> Innovations growing out of this basic technique depend upon the personality of the leaders. Dick Harvey has a radio quiz for St. Louis boys and girls. Glenn Wagner has a free canteen for service men, set up each Saturday night prior to the meetings. The Detroit "Voice of Christian Youth" features annual boat cruises on Lake St. Clair, banquets, and a Gospel Team ministry. Interesting advertising angle is their Sales Promotion Group, with

---

3. See page 20 of *Reaching Youth for Christ* for Johnson and Cook's diagnosis of the current crisis among the youth of America.

4. For more on Youth for Christ and the broader emphasis on meeting the cultural location of young people in the first half of the twentieth century, see Thomas E. Bergler, *The Juvenilization of American Christianity* (Grand Rapids: Eerdmans, 2012).

district managers in the various churches, serving under a regional manager, who in turn reports directly to the promotional chairman. Mailing groups, prayer groups, and personal workers are all handled under volunteer leadership. Philadelphia Youth Center allows two or three service men to call their homes—or sweethearts!—during the rally, telephoning directly from the platform.

The unifying factor of the entire movement, however, is the pull for souls. Every one of these groups is out for the salvation of the thousands who are tagged with the dreadful word, "delinquency." It is the passion for souls that is uniting American youth today.

Another critical youth outreach initiative was the Young People's Church of the Air, a radio broadcast that first began in 1931. These broadcasts, which imitated secular music programs of the era, featured a wide array of different instruments and ensembles that punctuated the testimonies, messages, and evangelistic invitations. In this source, the leader of the Young People's Church, Percy Crawford, introduces a hymnal filled with the new songs that he described as critical to the evangelistic success of his ministry.

Source: Percy B. Crawford, *Pinebrook Praises* (Wheaton: Van Kampen Press, 1943), Foreword.

One factor of great influence in turning the youth of our great nation back to God has been the Choruses sung at the Pinebrook Conference held ever Summer in the Pocono Mountains in Pennsylvania. Through the Young People's Broadcast of the Air these choruses are now being broadcast in the forty eight States of our great Nation and around the world by short wave, every Sunday afternoon on the Mutual Broadcasting System. It is hoped that you will not only be blessed through singing these choruses but that you'll soon come to see that the only thing worth while in this old life is to have Christ as your Saviour and thus have a hope beyond the grave.

Alongside these ministries that organized mass events for youth, a new movement emerged in this period that sought to enable the youth themselves to carry out evangelism that would appeal to their own generation. This was the youth musicals movement. In the period from 1967 to 1975, over seventy different musicals were written and eagerly adopted and produced by a host of churches. These musicals featured themes that were relevant to the youth of the day and also heavily featured folk and rock-influenced musical styles and instrumentation.[5]

Source: Mack Moore, "Current Trends in Youth Musicals," *The Church Musician* (July 1974), 54.

In 1968, Broadman Press released an innovative form of music which would hopefully turn the youth of our churches toward greater involvement in outreach. And, turn it did! With the advent of Good News, by Bob Oldenburg, came a period of unheard-of growth within music ministries throughout America. Youth became more excited about their faith through the vibrant sounds of "their" music. Churches saw a new day dawn in the lives of their young people. Consequently, many of these churches were filled with a new excitement and sense of need to share the good news of Christ.

Utilizing guitars, drums, string bass in addition to the usual piano, the new musicals allowed the youth to share Christ in their own, unique way. Using the form of the traditional cantata, a narration added special emphasis to the message being proclaimed. . . . They were in rebellion against many of the phoney attitudes of Christian people who loved and cared for them only when it was convenient. The impact was a tremendous one, and was effective in causing "John Doe—church member"—to see himself in the light of how men in the world saw him. The catchy rhythms, though unorthodox by most of our churches' standards, soon had the feet of young and old alike tapping. The melody and words of the Bill Cates song "Do You Really Care?" were soon heard on the lips of nearly everyone. There was a sense that a new era had arrived in church music.

While Youth for Christ rallies gathered thousands of young people in decades past, mass rallies of young Jesus People like Explo '72 in Dallas were making news headlines. Over time, youth-centered evangelistic programs beyond the church's walls began to shape the practice of musical worship in local church congregations. As you might expect, this was contentious. Pastors and musicians had to navigate these waters carefully to not alienate their older members

---

5. For this claim and for more information about the youth musical movement, see William R. Bishop, "Christian Youth Musicals: 1967–1975" (PhD diss., New Orleans Baptist Theological Seminary, 2015).

even as they reached out to younger people. Eventually, these disputes over musical taste would spill into the popular consciousness with the outbreak of the "Worship Wars" by the 1990s.[6] In this example from the 1970s, Pierson highlights the power of communicating with the adult congregants about the evangelistic intent to avoid misunderstandings about the purpose of the new music.

Source: Charles E. Pierson, "Right and Wrong Ways of Introducing Contemporary Music," *The Church Musician* (September 1973), 19–22.

If you are fearful about using any type of contemporary music, be reassured Mr. Average Church Member is more ready to listen to contemporary expressions than Tom Teenager is to hear the grand hymns of the faith. Mr. A. C. Member may be trying to say two things: (1) "Show me that this music is vital to our ministry to young people," and (2) "Don't expect me to enjoy all of the new music. I have my own tastes."

If particular groups in the church are likely to be uncomfortable, discuss the problems with them ahead of time. Prepare them to look for the message in the music.

Help them see that the introduction of new musical forms is not part of a campaign to take away the great hymns of the past or bring the world into the church. Space out special musical presentations so that members do not get the impression that the traditional is being supplanted.

... If your aim is evangelism, explain to parents and other adults that the music they will hear is the type to which young people will listen; that the songs are message-oriented, not just music; that there is a difference between not enjoying certain music and insisting that it is "wrong."

In a program of this kind, the message should come across clearly. The music used should be of the type that communicates to youth with no adaptation being made for adults in the audience. This type of ministry should therefore not be conducted during regular adult services.

If the purpose of the meeting is to edify youth, explain to adults as above

---

6. For more on the history of the Worship Wars, see Robb Redman, "Worship Wars or Worship Awakening?" *Liturgy* 19, no. 4 (2004): 39–44, https://doi.org/10.1080/04580630490490512; Lester Ruth, "The Eruption of Worship Wars: The Coming of Conflict," *Liturgy* 32, no. 1 (2017): 3–6, https://doi.org/10.1080/0458063X.2016.1229431. For longer treatments of the Worship Wars in context, see also Terry W. York, *America's Worship Wars* (Hendrickson Publishers, 2003); Anna E. Nekola, "Between This World and the Next: The Musical 'Worship Wars' and Evangelical Ideology in the United States, 1960-2005" (PhD diss., The University of Wisconsin–Madison, 2009).

that this is message-oriented music addressed to young people. Explain to the youth on the other hand that they should not be critical of the music adults find edifying—in fact they should learn to profit from it as well as their own music.

. . . If your purpose is to orient adults concerning contemporary Christian music, let adults know in advance that this is what you purpose to do. Lay the theological foundation well ahead of time. Explain in detail in advance the type of instrumentation that will be used, the type of singing, dress, and presentation. Keep things on a positive note. Discourage attendance for the sake of being shocked.

Starting in the 1950s, Robert Schuller shaped his ministry in southern California to be attractive to contemporary people, first with drive-in services and later with iconic architecture and television programming. Below, Schuller offers his thoughts to other pastors on overcoming the gap between worship and people. In addition to his writing, Schuller is perhaps most famous for his long-running television program "The Hour of Power," broadcast from the iconic "Crystal Cathedral," a glass structure capable of seating 2000 for worship services. Schuller was one of the first to so clearly link a numbers-based approach to worship to a duty to evangelize effectively, an approach that would crystalize in the subsequent decades through C. Peter Wagner as the "Church Growth movement."[7]

Source: Robert H. Schuller, *Your Church Has Real Possibilities!* (Glendale: Regal Books, 1974), 39.

Many churches are so dignified they're dull! The music is dull, the messages are dull, the architecture is dull; there is no excitement in the air! The worship service might be described as sleepy, quietly meditative and a perfectly tranquilizing arrangement—guaranteed to produce yawning and boredom.

There is absolutely no excuse for the bearers of the good news of the gospel of Jesus Christ to be anything but enthusiastic, exciting and dynamic!

---

7. For a larger review of the Church Growth movement and its connection to Robert Schuller, see Mark T. Mulder et al., *The Church Must Grow or Perish: Robert H. Schuller and the Business of American Christianity* (Grand Rapids: Eerdmans, 2025); Mark T. Mulder and Gerardo Martí, *The Glass Church: Robert H. Schuller, the Crystal Cathedral, and the Strain of Megachurch Ministry* (Rutgers University Press, 2020).

If the gospel is truly preached, it will be preached as exciting good news! Good news is never dull. If a service is dull, there must be no good news. If there is no good news, there must not be any gospel!

Among the most influential evangelical musicians of the 1960s was a composer with roots in Youth for Christ, Ralph Carmichael. After a career that saw success in writing secular music, Carmichael turned his attention again to the church in the mid-1960s. Carmichael became a prolific composer of new music for evangelistic ministries. As one of the most outspoken proponents of popular music, Carmichael was critical in eroding some of the resistance that evangelicals had with popular music styles in churches. For instance, in this source we see Carmichael questioning many of the aesthetic assumptions about what "good" music is. The following is a distillation of quotations taken from a talk that Carmichael first gave at Fort Wayne (Indiana) Bible College and that was later published in print.

Source: John Gillies, "What's So Sacred About Music," *The Church Musician* (May 1974), 50–51.

What's "Good" Music?

Good music is good timing and good pitch. It hasn't anything to do with form. Good music simply has to be effective and relevant. And good music can sell anything.

Things—including music—aren't good or bad in themselves. Things become good or bad, depending upon how they are used.

On Relevance

So what is relevant music? It's music that helps meet whatever crisis has to be faced. Now there's a real challenge for Christians!

I'm not out to create a new musical trend. I'm just going where the music is going—where the action is; where the kids are; where the people are.

I am going to remain open to different styles of music. Sure, I have my personal preference. But they're none of your business. Likes—preferences—shouldn't ever get in the way of a music communicator. And likes have something to do with one's mood, you know. So they can get in the way of honest communication....

Isn't All of This Just Plain Syncopation?

Ah, that nasty word! Some people still wonder whether syncopation has a place in church. Well, friend, how do you talk? In even half notes? In even whole notes? No sir. Listen to yourself talk. You talk in all kinds of jerky, rhythmic patterns. You talk in syncopation—and you'd sound might silly if you didn't. So what's wrong with it?

Movement is what's behind the new rhythmics—and the new music. I don't feel worldly when I talk. Why should I feel worldly when I sing? or play?

The success of the efforts of figures like Ralph Carmichael and many others can be seen in the source below. This hymnal published by the major evangelical publisher Zondervan does not evidence the need to theologically justify its embrace of country and western music—the music of the "common people." Moreover, the source expects that many churches will have worship contexts (such as Sunday evening services) where such a hymnal will be a valuable addition.

Source: *Country and Western Hymnal*, comp. Fred Bock (Grand Rapids: Singspiration Music of the Zondervan Corporation, 1972).

Some call it "southern gospel." Others think of it as "shape-note music." The younger generation may identify as "the Nashville sound." We've chosen to label it "country and western." Whatever the name, the overall style is unmistakable, for in recent years it has swept across our country to capture the attention and the devotion of millions of Americans from all walks of life. You hear it not only in the deep south, or on the midwestern prairies, or in isolated mountain communities, but just as frequently in the great urban centers from coast to coast. Harmonically it is simple and unsophisticated; poetically it is direct and down-to-earth. It is the music of the common people, music of the heart, with roots buried deep in the musical traditions of the past hundred-and-fifty years.

Here for your inspiration and blessing, is a selection of 117 of the finest and most popular of these hymns and gospel songs. . . .

Many will select this book for use with a choir. Often it will serve as a resource for solo or quartet performance. But it is primarily designed as a hymnal—perhaps as a supplementary hymnbook in your church for use in Sunday evening song services or for sing-alongs in the home or smaller church gatherings.

Not all evangelicals were in favor of the growing use of popular music styles. A.W. Tozer raised his voice in protest against what he saw as the overly-sexualized nature of the music deployed in certain services. Many later worship leaders and thinkers in the Reformed and evangelical traditions would point back to Tozer as an early, authoritative source—especially his booklet Worship: The Missing Jewel of the Evangelical Church *(1961).*

Source: A.W. Tozer, *Born After Midnight* (Harrisburg, PA: Christian Publications, 1959), 37–39.

The cult of Eros is seriously affecting the Church. The pure religion of Christ that flows like a crystal river from the heart of God is being polluted by the unclean waters that trickle from behind of altars of abomination that appear on every high hill and under every green tree from New York to Los Angeles.

The influence of the erotic spirit is felt almost everywhere in Evangelical circles. Much of the singing in certain types of meetings has in it more of romance than it has of the Holy Ghost. Both words and music are designed to rouse the libidinous. Christ is courted with a familiarity that reveals a total ignorance of who He is. It is not the reverent intimacy of the adoring saint but the impudent familiarity of the carnal lover. . . .

If my language should seem severe, let it be remembered that it is not directed at any individual. Toward the lost world of men I feel only a great compassion and a desire that all should come to repentance. . . .

When God's sheep are endangered the shepherd must not gaze at the stars and meditate on "inspirational" themes. He is morally obliged to grab his weapon and run to their defense. When the circumstances call for it, love can use the sword, though by her nature she would rather bind up the broken heart and minister to the wounded. . . . For the last three decades timidity disguised as humility has crouched in her corner while the spiritual quality of evangelical Christianity has become progressively worse year by year.

Adapting to the Cultural Revolution: Catholic and Mainline Churches Experiment with "Contemporary Worship"

It was not only evangelicals who came to see popular music as a possible solution to the problems they were facing. The cultural and social changes in the 1960s led some Mainline and Catholic Christians to worry that a significant gap was emerging between older ways of worship and contemporary people, especially youth and young adults. The sources below from a variety of Mainline authors reflect a general anxiety that motivated the first wave of so-called "contemporary worship" among these churches in the 1960s and 1970s. (This was the first time that the phrase "contemporary worship" was used). This era of contemporary worship was marked by a highly experimental approach towards all aspects of Christian worship. However, experimenting with popular music was invariably a key part of the wider campaign for modernization. Although this intense period of experimentation settled down after the 1970s, the underlying anxiety that Mainline worship (and its music) did not reflect the needs and concerns of the contemporary person persisted.

James F. White, a young professor of worship at a Methodist seminary in Texas, draws upon the insights and categories of Marshall McLuhan, one of the most prominent writers on communication in the 1960s (and the originator for the famous statement "the medium is the message"), to argue that a generation formed by television will be disengaged from forms of worship that mostly talk at them. White utilized opportunities at his seminary chapel and his home church to engage in new forms of "experimental" or "contemporary" worship.

Source: James F. White, "Worship in the Age of Marshall McLuhan" in *Christian Worship in North America: A Retrospective: 1955–1995* (Collegeville: The Liturgical Press, 1997), 135–41. Originally published as "Worship in an Age of Immediacy," *The Christian Century* 75 (February 21, 1968): 227–30.

It is the young who find the present forms of worship so intolerable. They're frank about it: to them worship is basically boring. And I, too, admit that the dullest hour of the week is the one I spend in church. I'm sure dullness is not intrinsic to worship since some of the most exciting moments of my week are those spent at seminary services. The word-package that constitutes most of Protestant worship just isn't turned on for a generation accustomed to participation and involvement. If "the medium is the message" then much of Protestant worship indicates that the message is not very vital or relevant.

There are groups in our society in which worship is definitely of a turned-on variety: many of the African American churches, the Pentecostal groups and churches retaining a strong revivalistic fervor. There one finds no lack of participation in the worship; the foot-tapping music leaves no doubt about that: you "get with it" in a hurry. And something happens—maybe not just what we might like, but undeniably each service is a happening. Many of the large American denominations once had those qualities in their worship. Whatever we may think about revivalism, its advocates know that to move people spiritually you must move them physically. Most of us long since became too sophisticated for that. Our problems in worship today are often the result of middle class self-consciousness; metaphorically, we got shoes—and our respectability has been pinching us ever since. In a literal sense the most exciting service I've seen in a long time occurred when the celebrant took off his shoes and danced in a procession to music from Zorba the Greek.

For one pastor and professor at Vanderbilt, the new era was marked by an exciting new aesthetic. The church's worship failed to reflect this new style and mood and so risked becoming increasingly irrelevant.

Source: John Killinger, *Leave It to the Spirit: Commitment and Freedom in the New Liturgy* (New York: Harper & Row, 1971), xiii, xviii, 7.

We live in a Peter Max[8] world of exciting colors and configurations. We listen to music that is produced both electronically and atonally. We read novelists who write cryptically and suggestively, so that we are forced to puzzle over their meanings or else despair of their having any meaning. We produce and watch television shows and movies that are so weird or

---

8. Peter Max was an artist who used bright colors in his work. In the 1960s his work was popular among forms of psychedelic art and pop art.

imaginative as to defy our intelligence and appeal only to our emotions. But for some reason we have not brought our every day way of life into the sanctuary of the church. We have a syncopated, rock-and-roll, electronic consciousness for most of the week and a funereal, four-four attitude toward Sunday morning. And what it means is that Sunday morning is where least is happening in our lives.

If modern-day worship was the problem, the solution that some leaders like James White offered was to adopt a greater flexibility and diversity in worship. He sought wisdom for the church's worship in business practices. Noticing how companies had shifted their practice to attract consumers to buy their products, White argued that the church needed to adopt a similar approach—an approach that many of his evangelical counterparts had championed already and would continue to into the twenty-first century.

Source: James F. White, *New Forms of Worship* (Nashville: Abingdon Press, 1971), 33–34.

The splintering of society means that to be true and relevant to people as they now are, we will need to be all things to all people. In the past we have offered what businessmen call a manufacturing mentality. We produced a product and then looked for someone to take it. Now, instead, we need a marketing mentality. Businesses operating on a manufacturing mentality are not apt to survive since their competitors can produce something that people really want. Yet such has been the mentality of the church. A marketing mentality searches for what people want and need and then resolves to satisfy that need. Our pastoral norm emphasizes the need to recognize the great variety of persons in the church today and their varying conditions of life. This almost automatically demands a greater number of choices of types of worship. Henry Ford is reputed to have promised the customer any color as long as it was black, but Ford Motor Company would not be in business today if it had kept that policy. . . .

Our worship must be constructed around a healthy respect for the varieties of people who will be worshiping either in homogeneous or heterogeneous groups. What is appropriate worship for children may not be so for teenagers or for their parents. No longer can we afford to offer a menu with one dinner on it.

The response of Mainline churches to the growing sense of crisis was to experiment in many diverse ways with their worship. These experiments incorporated many artistic mediums running the entire spectrum from the kitsch to the profound—puppets, clowning, dancing, dramatic skits, poetry, and visual art. Using popular music was a recurrent emphasis of these experiments though. This source is from the introduction to a collection of contemporary worship services. In it, the author explains the ethos of the new movement for contemporary worship.[9] This movement strove to use contemporary thoughts and words, to reclaim a celebratory aspect to worship, and to express the needs of modern-day worshipers. He then proceeds to explain what these services look like.

Source: James L. Christensen, *Contemporary Worship Services: A Sourcebook* (Old Tappan, NJ: Fleming H. Revell, 1971), 11–12.

Contemporary worship . . . is characterized by a focus upon life and the social applications of faith, in contrast to the other-worldly emphasis. A basic premise is the view that the church is servant, and a leaven in the world. The Christian lives in a secular world and contemporary worship trains the Christian for witness in such a responsibility.

To accomplish these purposes, contemporary worship utilizes new forms, modern ballads, varied instruments, light, color, all kinds of arts, movements, dance, recorded music, films, picture projections, clapping, Scriptures and prayers with words that are in current usage, and varied sermon methods. Popular music usually accompanied by guitars and ukuleles, and occasionally trumpet, drums, vibra-harp or accordion is typical of most modernized services.

Varied environments are accomplished by changing lights, artificially controlled with rheostats and mirrors, and photographs shown rapidly upon a screen. . . . Consciousness is also expanded by bodily movement accomplished in interpretive ballet.

One of the most apparent and necessary innovations of the contemporary service is the translation and paraphrasing of Christian traditions, Scriptures, and prayer into words of daily vocabulary and modern images and idioms. Much of Christian tradition is an archaic language. Contemporary worship seeks to make the language of worship the language of life.

---

9. The popularity and influence of this volume is suggested by the fact that two years later, Christensen published another volume of services: James L. Christensen, *New Ways to Worship: More Contemporary Worship Services* (Old Tappan, NJ: Fleming H. Revell, 1973).

Now these innovations may shock and excite many tradition-oriented members. Therefore, the worship leader must keep balance and avoid extremes as a regular diet. If he is steeped only in the traditional forms of worship, he risks being irrelevant to the twentieth-century mind. On the other hand, if he is extremely far-out he risks losing the historical perspective and the tradition-oriented segment of the congregation. Both results are unfortunate, and to be avoided if possible.

This source, describes one such experiment with a new, contemporary service called "Church-O-Theque." (The name is a play on "discotheque.") What was meant to be an experimental trial run of four weeks during the lull of summer became something much more established as the service proved wildly popular. This evening service quickly jumped from thirty people to three hundred.

Source: Floyd E. Werle, "Church-O-Theque," *Music Ministry* 9, no. 6 (February 1968): 3, 5–7.

In the effort to make Christian worship relevant and meaningful to twentieth-century man, more and more churches are turning to the latent possibilities offered in the involvement of contemporary art forms, notably jazz-folk-rock modern music, dance, film, et cetera, in various types of presentation. . . . Church-O-Theque, which made its debut in August 1966, at Mount Vernon Place Methodist Church in Washington, D.C. represents a successful attempt to utilize the "jazz mass" for public worship on a practical, continuing weekly basis. . . .

Our Church-O-Theque combo is known appropriately as the "Persistent Ciphers" and consists presently of electric guitar, electric bass, drums, and organ. All players are professional and able both to read and to improvise. This group can present small-combo jazz, the top-forty sound, or folk music with complete flexibility and authenticity. In the initial services only jazz was used; we are now moving more and more to top-forty forms and laying ground-work for involvement of the vast army of teen combos. . . . The order of service in Church-O-Theque is indistinguishable from that of an ordinary worship service, reads the same way in the bulletin, and contains the same elements. It is normal practice to introduce at least one element besides music that is not commonly found in ordinary Victorian-style worship. This may be a film, filmstrip, recorded selection, dance, dramatic piece, dialogue, and so forth. Longer audio-visuals or dramatics often replace the sermon, and the latter when used is encouraged to be outspoken on vital topics. . . . [With respect to music, we] use only original tunes. These tunes are simple and designed to be picked up by the congregation on the spot with no prior rehearsal or instruction. A lead sheet containing the new tune (which is always unison), the chord changes (dance-style guitar), and the verses is prepared and enough copies duplicated for the choir. . . .

Within the format [of the service], the possibilities for communicating the Gospel in new ways appear limitless. . . . Some of our more outstanding main events in Church-O-Theque have included a joint holy communion with a Lutheran congregation, whose pastor played jazz clarinet; several tape, slide and film presentations; a chance drama; [a sevrvice led by] a Roman Catholic priest with the popular "Peanuts" theme; a university poet-in-residence, who provided original hymn material; and the resident bishop, John Wesley Lord, who told a packed house that the church must change its ways or perish.

Within the Catholic Church, the Second Vatican Council from 1962–65 (often called Vatican II) unleashed a wave of liturgical reform within many parishes across the United States. One of these developments was the embrace of new musical styles and instrumentation within the Catholic Mass. The official documents of Vatican II itself charted a conservative line, arguing that Gregorian chant should be given "pride of place in liturgical services" and highlighting the pipe organ as the most suitable instrument for Christian worship. However, the key Vatican II document on liturgical reform, Sacrosanctum Concilium *(the Constitution on the Sacred Liturgy), also cracked open the door to modern instruments and contemporary music by allowing local musical traditions to be incorporated into worship—especially in missional districts.*[10] *The source below is from the album cover of one of the first post-Vatican II recordings of a new collection of folk-music for use in Catholic liturgy. While it notes that folk music in worship was still controversial, it justifies the new music by arguing that it speaks the language of the people—especially young people.*[11]

---

10. Second Vatican Council, *Sacrosanctum Concilium* [Constitution on the Sacred Liturgy], December 4, 1963, paras. 112–21, Vatican.va, https://www.vatican.va/archive/hist_councils/ii_vatican_council/documents/vat-ii_const_19631204_sacrosanctum-concilium_en.html.

11. Numerous other recordings, hymnals, and song collections were produced in the same period after Vatican II, demonstrating the eager embrace of the new musical styles by

Source: Ray Repp, Liner notes to *Mass for Young Americans* (FEL Publications, 1966).

Certainly one of the reasons for the popularity and wide acceptance of Mr. Repp's music, especially among young people, is that its language is a language of the people. The texts . . . express in a manner just as simple and meaningful as the music the soul of the modern psalmist. . . .

We think that the listener will find in this album an expression of youthful, vigorous religious feeling, for, as the composer states, "My music was written for Young Americans and people with young American ideas who want to glorify God and "sing a new song to the Lord."

Vatican II had not just opened the way for new musical styles to be incorporated into worship. In a similar vein to "Church-O-Theque" (above), other liturgical innovations also followed. This source describes the folk masses[12] at the campus ministry at the University of Michigan, which contained both contemporary renditions of classic liturgical texts as well as music pulled from the Beatles. In this case, there isn't just an updating of the styles of music for Christian lyrics, but the inclusion of a popular song from the radio. (Much later, the U2charist would take that approach to its most elevated level.) Notice that the innovations of this service extend far beyond only music. In this service, there were mime troupes, journalism, drama, and film.

Source: Myron B. Bloy, Jr., ed., *Multi-Media Worship: A Model and Nine Viewpoints* (New York: The Seabury Press, 1969), 7–8, replicating the account from the October 25, 1968 edition of the student newspaper, *The Michigan Daily*.

Last Sunday, the folk mass was enriched by members of the San Francisco Mime Troupe and the first showing of a film by Craig Hammond, one of the two Episcopal ministers who direct the center.

The service was a mixed-media exercise. A folk trio . . . accompanied the singing of formal parts of the mass and folk counterparts of hymns

---

some in the church; see Joe Wise et al., *Young People's Folk Hymnal*, vol. 1; *25 Guitar Songs for Use in Worship Services* (Chicago: World Library Publications, 1965); Roger D. Nachtwey ed., *Hymnal for Young Christians*, vol. 2 (Los Angeles: FEL Publications, 1966).

12. For a broader description of the folk mass movement during the 1960s see Ken Canedo, *Keep the Fire Burning: The Folk Mass Revolution* (Portland, OR: Pastoral Press, 2009).

or anthems. In one scene, the Mime Troupe moved to the rhythm of one drum and a brief narration from *Time* magazine about prosecution of the Catonsville nine[13]; in another, a "crankie" of rolled paper illustrated the tale of a soldier told by an actor and punctuated by two recorders. The color film combined an excellent spatial collage for an episode with the people themselves and their best communicators, children. A musical track accompanied the film, introduced by the Beatles singing "Fool on the Hill." . . .

Hammond read the epistle to the trio's quiet playing and humming of "Hey Jude," and people were asked to participate in the prayer of intercession. One man said, "Prayer is so often a downer, I pray it would be otherwise." And communion was celebrated with round loaves of bread in baskets, and wine in earthenware goblets passed among the people.

The focus was constantly shifting and the scene changing during the service, but nothing seemed to be forced upon the people—things were being done their way and the points were made. Dan Burke, the minister who officiated at the folk mass, was silent for a moment after the gospel was read, then he said, "You can hardly avoid it, but touch each other." Then louder, "Come on, touch each other." Two hundred and fifty people sat on the floor and the stage, leaned against walls and railings, hand in hand. Communication became fellowship.

In the early 1970s, the pastor of a Presbyterian church in Port Jervis, New York, wrote a report of the worship changes he had seen. His report named the standard components of "experimental" or "contemporary" worship at the time. Many of these features fell by the wayside (and are not practiced in current Contemporary Praise & Worship). Others though—for instance, increased lay participation—became mainstream. An especially important legacy of this period of experimentation was the centrality of creativity in order to match Christian worship to contemporary people. The perspective would carry over to a second round of "contemporary worship" among Mainline congregations in the late 1980s and 1990s.[14]

---

13. The Catonsvillle nine were a Catholic group that destroyed some draft files in a war protest.

14. One of the earliest secondary sources documenting the adoption of Contemporary Praise & Worship into Reformed and other Mainline contexts is Robert Webber, "Enter His Courts with Praise: A New Style of Worship Is Sweeping the Church," *Reformed Worship* 20 (June 1991): https://www.reformedworship.org/article/june-1991/enter-his-courts-praise-new-style-worship-sweeping-church.

Source: Richard K. Avery, "The Church Is Alive and Singing," *Presbyterian Life* (October 15, 1971), 9–10.

One of the most interesting phenomena in the life of the Christian church today is a growing interest in creative worship, especially in new music. Traveling around the country now one hears quite often about balloons, posters, parades, banners, dialogue sermons, prayer on film, acted-out sermon illustrations, and dance all being used reverently and effectively in services. And the creation and use of new music amounts to nothing less than an explosion. . . . For many people, the church's pre-occupation with postures and expressions of solemnity, guilt, and propriety in worship has been carried too far. See what's happening now. See Christians clapping and snapping and swaying and laughing to God's glory. Mark the rediscovery of foot-tapping gospel songs. Share our amazement at the international popularity of our happy, calypso-rhythm settings of the "Gloria Patri" and the Doxology. . . .

But many people, old and young, are finding themselves excited by the new rhythms of praise, moved by the fresh melodies of devotion, and stimulated by new words about faith and morality. Along with a rediscovery of the variety of musical instruments to glorify God, all this is causing us to see goose bumps, tears, tapping feet, smiles, and eager listening again on Sunday mornings. Now that people are thinking more and more of the church as a family, a body of people rather than an institution or a clerical establishment, members of the family to share actively in worship, to be mere observers no more. Indeed, the desire has become a demand by people to speak, move, and sing for themselves and to have worship represent their feelings.

Discussion Questions

- Consider your own local worshiping community that you participate in. Can you think of any specific examples where your community's worship may be influenced by pragmatism (an orientation towards prioritizing what "works")? What are the theological risks or benefits of thinking pragmatically about worship?

- Many of the leaders that we have heard in this chapter believed that worship should reflect the aesthetic and cultural sensibilities of their time. Are there ways in which the influence of cultural values may be dangerous or malformational for Christian worship?

- Catherine Booth argued that as long as the message of the gospel was left intact, Christians are free to use whatever cultural tools or practices they have at their disposal to evangelize. How do you assess that argument?

- What challenges might be present in using music as a tool for evangelism in Christian worship?

- Which of the arguments or sources that you have encountered in this chapter do you find most persuasive? Do these voices come from traditions that you are part of?

CHAPTER 2
POPULAR: USING CONTEMPORARY MUSIC IN WORSHIP

Part 2: The Jesus People and Beyond

In part 1 of "Popular," we showed that the incorporation of popular music in Christian worship was rooted in a tradition of pragmatism that extends back (at least) into the nineteenth century. However, if you ask many scholars or church leaders today where Contemporary Praise & Worship comes from, many would likely tell you a story that started with the Jesus People movement.

The story goes something like this: in the counterculture of Southern California in the late 1960s, there were a group of hippies who gave their lives to Jesus and became the Jesus People. These hippies began to blend the counterculture with their newfound Christianity and expressed themselves in folk and rock songs. They kept their guitars, but they started singing to Jesus.[1] The churches with which they were affiliated—especially Chuck Smith, Sr.'s Calvary Chapel—began to develop resources and institutions to disseminate the music that was being written in their congregations. Maranatha! Music was founded in the early 1970s, and by the 1980s, the Vineyard churches also launched Vineyard/Mercy Re-

---

1. Adam Perez has discussed the role of instrumentation in the history of Contemporary Praise & Worship music, namely the guitar and the keyboard. See Adam Perez, "Beyond the Guitar: The Keyboard as a Lens into the History of Contemporary Praise and Worship," *The Hymn* 70, no. 2 (2019): 18–26.

cords. The influence of this music spread ever outward and many churches started singing their music in Sunday worship services.

While the Jesus People movement is not the only genesis point for Contemporary Praise & Worship, it is a significant point in its development. In the second part of this chapter we pick up the story at the point where popular music starts to become widely accepted and adopted throughout a broad swathe of churches.

Alongside the rise of new church networks like Calvary Chapel and the Vineyard, other movements were coming to the fore that would aggressively promote the necessity of using popular music. The Church Growth movement was another critical catalyst. Robert Schuller, who we heard from in the previous chapter, was an important forerunner. The Church Growth movement encouraged churches to strategically adapt all aspects of their congregational life, especially their worship services, to better reach out to the unchurched. Introducing new Sunday services that were defined by their use of popular music—sometimes called "seeker" or "seeker-friendly" services—was a primary way churches sought to do this. The megachurches that grew from this logic became some of the most important models and operated as hubs for the dissemination of the movement's teachings (e.g., Willow Creek Community Church, Saddleback Church, Community Church of Joy, and others).[2]

The adoption of popular music to help the church's outreach was by no means universal. By and large, Pentecostals remained highly suspicious of music that had associations with the secular world. A favorite verse for many Pentecostals was that a bad tree could only produce bad fruit (Matthew 7:17), and many thought that rock music was a tool of Satan. The story is more complicated. Along with African American churches, white Pentecostals had long embraced a wide range of instruments as not only allowed in Christian worship but commanded by Scripture. Scriptural examples made room for organs and choirs, but Pentecostals also made use

---

2. For a sense of the widespread influence of the megachurch movement, see Gordon W. Lathrop, "New Pentecost or Joseph's Britches? Reflections on the History and Meaning of the Worship Ordo in the Megachurches," *Worship* 72, no. 6 (1998): 521–38. While Lathrop is highly critical of the megachurch movement he describes, he offers an early overview of the forms of worship becoming increasingly normalized in these settings.

of orchestras and guitars. Gradually, the new popular music flooding the airways from the Jesus People began to erode Pentecostal concerns about rock music.

Our chapter ends with a variety of contemporary excerpts that show the ongoing evolution and spread of popular music. The popular music common to Contemporary Praise & Worship repertoire is not the only form in practice today. Some Mainline churches, for example, began to experiment with secular music in their liturgies. Other church movements emerged that incorporated an even broader variety of musical styles. Because popular music is constantly changing, the church's musical style is perpetually evolving.

"A Fire Marshal's Nightmare and a Jesus Freak's Dream": Worshiping in the New Paradigm Churches

The emergence of the Calvary Chapel and Vineyard churches in Southern California marked a paradigm shift in American evangelical worship. This is reflected in the name coined for them by sociologist Donald Miller: "New Paradigm" churches. With both networks having connections to the hippie counterculture of the late 1960s and early 1970s, the band-based rock and folk music that was common in that counterculture was made mainstream throughout these networks.[3]

In Chuck Smith, Sr.'s 1972 reflection (he served as pastor of Calvary Chapel in Costa Mesa, California), he notes the evangelistic power of using the music of youth in their church's ministry. This new music was not used in the congregation's Sunday morning services, but it was used in special concerts and in evening Bible studies. The church spawned many church plants, many of which used the new music for their main services as well. Note how this excerpt attributes the songs to God while also acknowledging a sense of a biblical

---

3. For documents on the Jesus People movement, see David Di Sabatino, *The Jesus People Movement: An Annotated Bibliography and General Resource* (Greenwood Press, 1999).

mandate to adapt to culture for the sake of evangelism, citing the banner verse for this evangelistic logic, 1 Corinthians 9:22b.

Source: Chuck Smith and Hugh Steven, *The Reproducers: New Life for Thousands* (Glendale, CA: G/L Regal Books, 1972; Philadelphia: Calvary Chapel of Philadelphia, 2011), 79–80.

I'm not a rock festival fan. I'm a conservative missionary pilot from Rhodesia. But I've been concerned for churches and Christians to come back to a biblical concept of what Christianity is all about. I believe the Jesus Movement with their music and witnessing, their ability to look past outside appearances, and the emphasis on the Word is a beautiful expression of what the true gospel is all about. . . .

There were and are many like this missionary who find the new approach to music difficult to understand and digest. But the music is composed and played for the youth of the seventies. And for every adult who can't understand, there are thousands of the youth who do.

"And," said Bob Wall, current lead guitarist for [the musical group] the Love Song, "we want to reach the kids who listen to Led Zeppelin and the Rolling Stones. They offer a beat. But we have a message given to us by God and it's all about His Son Jesus Christ."

"Bob is right," said Chuck Smith. "The Love Song does have a message. After they accepted the Lord and began sharing their talents in the Chapel and special concerts, the Lord gave them fantastic new songs. This immediately opened up a whole new dimension at Calvary. In a sense we became all things to all men in order to win them. Kids started coming in tremendous numbers just to hear the music. Whenever they take part in the service or hold concerts, the young musicians always give their personal testimonies and an opportunity for people to accept Christ."

Love Song not only attracted large groups of young people to come and listen to their music; they inspired other talented groups to form and begin using their talents for Jesus.

This source provides a firsthand account of what the meetings within the Jesus People movement looked like, especially in their use of music. These services included a mixture of older hymns and new songs, congregational songs and soloist numbers. Despite the more performative nature of the music, the source makes clear that the young people who attended these meetings felt highly involved in the meeting throughout—moving, gesturing, singing. Also notice the quantity of music in these meetings (over two thirds of a three-hour gathering would be music and testimony).

Source: Ronald M. Enroth, Edward E. Ericson, Jr., and C. Breckinridge Peters, *The Jesus People: Old-Time Religion in the Age of Aquarius* (Grand Rapids: Baker, 1972), 86–87.

The midweek Bible studies are a fire marshal's nightmare and a Jesus Freak's dream. Not only are the pews packed with the faithful, but the aisles and any other available spaces are filled with young bodies, many of whom sit cramped for an hour or more before the service begins reading their Bibles, quietly chatting with friends, and checking out the most interesting looking members of the opposite sex who file into the chapel. Most of the midweek attenders appear to be in junior and senior high. There is a sprinkling of straight adults in the audience.

The young people are attired in the garb of middle-class California casual types: long dresses, levis, football jerseys, T shirts (some with "One Way" inscribed on the back), patched blue jeans, and hot pants. Nearly all carry a Bible. The format of the service varies little from night to night, and the music is a combination of old-time choruses and the new hip evangelical sound. The entire youthful congregation joins in singing "Pass It On" or a similar song that often includes swaying with the music, arms interlocked. Individual soloists perform, accompanied by a guitar, and share music received "from the Spirit." Some of the musical groups—like Country Faith and Blessed Hope—are somewhat more enthusiastically received and enliven the tempo of the evening. As each song ends, members of the audience point their forefinger heavenward in the Christian sign meaning that there is only one way and it is through Jesus Christ. After approximately two hours of music and testimony, the Bible study begins. In another forty-five minutes or so the meeting is dismissed, and the young people go to their Orange County homes—or to Christian communes.

These youth meetings combine 1950-vintage Youth for Christ rallies with 1970 rock festivals.

Few persons had as good a front row seat to see the developments at Calvary Chapel than Chuck Fromm, the first executive of Maranatha! Music and Pastor Chuck Smith's nephew. In his later academic writing, Fromm pulled from his first-hand knowledge and access to early participants in his reflection on how the popular music of the hippies became staples in the congregation's communal homes, concerts, and Bible Studies. Note how Fromm sees a distinction between simply "mimicking songs from the culture" and allowing one's personal engagement with God to find voice in the music of that generation.

Source: Charles E. Fromm, "Textual Communities and New Song in the Multimedia Age: The Routinization of Charisma in the Jesus Movement" (PhD dissertation, Fuller Theological Seminary, 2006), 176, fn. 7.

For some the singing of Jesus lyrics to secular jingles was not acceptable. A value emerged at The House of Miracles[4] that creating music out of your own experience with God, rather than simply mimicking songs from the culture was seen as a more authentic expression of one's faith. . . . This was a pivotal value, fueling the velocity of new songs. . . . John Higgins related the following in an interview in 2000: "People were taking the songs like 'We're the Pepsi Generation coming at you' . . . putting Jesus words to it: 'We're the Jesus Generation coming at you.' . . . It was getting kind of offensive to a bunch of us. And we were saying . . . if these other guys wrote these songs, like 'Great is Thy Faithfulness' and 'Amazing Grace' . . . all the old hymns, we knew that they had an experience with Christ and out of that experience came this music. . . . We banned the singing of the songs like 'It's a Small World.' We said 'no singing that stuff, let's not do that. Let's work hard, let's let our lives express Christ and let's write songs that come from our life and our experience rather than copying the world.' . . . They were songs that were written from the heart."

Although John Wimber was not the originator of the Vineyard Fellowships (that honor belongs to Kenn Gulliksen), he became its leader early in the 1980s and helped to grow the Vineyard movement into prominence until his death in 1997. Having started his career as a professional musician, Wimber was well-versed in popular music styles and incorporated them freely into worship. For Wimber, this was strategic in helping churches reach younger generations. (Notice the influence of generational thinking that may have been directly influenced by the church growth and youth evangelism proponents of the prior generation.[5])

---

4. The House of Miracles was a collection of Christian communes that organically took shape under the leadership of Lonnie Frisbee (a key leader in the Jesus People) and Chuck Smith.

5. Wimber was also a student of, and collaborator with, C. Peter Wagner, an important popularizer of church growth methods. For more on this history, see Glenn Stallsmith, "The

Source: John Wimber, "Zip to 3,000 in 5 Years," *Christian Life* 44, no. 6 (October 1982), 22.

Today in America, 78 million people are packed between the baby boom ages of 17 and 35. An additional 54 million are under the age of 17. These 132 million people will determine the future of the American church in the '80s and '90s.

When our church began, the average age was about 19. Today, it is up to about 21. We are a young church.

For the most part, the organized church in America is not relating to the younger generation.

The pre-war generation is beginning to pass from the evangelical church scene without replacing itself. Few churches are effectively reaching the young—those who do not feel comfortable with the lifestyle, music or jargon of establishment Christianity. We are reaching them. As a young church, we experience all of the opportunities and problems which accompany youth. Our young 18- to 25-year-old attenders are providing the spiritual dynamic which enables us to reach out to a young culture and relate the Gospel to them.

Because we are young, we are current. We speak the language of these people. Our sermons and songs are familiar and acceptable. We find ourselves communicating eternal truths in a contemporary style. We recognize we must answer the questions people actually are asking.

Within a short time, both the Calvary Chapel and Vineyard networks were developing resources to help other churches utilize band-based forms of worship and thus appeal to the youth. In the 1980s and 1990s, the publishing houses of these two networks were prominent in the promotion of, and training for, worship bands. Below is an announcement for a new resource from Maranatha! Music, the publishing outlet of Calvary Chapel, that offered resources for both training and congregational use. The transparencies and music books were offered alongside cassette or compact disc recordings.

Path to a Second Service: Mainline Decline, Church Growth, and Apostolic Leadership," in *Essays on the History of Contemporary Praise and Worship*, ed. Lester Ruth (Eugene, OR: Pickwick Press, 2020), 55–73.

Source: "The Praise Band," *Worship Times* (July/August 1989): 2.

In churches all across America, praise bands are earning an important role in leading congregations into worship. Their musical approach tends to be enthusiastic and simple; usually with guitars, piano, drums, and a small vocal ensemble leading the way. Maranatha! Music brings this new dimension of worship music to you with **THE PRAISE BAND**.

THE PRAISE BAND is a new approach to worship music, designed to appeal to teens and young adults. The arrangements are fresh and the music is filled with energy in an acoustic up-tempo style. **THE PRAISE BAND** is certain to play a major role in your music department, and in the church at large as you use them as a worship leading tool for your Sunday congregation, mid-week groups or youth meetings, or a stand-alone piece for your choir.

The music book includes all the vocal arrangements as well as cut-out pages with words and chord symbols for your instrumentalists. Also available is a set of transparency masters of all songs for overhead projection.

By the 1990s Calvary Chapels and Vineyards had become the subject of scholarly investigation. In the following passage based on interviews with people from these churches, a sociologist describes the importance, differences, and tensions found in their music. From their beginnings in the 1970s, both churches were major sources for contemporary worship music. Miller also captures the logic that new songs are required for keeping the "music fresh and distinctive" —that is, keeping up with culture.

Source: Donald E. Miller, *Reinventing American Protestantism: Christianity in the New Millennium* (Berkeley: University of California Press, 1997), 83–85.

According to Chuck Fromm, who was involved with Maranatha Music from its early days, the most powerful and enduring songs were written by nonprofessionals from the depths of their own experience. They were truckers, former strippers, and housewives who wanted to share their love of God and wrote songs such as "Father I Adore You," "Seek Ye First," and "Glorify Thy Name."

As we interviewed worship leaders at Calvary, Vineyard, and Hope[6]

---

6. Hope Chapels are another California-derived "New Paradigm" church but without the numbers and public prominence of the other two.

churches, it became evident that they knew each other's music and often typecast it in similar ways. Vineyard music, for example, is viewed as intimate and worship-oriented; Calvary music is identified as more upbeat and praise-oriented. Within a given church, there are typically also identifiable styles that reflect the various worship bands. . . . And sometimes the same music is played differently depending on the region of the country. For example, a worship leader from a Vineyard in Chicago told us that southern California Vineyard music is just too mellow for their taste, so they arrange it with a stronger beat and a more urban, "bluesy" flavor.

What is distinctive, however, is that these groups are constantly writing new music. Most of the music played on a Sunday is probably no more than three or four years old. Obviously this constant innovation keeps the music fresh and distinctive. . . .

Some new paradigm pastors are beginning to worry that their music has lost its contemporary edge. Christian bands are focusing too much on the Christian marketplace and are not connecting with youth who are nonbelievers. Within three decades Christian music has already become routinized, reaching an audience mainly of fellow Christians.

Playing the Organ under the Anointing: Pentecostals Gradually Acclimate to Popular Music

While new styles of music were gaining momentum among evangelicals and Mainline churches in the latter half of the twentieth century, Pentecostals—particularly in the Praise and Worship movement arising out of the Latter Rain revival—were generally slower to adapt. Though they shared the early Pentecostal emphasis on jubilant, expressive worship and embraced a variety of instruments, they also remained deeply wary of popular music, often due to the perceived demonic associations in rock music that came from the influence of fundamentalist postures toward culture.[7] Thus, even as the Praise and Worship movement was becoming increasingly influential, it remained stylistically conservative. Organ, orchestra, and choir remained common musical features for some time.

---

7. See also Anna Nekola, "'More than Just a Music': Conservative Christian Anti-Rock Discourse and the U.S. Culture Wars," *Popular Music* 32, no.3 (2013): 407–26.

Typical Pentecostal ways of envisioning congregational music could surprise you. A combined emphasis on ecstatic, Spirit-led improvisation alongside traditional instrumentation was not uncommon (nor the addition of bass guitar and drums to that ensemble). Baker, a prominent Pentecostal pastor and conference speaker, provides here one example of traditional anthems, organs, and orchestras all sounding together under the leadership of the Holy Spirit.

Source: E. Charlotte Baker, *On Eagles Wings: A Book on Praise and Worship* (1979; Shippensburg, PA: Destiny Image, 1990), 92.

Psalms 149 and 150 specify that the children of Israel used many instruments in worship: timbrels, harps, psalteries, stringed instruments, organs and cymbals. Today there are those who would remove from the Church the playing of instruments, but this is far from scriptural. As the Church increases in glory, there will be more singing and more instrumental music than ever before. There will not be the element of entertainment through natural talent, for there is a higher purpose in music and song than mere entertainment. Music is a vehicle through which God will express Himself to the Church, and through which the Church will express herself to God and to His people. The music of the last-day Church will ascend as a cloud of worship and blend with everything God is doing in the worship service. It is a wonderful blessing to find a pianist or organist who will abandon his or her talent unto God, and play anthems of praise under the anointing, while the congregation listens in quiet worship. There have been occasions when a pianist or organist has led an anthem of worship; as the playing progressed every instrument began to play under the same anointing, not following a musical score but playing spontaneously and forming an anthem of orchestral praise unto the Lord. With such worship heaven must be filled!

Following the broader traditions of Pentecostal and African American church music, this source demonstrates that a primary concern was for music to be joyful and loud in its praise of God. For Garlington, an African American pastor, praise in the temple/tabernacle of David and Solomon for which he was advocating cut a stark contrast to the "traditional" worship of other unnamed liturgical traditions that are marked by quiet reverence.

Source: Joseph L. Garlington, *Worship: The Pattern of Things in Heaven* (Shippensburg: Destiny Image Publishers, 1997), 26–28.

If the experiences of King David and King Solomon are any guide, God likes exuberant and elaborate praise with lots of dancing and excitement, and enough instruments to reach every eardrum for miles! . . . When King Solomon dedicated the temple at Jerusalem, the music team and singers included 120 trumpets blowing at the top of their lungs; an untold number of musicians playing cymbals, harps, lyres, and new musical instruments specially created by King David for the worship of God; and several generations of Levitical singers from three priestly families. . . .

Although the Bible is filled with rich references to exuberant praise and worship in prostration before God, countless modern church services are begun with the dry recitation of one Scripture verse: "But the Lord is in His holy temple. Let all the earth be silent before Him."

Somehow, this isolated verse has been elevated to the level of a church doctrine or ordinance of operation. The truth is that this verse is almost always quoted with no reference to context. . . .

Habakkuk is telling us to get silent for a moment so we can focus on the One we are going to worship. He also is making a point of saying that we need to be silent at times because, unlike the mute and man-made gods of wood and stone, this God is alive and at home. He speaks to His people! Once we have fixed our focus on Him, we are to worship Him with all of our might and strength!

Continuing the distinction we noted in chapter 1, white Pentecostals had long embraced diverse instrumentation even as they remained hesitant about popular musical genres. In the 1980s, Praise and Worship Pentecostals were continuing to negotiate this tension. The excerpt below is from a famous Pentecostal pastor whose ministry in New York during the 1960s was immortalized in the book The Cross and the Switchblade *(which was also developed into a movie). In this book, Wilkerson foretold a coming divine judgement against America and against the church for its manifold sins. Among these, Wilkerson highlights the use of popular music styles in Christian worship. Because, for Wilkerson, these musical styles have satanic origins, their use in the worship of God is akin to the strange fire that the sons of Aaron offered in Leviticus 10:1-3.*[8]

Source: David Wilkerson, *Set the Trumpet to Thy Mouth* (Lindale, TX: World Challenge, 1985), 86–87.

The ungodly music creeping into God's house today has to be the wonder of heaven, the disbelief of all that is celestial, the grief of the four and twenty elders around God's holy throne. The question in glory has to be, how can those who call themselves by Christ's holy name take coals off Satan's personal altars and bring them into God's presence, to lay them on His altar? The angels must be asking, "Are they so blind? Don't they know they are offering strange fire with strange coals? There is hellfire in each coal! There is damnation in it! Priests of God have been killed for such abomination! Don't they know God will destroy those who enter the holy place with strange fire? How can this be?" "But they set their abominations in the temple, which is called by my name, to defile it" (Jeremiah 32:34).

The following source from notable Assemblies of God minister Jimmy Swaggart, himself a gospel musician, renders a similar verdict to Wilkerson on the evil influence of rock and roll music in the church. Despite recording several music albums that might potentially fall foul of his own teaching,[9] *Swaggart here denounces the common argument that had been made across evangelicalism that popular musical styles are necessary for evangelism.*[10] *(It is helpful to note that while some evangelicals were also concerned about the spiritual influence of certain popular music styles,*[11] *this concern for the spiritual influ-*

---

8. In another contemporaneous source, another Pentecostal preacher likened the new worship music to a new cart of the Philistines that David tried to transport the ark of the Lord on (1 Chronicles 13). Kevin J Conner, *The Tabernacle of David, Revised and Expanded* (Portland, OR.: City Bible Publishing, 1986), 214–18. Both biblical images speak of God's coming wrath against the church for its profane worship.

9. For more see John J. Thompson, *Raised by Wolves: The Story of Christian Rock & Roll* (Toronto: ECW Press, 2000), 31.

10. On the question of Christian rock music and the way it seems to have eclipsed the power of preaching in American Christianity, see William D. Romanowski, "Roll Over Beethoven, Tell Martin Luther the News: American Evangelicals and Rock Music," *Journal of American Culture* 15, no. 3 (1992): 79–88.

11. For example, figures like Bill Gothard who led the Institute in Basic Life Principles famously denounced the influence of rock music. For example, Institute in Basic Life Principles

ence of rock music was most prominent among Pentecostal and charismatic churches.) Here, Swaggart argues that evangelism through music is not only an unbiblical pattern, but it is also one that does not work!

Source: Jimmy Swaggart and Robert Paul Lamb, *Religious Rock 'n' Roll: A Wolf in Sheep's Clothing* (Baton Rouge: Jimmy Swaggart Ministries, 1987), 45–47.

The heart of the matter as it relates to religious rock is that people have brought a musical form, birthed in the seething cauldron of rebellion, into the church and attempted to identify it as a tool of evangelism.

Music is not for evangelism.

There is no biblical case for music to be used for evangelism as some proponents of religious rock would suggest. In fact, there is not one scriptural reference in the Bible tying music and evangelism together.

Music in the Bible in every instance is either used in praise and worship to God or to Satan. There appears to be no biblical ground for the use of music as a viable soul-winning technique. . . .

Evangelism, or soul winning, is always tied into the preaching of the Word. Although mentioned over 800 times in Scripture, music is never used as entertainment or an end within itself. The music medium can speak to us, soothe and challenge us, but it takes the preaching of the Gospel to transform a life. . . .

Ironically, most of the singers and musicians now playing religious rock were not won to Jesus Christ by the same tactics they now claim must be employed to reach young people. They weren't saved on a rock and roll gospel.

Yet virtually all these artists—some of which sport mohawk haircuts and wear chains and leather—insist that young people can be reached only through the medium of that culture, rock music.

Although many white Pentecostal denominations remained concerned about the influence of popular music, there was a marked softening through the 1980s. The new music being produced by groups like Maranatha! and Integrity's Hosanna! Music was growing in influence and attracted listeners, whether or not it was sanctioned. Increasingly, leaders recognized the power of music as

---

Advanced Training Institute International, *How to Conquer the Addiction of Rock Music: Written by Youth Who Have Found Freedom* (Oak Brook: Institute in Basic Life Principles, 1993).

a cultural form and were relieved that their youth were listening to Christian music.[12]

Source: Terry Raburn, "A Powerful Tool: Use It For God and the Gospel," *Advance* 26, no. 10 (October 1990), 9.

Music is one of the most loved and possibly least understood, of all the tools that touch the human mind and emotions. Beethoven is quoted as saying, "Music is the mediator between the life of the senses and the life of the spirit."

. . . It is important to remember music is not an event, person, or location. It is simply the tool used to imprint the happening onto the sense of the observer. Satan knows the power of this tool, and he uses it in the process of temptation. He has perverted music to become a companion of those who celebrate in darkness and places where sin is rampant.

But God also knows the power of music! That's why praise and worship are so powerful, church choirs so beautiful, and sacred music so meaningful. . . .

According to the latest survey of our youth, average Assemblies of God teenagers spend 10 to 15 hours every week listening to music. They dislike heavy metal, hard rock, country, or easy listening music. They like contemporary Christian music. They want their music to have a beat and high energy levels, but they want the lyrics to be about Jesus! In other words, our young people are imprinting their teenage memories inside a framework of Christian music. That's great!

Appealing to the Target Market: Popular Music in the Church Growth Movement

While the Jesus People movement was beginning to emerge, the Church Growth movement of the 1970s was also starting to influence how evangelical and Mainline churches viewed the use of popular music

---

12. Leah Payne discusses the way contemporary Christian musics were used by parents to help shield their children from popular culture. See Leah Payne, *God Gave Rock and Roll to You: A History of Contemporary Christian Music* (Oxford University Press, 2024).

in worship (admittedly, the two are not entirely distinct). Many of the earlier sporadic experiments with popular music (described in chapter 1) were increasingly caught up into this movement. Originally, the Church Growth movement was a North American application of the missiological theory originated by missiologist Donald McGavran. While the movement did not initially connect evangelism with Sunday worship, by the early 1980s, its proponents were considering evangelism as the central goal of the church's worship services. Out of this emerged a consistent position about the church's music: churches need popular forms of music in order to grow. This idea came to exert influence upon a wide variety of churches—traditional, evangelical, Mainline,[13] and even some Pentecostal churches.

This passage comes from Donald McGavran, the founder of the Church Growth movement, and his former student, George Hunter, a United Methodist evangelism official. It is significant because it was one of the first times that Church Growth theorists mentioned worship. McGavran and Hunter note the problem of a gap between older forms of worship and contemporary people to argue for an openness to liturgical change for the sake of strategic evangelism to a "target subculture."

Source: Donald McGavran and George G. Hunter III, *Church Growth: Strategies That Work* (Nashville: Abingdon Press, 1980), 107–8.

As generation succeeds generation, most denominations settle into cultural forms of worship usually quite appropriate to the people they have become, a dignified procedure for the worship of God. Majestic worship, quiet reverent prayer, tuneful singing, impressive organ music, an aesthetic experience characterizes their worship. Since only a small part of the total community

---

13. On the negotiation of worship music styles in Mainline Protestant contexts, see Deborah R. Justice, "Public, Private; Contemporary, Traditional: Intersecting Dichotomies and Contested Agency in Mainline Protestant Worship Music," *Folklore Forum*, April 19, 2010, http://folkloreforum.net/2010/04/19/public-private-contemporary-traditional-intersecting-dichotomies-and-contested-agency-in-mainline-protestant-worship-music/; see also Justice's broader dissertation project: Deborah R. Justice, "Sonic Change, Social Change, Sacred Change: Music and the Reconfiguration of American Christianity" (PhD diss., Indiana University, 2012),

"fits" worship forms like this, mainline denominations slide into assuming that only those who like majestic worship and elevated sermons are eligible for evangelization by them. But is this conclusion one that you will stand by? Would the Galileans have liked your liturgical life-style? Would your sermons have communicated with multitudes of the working classes in the Britain of Bunyan, or Knox, or Wesley, or Marx?

To put the question in a different form, suppose you could win large numbers of the American proletariat to the New Life [of Christ] by evangelizing them in less elevated ways and engaging them in a liturgical style quite different from your present practice, ways that "fit" them culturally. Would you do it? Would you cease importing culturally foreign music and worship into settings where those forms are not natural? Worship must be expressed in the "heart language" of the target subculture if its members are really to see it, to appropriate it, and to be involved in it.

By the 1990s, the Church Growth movement was influencing many church leaders to become more attentive to the people that they wished to attract to worship. Such attentiveness often led to the conclusion that having an appealing, popular form of music was one of the most critical things. This approach was advocated by the Lutheran pastor in the following quotation. Notice how differences in approaches to church music were dismissed as matters of individual aesthetics or personal opinion rather than a substantive concern about worship.

Source: David S. Luecke, *The Other Story of Lutherans at Worship: Reclaiming Our Heritage of Diversity* (Tempe, AZ: Fellowship Ministries, 1995), 11, 98–100.

Contemporary music in the current worship movement represents *popular culture*, which is usually different from high culture. Music you hear on most-listened-to radio stations is popular culture. Looking at "the charts" to see which praise songs are most frequently used in churches reflects a popular culture perspective in churches. You determine which music people like most in worship and do more of it.

There is usually a tension between preferences for high culture and for popular culture. This tension is often at the heart of conflict over worship in Lutheran churches today. There may be attempts to cover it with theological dressing, but in most cases the tension is basically over issues of aesthetics. . . .

Church leaders intentionally pursuing church growth strategies look for user-friendly forms and music that can support the worship experience of people with little church experience. Popular contemporary Christian music thus becomes attractive. Traditionalists often don't like this approach—for reasons that usually stay at the level of feeling that "church shouldn't be done that way."

The rationale for leaning toward popular culture expressions of music in church seems clear to me. This is a natural development for a church with a high priority on outreach and evangelism. The rationale for high culture in churches has something to do with offering "the best." But defining "the best" leads into some complicated issues that often are left unexamined until questions of purpose for a church's worship are raised.

As with earlier experiments with youth-centered music, updating the church's worship could often be a fraught process. Pastors had to be careful in navigating their church through a season of worship transition that wrenched lay worshipers and professional musicians away from the forms of music that were well-loved. Yet, the author of the source acknowledges that new music led to growth and shows awareness of the power of strategic thinking about demographics.

Source: Carlyle Fielding Stewart, *African American Church Growth: 12 Principles of Prophetic Ministry* (Nashville: Abingdon Press, 1994), 59.

One preacher related the story of the trials he experienced in revitalizing worship services at his new charge. Tradition had entrenched itself and the choirs of the church sang only anthems. When the issue of gospel music was introduced, the members of the various choirs rejected the idea. Responses ranged from "We don't sing that kind of music here" to "Gospel music is too emotional." This minister happened to be serving a mainstream denominational black church in a predominantly black middle-income community. While the choirs prided themselves on singing anthems, which were good music, the pews on Sundays were only partially full because the music lacked inspiration....

To appeal to the younger segments of the community in which it was located, the church had to develop a worship format that included more inspirational, spiritual, and gospel music. After adding a good inspirational gospel choir, worship attendance began to increase. Now the church is full on Sundays.

In the 1990s, Mainline denominations started to prepare resources for congregations to implement contemporary worship. The first for United Methodists was written by two pastors in suburban Minneapolis, Minnesota. Following similar logic to that which inspired their evangelical peers at Willow Creek and Saddleback Church, these authors encouraged pastors starting a contemporary service to develop a clear idea of their "target population or market." This would enable them to adapt the dynamics of their worship accordingly. This kind of literature assumed that people were more likely to attend a church if they did not have to cross any cultural barriers, a clear influence from earlier strategic missiological thinking. Lyle Schaller, mentioned in the quotation, was a popular and influential church leadership consultant at the time (so popular by 1989 that he was voted the most influential Protestant church leader—even above Billy Graham!). Note, too, the emphases on presentation quality and bodily engagement.

Source: Cathy Townley and Mike Graham, *Come Celebrate!: A Guide for Planning Contemporary Worship* (Nashville: Abingdon Press, 1995), 28–29.

As you go through the visioning process for your worship, you will need to consider who will be the beneficiaries of your alternative worship service. We hope, in fact that the idea of ministering to a specific constituency was the main force behind your idea to start contemporary worship. . . .

Concerning an alternative worship style, then, we must ask, "Who is it for?" In other words, who is the customer or the target audience for this ministry? The customers exist within and outside your church, but probably share some characteristics. . . . Lyle Schaller comments that the generation born between 1955 and 1968 is coming back to church in large numbers, and settling in congregations that (1) place a premium on quality in everything, (2) offer a variety of choices to people, (3) provide a strong and meaningful teaching ministry to adults, (4) find a place for contemporary music and drama in the worship, (5) challenge people by setting high expectations, and (6) are open to creativity and innovation. Schaller goes on to say that motion and emotion in worship are replacing passivity and presentation.

Churches that offer contemporary worship provide a choice for these generations which approach church as consumers. [. . .] Again, it all comes down to listening to the needs of your "customers."

———— *Popular: Using Contemporary Music in Worship, Part 2* ————

As a sign of the groundswell of changes taking place in Mainline churches, the United Methodist denominational magazine, Circuit Rider, *devoted a whole issue to recent congregational experiments with contemporary forms of worship. The longest description—which you will read here—was of the new service at Lester Memorial United Methodist Church in northeast Alabama. This church was one of the first churches in the area to adopt a contemporary service. The article's author argues that the primary objective of this service was to reach new people—especially the boomer and buster generations. Their use of new forms of music did not emphasize sophistication or professionalization but congregational participation and worship that was appealing to all ages.*

Source: "The Pastor Wears Tennis Shoes," *Circuit Rider* 18, no. 10 (December 1994/January 1995): 14.

In Oneonta, Alabama, the local newspaper offers its readers lots of choices—which movies to see, which bargain to hunt—and which of two very different worship services to attend at Lester Memorial United Methodist Church.

At the 11 A.M. traditional service in the sanctuary, an excellent choir sings high quality anthems, usually with organ accompaniment. Everyone follows the order of worship in a bulletin and sings from the hymnal. . . . It is a very time-honored service with acts of praise, congregational prayer, and affirmations of faith. The people who choose this traditional worship service each Sunday are drawn closer to God through its richly textured liturgy and classic music.

Worshipers choosing the 8:30 a.m. contemporary service worship God in a different way. Formby (the pastor), dressed in jeans and tennis shoes, greets them in the Fellowship Hall. Almost all of the people are dressed casually. There is no choir. Individuals get up and lead the singing at microphones. An overhead projector shows the words of contemporary Christian music on the walls. A 10th grader plays the drums and an 11th grader plays bass guitar. No bulletins. No hymnal. No separate children's time is necessary because children love the whole service, sitting in the front row to clap and read the praise choruses. Their enthusiasm is contagious.

The prayers are spontaneous, and the pastor takes prayer requests. Some people move to the prayer bench at the front of the hall to pray with the pastor, while the congregation holds hands. "The whole service aimed much more at the heart than the head . . . ," says Gary Formby (the pastor). ". . . . Our goal was not to change worship. Our goal was to reach new people, and the new service has certainly done that! It also brought back inactive members. As expected, we have a lot of boomers and busters, but we were surprised that people of every age enjoyed coming. A number of our oldest members prefer coming to church early; some, I think, hear better in the Fellowship Hall with the microphones."

By the mid-1990s many Mainline and evangelical churches followed the advice of the Church Growth movement to add an additional contemporary option to their weekly service offerings. In the following passage, this Church Growth author describes numerous variables that pastors and musicians should consider when tailoring their music choices toward a target age group.

Source: Charles Arn, *How to Start a New Service: Your Church Can Reach New People* (Grand Rapids: Baker Books, 1997), 167–68.

Spiritual Variables
- The more unchurched your target audience, the more they will want to listen to the music. The more churched your target audience, the more they will want to participate in it.
- The more unchurched your target audience, the more the music style (rhythm, beat, instrumentation) should reflect their secular musical preference. The more churched your target audience, the more tolerant they will be of musical variety.

Generational Variables
- The older your target audience, the more important are the words. The younger your target audience, the more important is the rhythm.
- The older the generational group, the mellower the music should be. The younger the group, the harsher the music should be.
- The older the generational group, the longer the same song can be sung or played. The younger the group, the shorter the song should be.

Cultural Variables
- The stronger the cultural identity of your target audience, the more the music should be culturally appropriate. The weaker the cultural identity, the wider the tolerance of music styles.

- The stronger the cultural identity of your target audience, the greater their desire for participation in the music. The weaker the cultural identity, the less desire for participation.

Reaching Unchurched Harry and Mary: Megachurches Model the Use of Popular Music

It is one thing to hear someone advocate for the use of a popular style of music in worship and another to actually see it, especially when the new music is successfully attracting large numbers of people. In the late 1980s into the 1990s, key megachurches in the U.S. used conferences and media products to model popular music as one key to their numeric success. At the time, the most prominent of these churches was Willow Creek Community Church in the suburban Chicago area. Other notable examples included Saddleback Church in California, Community Church of Joy (Lutheran) in Arizona, and Ginghamsburg United Methodist Church in Ohio.[14]

In the 1990s, Willow Creek Community Church was perhaps the best-known and most influential megachurch in the United States. Its influence stemmed from its numerical growth and scale of operations as a result of its "seeker service" model. These services were aimed at "unchurched Harry and Mary," the imagined Chicago suburbanites that this congregation felt called to evangelize. In the following piece, Lee Strobel, one of the teaching pastors at Willow Creek, stressed the importance of using popular forms of music (i.e., the type of music that an unchurched person listens to).

Source: Lee Strobel, *Inside the Mind of Unchurched Harry & Mary: How to Reach Friends and Family Who Avoid God and the Church* (Grand Rapids, MI: Zondervan, 1993), 180–81.

---

14. See also this broader evaluation of the suburban megachurch phenomenon in Justin Wilford, *Sacred Subdivisions: The Postsuburban Transformation of American Evangelicalism* (NYU Press, 2012).

Let's face it: Unchurched people don't spend their spare time listening to organ music, unless they've tuned in an oldies station and happen to hear the 1960s classic "96 Tears" by Question Mark and the Mysterians. Look at what sells in music stores—pop and rock are biggies; classical and gospel music have only modest market shares. And yet most churches highlight classical and organ music.

The reason, of course, is that Christians like that kind of music. Unchurched Harry and Mary, though, have their car radios tuned to more mainstream entertainment. But I can tell you from personal experience that when their favorite style of music is wed to Christian lyrics, the combination can have a strong impact on furthering their spiritual journey.

What we as Christians have to do is crack our society's cultural code. We need to determine what style of music appeals to the Unchurched Harrys and Marys whom we're trying to reach. Are they into rap, country, rock, pop, or jazz? It's easy to determine by checking the ratings and demographics of local radio stations. And once we do that, we can work on harnessing that mode of music for Christ.

In his Doctor of Ministry thesis, Rick Warren, pastor of the influential Saddleback Church in southern California, argued for the value of using rock-based music in order to reach unchurched Baby Boomers. Warren's thesis reads like an early draft of his best-selling book, The Purpose Driven Church *(Zondervan, 1995). In both, he moves between describing his own congregation and prescribing practices for others, revealing his strategic demographic thinking and appeals to basic pragmatism.*[15]

Source: Rick Warren, "New Churches for a New Generation: Church Planting to Reach Baby Boomers: A Case Study: The Saddleback Valley Community Church" (D.Min. thesis, Fuller Theological Seminary, 1993), 37–38, 280, 283, 285–86.

Over 80 million people in America were born between 1948 and 1968. This is the Baby Boom generation. Baby Boomers make up the largest single segment of our society. Baby Boomers also form the largest group in the Saddleback Valley [the location of Warren's church]. . . . [I]f you are going

---

15. Today's megachurches employ different approaches to music and worship while also engaging with the industry and media in novel ways. See Adam Perez et al., "'Do It Again': Chart-Topping Worship Songs and the Churches Behind Them," *Liturgy* 38, no. 4 (2023): 31–40, https://doi.org/10.1080/0458063X.2023.2259766.

to reach the unchurched Baby Boomers, you must use the kind of music that they understand and relate to. You can't use music that sounds like the fifteenth century or sixteenth century. That is just as foreign to their ears as if you used oriental music or delivered the sermon in Latin.

Sometimes I am asked, "Why doesn't your church ever use classical music?" I reply, "Because only 2% of all the albums sold in America are classical. I'm not interested in using a music style that appeals to only 2% of the population!"

When we first began worship services we tried to appeal to all the different kinds of musical tastes. We used everything from Bach to rock. We would mix and mingle several different styles of music in an effort to attract and please everyone. Frankly, it didn't work! Not many people would listen to a radio station that kept switching its format with every song. If a radio station tried to play jazz, rock, country and western, classical, and easy listening in the same hour it wouldn't have any audience left at the end of the hour!

In 1984, we took a survey of those who attended our church. We asked everyone to list the call letters of the radio station they listened to most often. Almost all our people were listening to contemporary stations. When we saw the results of that survey we quit trying to please everyone and changed exclusively to contemporary music. . . .

You will want to match your music to the people you want to reach. The main positioning tool in your church is music. More than anything else, your music determines who you will reach and who you will never reach. When I started Saddleback, I made two mistakes, the first of which was that I underestimated the power of music. Music has the power to make or break a service, the power to change lives, to bypass the intellect and go straight to the subconscious. Music has the power to shape character. Today rock music is universally accepted. For the first time in the history of the world, you can turn on a radio anywhere in the world and hear the same contemporary music, baby boomer music. If you want to reach baby boomers, that is anybody under 45, you must realize that they do not understand any music that was produced before 1960, much less in the sixteenth century. Your church music must have a beat. . . .

Speed up your church's music. Many churches sound like a funeral march when they drag the tempo. The whole world sings in 1/8 notes, and many churches still sing in 1/2 notes. Never make the mistake of singing a song in a minor key. Americans prefer bright, cheerful, happy music, so keep it positive and upbeat. In Psalm 95:1, the Bible encourages us to make a joyful noise unto the Lord and Psalm 115:17 says "Dead men do not praise God." Neither do dead churches praise God. . . .

We also decided to replace the organ with a band. How many people do you know who listen to organ music on the radio? I do not know of many churches in America reaching baby boomers that are using a pipe organ. With this suggestion, I once saved about a million dollars for one of the largest churches in America. The pastor and I were in a meeting together when he said his church was planning to buy a pipe organ. I said, "Don't do it! For a third of the price you can buy the best synthesizer system in the world, and it will produce every sound that a pipe organ will."

"Popular Music Styles Don't Usually Stay Popular for Long": The Continuing Search for New Music

Worship pragmatists inevitably discover that the search to find what "works" in worship is a never-ending one since cultures and their music continue to change and evolve. And so, lest the church become attached to stale, antiquated forms of music—which must have been fresh and attractive at one point in the past—there are those who continue to try new approaches to making music in worship.[16] The following are a sampling of viewpoints from those feeling a continual hunger to make a musical connection with people today.

The source below provides a rationale for the constant renewal and updating of Christian worship music. The authors rejected any argument that there was any one particular style that was good or hallowed in its own right. Instead, there was a foundational principle that Christian music needs to stay up to date to have impact. Jimmy and Carol Owens are longtime songwriters of Christian musicals and other projects for children and worship.

---

16. On the topic of music style and its significance in shaping culture and identity, see Monique M. Ingalls, "Style Matters: Contemporary Worship Music and the Meaning of Popular Musical Borrowings," *Liturgy* 32, no. 1 (2017): 7–15, https://doi.org/10.1080/0458063X.2016.1229435.

Source: Jimmy Owens and Carol Owens, *Words and Music: A Guide to Writing, Selecting, and Just Enjoying Christian Songs* (Waco, TX: Word Music, 1984), 114–15.

But here we come to the problem: while some musical styles are timeless (many of our great two hundred to four hundred fifty year old hymns, for example), other styles are not. Those nineteenth century gospel songs were deliberate attempts to communicate with a generation in the musical styles of their own day. And we all know that popular music styles don't usually stay popular for long. The church, on the other hand, has an unfortunate penchant for latching onto something that works for a time and trying to immortalize it. That's exactly what they did with these songs. It wasn't long before the popular song styles of the late eighteen hundreds had become "funny" and out of date, quaint reminders of a past era when people were strange and different from the moderns of the twentieth century.... Of course what the church failed to recognize was that it was not the songs that worked; it was the principle: using current popular song styles to speak to its generation. Had the illustrious fathers lived on, they no doubt would have continued to write new songs in the new styles, discarding the old when they became stale and ineffective....

There is also a certain brand of music from the gospel youth rally days of the 1940s, '50s and '60s that may be past due for retirement. These songs were once considered touching or inspiring, but many of them now range from faintly amusing to genuinely funny. They are almost totally foreign to the youth culture of today, Christian or otherwise, not in message but in style.

In the 1990s, Mainline churches started to experiment with incorporating different popular music artists with traditional liturgy. In a way, this was a continuation of the first wave of Mainline experiments with contemporary worship that drew on jazz and blues in the 1960s–1970s (see chapter 1). Although both forms of experimentation have sought to help the traditional liturgical text find new resonance through the use of contemporary popular music, the distinctives of recent experiments has been a much higher quantity of music (arguably, the service has become about the music) and a more singular focus on a specific secular artist. One of the earliest versions of these contemporary experiments was a Eucharistic service organized around the music of Duke Ellington's Sacred Concert that was performed in the early 1990s at

Durham Cathedral in the UK.[17] Better known were the later iterations of this same idea using the music of U2 or Beyonce. In the source below, the author described the process and the practical decisions that went into performing their first U2charist.[18]

Source: Paige Blair, "What Is a U2 Eucharist (or U2charist)?" at http://s3.amazonaws.com/dfc_attachments/public/documents/414/What_is_a_U2charist.pdf (accessed 11 June 2024).

The background in brief: my parishioners and I noticed that U2 was popping up in conversation at the church in many different settings—adult education classes, meetings, coffee hour—and we kept finding ourselves talking about how U2 had been important on our spiritual journeys. I had just read *Get Up Off Your Knees*, a collection of sermons based on U2 lyrics,[19] and floated the idea of a service in which all the music, from hymns to "service music" (like the *Gloria* or *Kyrie*) would be by U2, and a number of parishioners in different generations were really excited. So we built a team to design the liturgy and choose the music, and to ask questions like, How do we get the sound loud enough? and How do we play the music? a DJ? A CD? Powerpoint? We chose Powerpoint since we figured we'd want the lyrics visible and for people to be hands-free for dancing and clapping if possible. . . .

The first U2charist service here at St. George's was July 31, 2005, and it was a roaring success. Over 130 people came, many people from outside the church as well as regular members. Youth and young adults and even older adults singing and dancing in the aisles and praising God at the top of their voices to the song Yahweh, among others. . . .

The liturgy itself is pretty traditional—it has all the usual required elements: a Gospel reading, prayers, and communion from an authorized prayer book. The music is really what is different. And yet not so different. It is rock, but it is deeply and overtly spiritual.

---

17. For more details, see Bill Hall, "Jazz - Lewd or Ludens?" in *Creative Chords: Studies in Music, Theology and Christian Formation*, ed. Jeff Astley, Timothy Hone, and Mark Savage (Herefordshire: Gracewing, 2000): 194–209.

18. For a discussion of the U2charist, among other types of fusion approaches to worship styles, see Bryan D. Spinks, *The Worship Mall: Contemporary Responses to Contemporary Culture*, Alcuin Club Collections 85 (SPCK, Society for Promoting Christian Knowledge, 2010).

19. Raewynne J. Whiteley and Beth Maynard, eds., *Get Up Off Your Knees: Preaching the U2 Catalog* (Cambridge, MA: Cowley Publications, 2003).

The emerging church movement in the late 1990s–early 2000s was a reaction against many of the seeker-sensitive trends towards outreach and evangelism that had become prominent in the 1990s.[20] *The emerging church advocated for the broadening of church music into even more experimental and underground musical styles that infused popular music with other elements. Note that David Crowder, a well-known Christian musician who has experimented with creative styles, wrote the foreword to the book quoted below.*

Source: Dan Kimball, *Emerging Worship: Creating New Worship Gatherings for Emerging Generations* (Grand Rapids, MI: Zondervan, 2004), 83–84.

Musical worship styles are usually a reflection of a specific community. Most emerging worship gatherings are moving beyond Christian-pop and moving into a post-Matt Redman form of musical worship combining the ancient with pop rhythms, global music, and other forms of eclectic and ambient music. An emerging worship gathering in the city of Chicago fuses hip-hop with the ancient and with pop. An emerging worship gathering in Minnesota focuses primarily on songs the community writes and is more folk-sounding.

In Vintage Faith Church, we use an eclectic blend of the ancient with contemporary pop. We have even formed a choir to sing ancient choral songs and Taize-style chants fused with contemporary pop. . . .

Music is not categorized in emerging church worship since it is a reflection of the church community and not simply repeating whatever top ten worship songs are playing on Christian radio stations. DJs with turntables are sometimes used in the band adding layers of sound and rhythm to the worship music. Many times ambient music is played for reflection during worship. There is some global music influence and definitely an eclectic feel to the worship music during a gathering.

In the following source, one Vineyard worship leader notes the tension present in staying contemporary and relevant in the church's music while also staying connected to the church's historical forms of worship. The answer that this worship leader reaches is a blending of old content with contemporary styles,

---

20. For a broader history of the Emerging Church movement, see Phyllis Tickle, *Emergence Christianity: What It Is, Where It Is Going, and Why It Matters* (Grand Rapids: Baker Books, 2012); Randall Reed and G. Michael Zbaraschuk, eds., *The Emerging Church, Millennials, and Religion.* vol. 1: *Prospects and Problems* (Eugene: Cascade Books, 2018).

employing a well-trod distinction between the musical sounds and the lyrical content.

Source: Dan Wilt, *How to Lead Worship Without Being a Rock Star: An 8 Week Study* (Wild Pear Creative, 2013), 32–33.

We live in a time and in a place in history. We embrace, to one degree or another, the sounds and musical textures of today's music, choosing to be true to who God has made us to be, and true to the communities we are seeking to reach. For that reason our music is not dated in its sound (though in some settings this may be appropriate) but is current with the kinds of sounds today's listeners, and worshipers, love to hear. We use video and other forms of cultural communication to connect with our attendees and our neighborhoods. In considering the value of cultural connection as it relates to worship leading, we must hold some truths in tension. As a worship community we don't want to contrive our sound, making music we're not comfortable with, always trying to "keep up" with popular culture. At the same time, we hold this in tension with the reality that we want to avoid "churchy" or "Christian sub-culture" musical styles that seem disconnected from the daily musical experience of the average person on the street. What is the answer? We seek in our worship expressions to reflect the demographic of our local community (both inside the church and outside), and this means that we choose the music of today's culture with which to worship, integrated with the familiar music of the Church historic (i.e., hymns, etc.). The sound that results from this quest is usually very culturally current music, that sounds like the tunes one might hear on the radio on any given day—but with lyrics that focus us Godward.

An important emerging trend in recent discussions about Contemporary Praise & Worship music is its growing global diversity. The author highlights that this genre presents exciting opportunities to reflect the worldwide nature of today's church.

Source: Brian T. Russell, *The Complete Contemporary Worship Handbook: How to Build and Sustain Meaningful Worship in Modern Denominational Churches* (Austin: Langmarc Publishing, 2016), 37–38.

The center of gravity in Christianity is shifting from the North Atlantic world of Europe and North America to the Southern Hemisphere. In order to function as globally aware and welcoming members of the Christian faith, we should be proactive in incorporating cultural influence from our increasingly-less-foreign Christian family in Africa and Central and South America.

Contemporary worship music provides a terrific avenue for this initiative. With a more diverse portfolio of instrumentation, contemporary worship music can add instruments from different cultures more easily. Contemporary music, which is way more likely to use drums than traditional music, is a closer relative to the more rhythmic sounds from African and Latin churches.

With respect to forms of popular music in worship, how far can one go if they still perceive a gap between worship and contemporary people? One Minneapolis pastor who leads a church built on hip-hop argued that most churches, even though doing some form of "contemporary" music, have not gone far enough to bridge the gap to the current generation and to turn around the decline in church attendance.

Source: Stacey B. Jones, *(i)Pastor Hip-Hop: Bridging the Gap Between Hip-Hop and the Christian Faith Community* (One Communications LLC, 2020), 12–13.

There is no exclusive piece of work or a single answer as it relates to the decline of Christianity and church attendance in America and Western soil, but there are critical reasons that we as followers of Christ tend to neglect, overlook and refuse to take into consideration as we examine this rapid decline. One main reason that sounds absurd to many people is the Church's refusal to maintain a healthy and holistic engagement with Hip-Hop culture. I applaud the attempts over the recent years, however, our misguided sincerity at best has done nothing more than contribute to the colonization and exploitation of Hip-Hop.

To many people's surprise, Hip-Hop has crossed every social, economic, racial, and gender barrier. Furthermore, it has a major influence on young people. For some odd reason, major business industries such as the tobacco and alcohol industries do a better job than the Church at maintaining engagement in this area. They seem to understand the necessity of investing in young people for the sake of longevity. . . .

For some unusual reason (excuse the sarcasm) one would automatically assume the Church would see the need for engaging and providing an example of utilizing this sub-culture in healthy ways, without exploiting it. Yet, it is the exact opposite. Some churches will not utilize Hip-Hop, thinking that it's not necessary and believing Christian Contemporary Music and Black Gospel will appeal to the average Millennial and late Generation Xer. When adult church folk speak and use statements like, "Our young people are the Church of the future," it might speak to subconscious notions of youth being an afterthought today.

Discussion Questions

- Many of the voices within the "New Paradigm" churches were concerned that their worship should not be jargony or representative of establishment Christianity but instead, ought to be the fresh and authentic expressions of the contemporary church. Is there a connection between the style of our worship and the concept of authenticity? Do you perceive some styles of music to be more "worshipful" than others?

- What theological concerns shaped the Pentecostal (and sometimes evangelical) resistance to the adoption of popular music styles in worship? Is there any wisdom in their concerns that we should learn from today?

- Some of the sources that we have read in this chapter argued that churches should actively survey the musical tastes of their local communities to shape the kind of music they incorporate into worship. What are the strengths and limitations of using this kind of market research to guide Christian worship?

- Given that the last section of the chapter highlighted how the genre of popular music is an ever-moving target, how should today's worship leaders respond? Should we seek to stay relevant to cultural sounds? Is there something gained (or lost) in "bucking the trend" and seeking to be rooted in the musical and cultural styles of your tradition?

- How do your worshiping communities navigate their relationship with popular music? Do you see the influence of particular streams from this chapter in your church's worship?

CHAPTER 3
POWER: CREATING DIVINE ENCOUNTERS THROUGH MUSIC

Consider the testimony of this worshiper deeply moved by the music of his church as he prayed to God: I was "keenly affected by voices of your sweet-singing Church! Those voices flowed into my ears, and your truth was distilled into my heart, and from that truth holy emotions overflowed, and tears ran down, and amid those tears all was well with me." Where does this testimony come from? The Great Awakening in the eighteenth century? The Azusa Street Revival in the early twentieth century? Bethel music, 2020? No, no, and no. Instead, the quote comes from North Africa, ca. 400 AD.[1] This famous testimony comes from St. Augustine—perhaps the most influential theologian in the early church—as he reflected on his experience in becoming a Christian. What St. Augustine described sounds a lot like many of today's worshipers who expect to be moved by the power of music.[2]

This chapter presents two prominent ways that Christians have experienced music's power to move.

---

1. Augustine, *The Confessions of St. Augustine*, trans. John K. Ryan (Garden City, NY: Image Books, 1960), 9.6.14 (page 214).

2. For another example of a prominent leader in the church who extolled the power of music, see Martin Luther's "Preface to Georg Rhau's Symphoniae iucundae" in Martin Luther, *Luther's Works*, vol. 53, *Liturgy and Hymns*, ed. Ulrich S. Leopold (Philadelphia: Fortress Press, 1965), 321–24.

In part 1 of this chapter, you will encounter sources that reflect on music's ability to stir worshipers' hearts. Across the twentieth century, many Christians (representing a variety of traditions) have been highly aware of worship music's ability to kindle holy affection for God.[3] This view has not only been held among evangelicals and charismatics but has found acceptance among Mainline Protestant and Roman Catholic Christians as well.

In part 2 of this chapter, we survey the distinct theological stream that has emphasized music's power to make God present to worshipers. This stream finds its source in the Latter Rain revival of the mid-twentieth century and highlights the capacity of musical praise to create "the dwelling place" for the manifest presence of God. Some of the Pentecostal authors represented in part 1 may also ascribe to the theology of presence outlined in part 2. We should not assume that these two views of music's power are opposing theologies. Instead, they are often additive; music's power to move the emotions can also contribute to an experience of God's presence in worship.

Many worshipers today implicitly acknowledge that something powerful occurs during times of musical worship. The question of *what* and *why*, however, remains more elusive. In the Mississippi River that Contemporary Praise & Worship has become, these two streams flow together (see the introduction for a description on this river analogy). Many worshipers experience something of both movements, where music both moves worshipers' hearts and enables a special encounter with, or sense of, God's presence.

---

3. This feature in American Christianity goes back at least to the camp meetings of the early nineteenth century. See Wheeler's account of the music at those gatherings: Anne P. Wheeler, "The Music of the Early Nineteenth-Century Camp Meeting: Song in Service to Evangelistic Revival," *Methodist History* 48, no. 1 (2009): 23–43.

Part 1—The Power of Emotions: General Expectations about Music's Effect on the Human Heart

The past century has witnessed a growing, general awareness of music's capability to stir human hearts.[4] Part 1 of this chapter offers a broad cross-section of the voices that have sought to put language to the work that music does. Reflections on the power of music have often been accompanied by an effort to harness that power towards some particular end. The sources in this section offer multiple practical outworkings of music's power. Some have been interested in music's evangelistic possibilities. Others have thought more broadly about individual and corporate Christian renewal. Some voices you will encounter have argued that music helps Christians to learn doctrine. Finally, others have reflected on how the right music can predispose the heart to a spiritual connection with God.[5]

In the nineteenth century, evangelistic ministries contributed in a significant way to the heightened role of musicians in Christian ministry. Revival musicians and composers like Ira D. Sankey became influential through their collaborations with traveling evangelists (see chapter 4). In this introduction to a collection of evangelistic songs, George F. Pentecost, a contemporary of the great evangelist D. L. Moody, reflects on the power of song for the conversion of souls. Where words and prayer alone had failed, song was the key that could unlock the seeker's heart to receiving Christ.

Source: George F. Pentecost, introduction to *Song Victories of "The Bliss and Sankey Hymns," Being a Collection of One Hundred Incidents in Regard to*

---

4. For a broader approach to music's power to shape emotion and identity in a contemporary worship context, see Nathan Myrick, "Relational Power, Music, and Identity: The Emotional Efficacy of Congregational Song," *Yale Journal of Music & Religion* 3, no. 1 (2017), https://doi.org/10.17132/2377-231X.1060.

5. This has been explored in Sarah Koenig, "'This Is My Daily Bread': Toward a Sacramental Theology of Evangelical Praise and Worship," *Worship* 82, no. 2 (2008): 141–61.

the Origin and Power of the Hymns Contained in "Gospel Hymns and Sacred Songs" (Dover, NH: D. Lothrop and Co., 1877), 17–18.

I said above that I have known a hymn to be used of God for the conversion of a soul where every other means had failed to bring light into the darkened and troubled heart. Once I was detained after prayer meeting with a few others, to converse and pray with a young woman who was under deep conviction, and who refused to go away from the place of prayer until she had found Jesus. It seemed to be all in vain that I talked with her, explaining the atonement, quoting the simplest and strongest promises of the gospel, and urging her to an immediate and simple faith; it was all in vain that I prayed with and for her. At last, because—as it seemed—I could do nothing else, I began to sing that little hymn, the last verse of which goes,—

> "Oh! bear my longing heart to Him
> Who bled and died for me
> Whose blood now cleanses from all sin,
> And gives me victory."

We had sung the whole hymn through, and were hushed into silence by the Spirit. During the singing of the last stanza, our friend had lifted her weeping face toward mine, and was looking intently and eagerly at me, as though she would fain drink in the words and power of the song. And now in the hush that was upon us, reaching out both her hands to me, she said, in a plaintive kind of whisper,—

> "Please sing that last verse again."

And again we sang, softly and tenderly,—

> "Oh! bear my longing heart to Him
> Who bled and died for me
> Whose blood now cleanses from all sin,
> And gives me victory."

As the words and melody died away, the expression of her face changed; the darkness was overpast, and the light and gladness of His peace had come in the place of it; and with a cry of joy she turned and flung herself into the arms of her sister, who was standing near, exclaiming, "I am saved! I am saved!! Oh! blessed Jesus," &c.

Incidents of this kind might be multiplied, but this one may suffice to illustrate the power of song in the conversion of souls to God.

This next source expresses a similar recognition of the evangelistic power of music that figures like Moody and Sankey were starting to realize. In this hymnal, Baptists were working to incorporate a wide variety of musical styles—most notably, the music of African American spirituals—with the expectation that these songs have the power to work upon the hearts of hearers to experience the gospel.

> **Source:** Music Committee of the Sunday School Publishing Board, *Gospel Pearls* (Nashville: Sunday School Publishing Board [of the] National Baptist Convention, U.S.A., 1921), preface (no page number).
>
> "Gospel Pearls" [the name of the hymnal] contains more than half an hundred familiar hymns and tunes that cling so closely to the heart, that try as you may, you cannot get away from them; then comes a collection of the standard old songs, gathered with great care and especially adapted for soul-winning, as well as the very latest and popular works of the very best composers of sacred song, and a collection of Jubilee songs known as Spirituals—the rarest and prime favorites. . . . These songs may be used in every phase of public worship and will prove to be of untold value in Revivals and Evangelistic Services. They are tried and true . . . it is a tribute to Christ we bring and it is our fondest hope that "Gospel Pearls" may enjoy the widest possible circulation and use, inspire the believer, convict the sinner, and cheer many a weary traveler.

Often, theological reflection on the power of music has struggled to articulate why music has the effect that it does. This source—an excerpt from an early Pentecostal magazine—reflects this difficulty. Although the author notes that music's power is felt in many places in normal human existence, ultimately, he describes its power as having a magical quality to it. Music is nothing less than a living character that speaks its own language that the heart understands.

> **Source:** R. H. Morrison, "The Foursquare Conservatory of Music," *Foursquare Crusader* (February 6, 1929), 12.
>
> Music has many magic powers. The majestic march of the band stirs the soul's direction. Armies have conquered, battles have been won because the soul of the soldier was aroused. Music also calls the soul to sobriety and restraint. The soft appealing tones of the flutes, the bells of the organ at

eventide call to quietude, repose and meditation. All the arts of the age put together cannot compete with music. It lives, it speaks! It is a language ever appealing to the senses of love, joy, sorrow, loyalty-creating new ideals and inspirations.

The compiler of an early twentieth-century hymnal targeting youth (see chapter 1) reflects on how music arouses the emotions in worship. For this author, not only does music draw the worshiper into the spiritual experience of worship, but it orients them toward a "higher" experience: that of carrying out God's mission in the world.

Source: H. Augustine Smith, *The New Hymnal for American Youth* (New York and London: The Century Company, 1930).

There will probably never be a time when music will not be a vital part of the acts of worship. The functions of worship includes the working of those mysterious elements of human feeling which may not be accurately measured or controlled, but which must nevertheless be recognized, and used if possible, in the development of the finest and best that worship can give. The emotional element in worship, properly aroused, leads to the higher and fine form of religious experience which may be called fruition. Worship merely as contemplation would never lead out of itself. Music affords a universal means of expression, either actually, or vicariously, and its use guarantees to religion of the greatest ministries, leading out of self to the great world where love and service unite for the building of the Kingdom of God.

Another mid-century voice—one from the Seventh-day Adventists—testifies to the power of music for religious revival. Citing Martin Luther and Charles Wesley, this source argues that music carries the work of spiritual awakening alongside, and perhaps more effectively than, the preaching of the Word alone.

Source: J. Harker, "Music of the Message: Music in Present-Day Evangelism," *The Ministry* 12, no. 9 (September 1939): 13.

Next to the preaching of the word of God's appointed messengers, there is no greater or more potent agency for reaching the hearts of men with the gospel than the simple singing of sacred songs. The power of music was well understood by the Reformers, especially Luther. He not only gave the people the Bible in their own tongue, but he also gave them a hymnbook. He built up a new style of congregational singing such as would enable them to express in song their newly found faith. In this work he did not hesitate to use many of the popular tunes of his time. It is said that the Reformation produced no fewer than one hundred thousand hymns in Germany alone.

Later on, about the middle of the eighteenth century, Methodism began its great work in this country. Here again, the Wesleys saw the great value attached to hymn singing. Within half a century, the "King of Hymn Writers," as Charles Wesley has been styled, is said to have provided approximately five thousand hymns—a collection that covered the entire range of Scripture.

In both of these periods of spiritual awakening, it is asserted that *the singing of hymns* did more to spread the revival spirit and indoctrinate the people than the preaching of the Word. We must use our judgment as to how this is to be interpreted, but the fact remains that the tremendous volume of exultant song which characterized these two movements, carried the work of God forward as on wings.

In this source, three highly successful Contemporary Praise & Worship songwriters describe the art of how to write and compose songs for Christian worship. The quotation provided below comes from near the beginning of the book as the authors seek to establish the foundational rules of good songwriting. Notice that not only do they assume that a song will have the ability to impact emotions. They go so far as to argue it is core to the very meaning of songs. Good songwriting should aim to impact the emotions by uniting the tone of the music to the message of the words.[6]

Source: Paul Baloche, Jimmy & Carol Owens, *God Songs: How to Write and Select Songs for Worship* (Lindale, TX: Leadworship.com, 2004), 43–44.

First let's consider what makes a successful song of any kind. Then we'll examine those specific things a good worship song needs to accomplish its purpose.

This brings us to what we call the Cardinal Rule of Songwriting. Well—it's not really a rule. Nothing we say here is a rule. But frankly, any song that

---

6. This source re-expresses a similar cardinal rule of songwriting that Jimmy and Carol Owens had established twenty years earlier in Jimmy Owens and Carol Owens, *Words and Music: A Guide to Writing, Selecting, and Just Enjoying Christian Songs* (Waco, TX: Word Music, 1984), 29.

doesn't follow it doesn't do a very good job of communicating its message and probably won't get far. It's so important that it needs a billboard, or at least a panel of its own:

Make all the elements work together to enhance the *feeling* of the message.

Songwriting is an emotional medium, a vehicle for the expression of feelings. Think about it. If your message consists only of a series of facts and makes no emotional impact, you would do better to present it not as a song but as a list or paragraph. Try to match the mood of the music to the meaning of the message, so the listener can feel it. This way, the song becomes more than the mere transfer of data—it becomes an experience. Emotion is the soul of a song. That's why computers can't write songs. Even if they can be programmed to think, they still can't feel.

This source provides a firsthand account of the kind of divine encounter that worshipers have often testified to. As this author—a charismatic vicar in the Church of England—notes, something mysterious about the combination of the words and the music in the context of worship gave him a vivid and deeply personal experience of the love of God.[7]

Source: Mark W. G. Stibbe, *From Orphans to Heirs: Celebrating Our Spiritual Adoption* (Oxford: Bible Reading Fellowship, 1999), 84–85.

The biggest breakthrough came when I took my youth group to a rally in Derby in about 1987.... My motive for taking them to the rally was to expose them to large numbers of teenagers who were enthusiastic about God and expressing that enthusiasm in heartfelt adoration.

In the event it was me rather than them that was touched and changed. I remember very vividly standing up with my youth group as the first song struck up....

There was something not only in the melody but also in the words that moved me at first. Having been abandoned as a baby at birth, I have always been particularly sensitive about being alone. The thought of the Father being always with us was hugely encouraging and heartwarming. But what

---

7. In his ethnography of a Latino Pentecostal congregation, Ricardo Alviso describes a similar understanding of the way music is used not to just connect spiritually with God, but to allow worshipers to give themselves fully to God and make the Spirit present. Ricardo Alviso, "Feel the Power: Music in a Spanish-Language Pentecostal Church," *Pacific Review of Ethnomusicology* 10 (Fall/Spring 2001–2002): 62–79.

struck me most was the statement about being "adopted" in God's family. I had never before sung a hymn or a song in which that word had appeared. As I sang out my praises to the Father for adopting me and making me his son, something was released inside me. I felt my knees turning to jelly and I sank to the ground in front of my rebellious youth group. I was in floods of tears and I couldn't do anything about it. Nor did I want to do anything about it. I knew what was happening to me was the work of the Holy Spirit and that it was about the healing of lifelong wounds.

Pentecostal pastor Jack Hayford's teaching represented an important development in the Pentecostal teaching on the presence of God in musical worship. Hayford did not necessarily follow the earlier Latter Rain teaching (described in part 2 below) that viewed musical praise as the instrumental cause of God's presence in the church. Instead, Hayford emphasized that God was enthroned by the church's praise. This is a subtle distinction but an important one. For Hayford, musical praise did not cause God's presenc,e but neither was it unconnected. In this source, Hayford describes how the power of God's presence and activity could be experienced within times of musical worship.

Source: Jack W. Hayford, *Explaining Worship* (Tonbridge, England: Sovereign World Ltd, 2000), 37–38.

The Bible tells us that singing brings forth life, overcomes obstacles, releases victory and is creative in its impact.

In Isaiah 54:1, song is linked with the birthing of new life. . . . What do you want to see brought forth in your life? Sing about it to the Lord. Let the creativity of His vital power surge through you, and His Spirit fill you to overflowing.

Singing breaks down walls and opens doors. Paul and Silas were chained in a prison cell in Philippi, but when they sang praises the Lord brought release. . . .

People who sing in the midst of bondage can find that deliverance comes through the power of a song. Psalm 32:7 says, "You are my hiding place; You will protect me from trouble and surround me with songs of deliverance." God hides us and preserves us from trouble by encircling us with songs of deliverance!

Singing is a way to gain victory, even when we face tremendous opposition. Second Chronicles 20 tells us how King Jehoshaphat and the nation of Israel, though greatly outnumbered by their enemy, went out to battle with the choir leading them. Their song of victory brought confusion to their adversaries, so the enemy was confounded and actually turned on each other. . . .

Song is creative. In Job 38:4-7 we are told that the original work of God's creation was accompanied by the singing of the angelic hosts. "The morning stars sang together and all the angels shouted for joy" (verse 7).

What is there in your life that is yet to be created? What needs to be brought into being where now you see nothing? Sing! And see the creative power of God burst forth to that accompaniment.

One of the perennial tensions that worship leaders have encountered as they have embraced the power of music is the charge of emotionalism. Some critics have worried that Contemporary Praise & Worship attempts to manipulate worshipers by using the inherent power of music. While this source does not speak directly to this critique, it illustrates a key argument that many worship practitioners today have embraced: that music is God's good tool, given to creation to draw people into relationship with God. Alongside his recognition of music's power to move human emotions, Baloche also suggests that music provides a means of connection with God's divine nature. This idea is a faint echo of the theology more concretely expressed by the voices featured in part 2 of this chapter.

Source: Paul Baloche, "Revealing the Divine," *Worship Leader* 18, no. 1 (January/February 2009), 10.

From my own experience, my guess is that the profound nature of music lies in its connection to our emotions—our response to this divine expression. . . .

The nature of music is that it expresses something that we as humans have a hard time putting our finger on. God created music, but He has also invited us to join His symphony with our musical compositions. And our creations have the ability to pull our emotions, invade our experiences, and transform our relationship with the divine. . . .

It seems to be a common theme that music touches people in a very different place than the rest of the sensory world can. It impacts us on a level that is just as hard to describe as our spirituality. And it is with its beautiful and mysterious existence that music reveals a part of God's character. Like music, He is mysterious and able to affect us beyond what words have the ability to describe. And just as God breathed the world into existence, it seems He also threaded music into the fabric of our being. The ultimate musician and music lover, God made us like Him.

We serve a God who is so profound, mysterious, creative and unique that our confined understandings cannot possibly comprehend Him. I think there is no stronger proof that music reveals a part of God's divine nature than the fact that it evokes that same profound response. There is something in it that is above our understanding. Perhaps this is the definition of art, of truth, of divinity. Either way, we are participating and experience a truly timeless and heavenly expression.

The worship coordinator at one of Methodism's leading churches in the latter half of the twentieth century makes a bold claim about music's potency: music is where God and humanity exchange love. In this source, you can see how music's power not only moves the emotions in response to God but enables one to experience the touch of God and God's presence in worship.

Source: Kim Miller, *Redesigning Worship: Creating Powerful God Experiences* (Nashville: Abingdon Press, 2009), 74.

Music is a powerful form of connection and communication as it plays to both sides of the brain at the same time. The tones keep the right side busy so that the messages can be absorbed into the left. Our team works hard to identify the musical styles that will enable the maximum number of people to connect to the celebration, to the message, and ultimately, to Jesus.

How is it possible to find music that will pour God's love into the hearts of worshipers needing a divine touch? And conversely, how can we create atmospheres of worship where our congregations passionately communicate the depth of their love to God?

Part 2—The Power of God's Presence: God Inhabits the (Musical) Praises of His People

Within the history of Contemporary Praise & Worship one specific theological notion has been particularly important, namely, that God becomes present or is manifested when worshipers praise. One biblical passage is the cornerstone of the theology: "But thou art holy, O thou that inhabitest the praises of Israel" (Psalm 22:3, KJV).[8] While some earlier figures in the twentieth century had briefly and sporadically reflected on the importance of Psalm 22:3,[9] it was the Latter Rain revival of the late 1940s that cemented this verse as a foundational concept for worship. In the decades that followed the initial revival, its theological descendants developed a complex biblical theology that connected the presence of God to the practice of praise—still grounded in Psalm 22:3—and increasingly highlighted music as the most potent form of praise.

In the latter twentieth century, this "Praise-Presence" theology helped to standardize a set of musical worship practices among Pentecostals, charismatics, and evangelicals. By the 1980s and 1990s, the Praise-Presence theology had moved to the center of many worship traditions around the globe at the same time as many communities adopted band-based music leadership. The views of leaders and teachers in this stream are similar to, but distinct from, the voices we have heard in part 1. While for them, music may have an ability to stir up the affections of the heart, music also provided a biblically ordained pathway for encountering and experiencing the manifest presence of God.[10]

This second part of the chapter highlights three phases in the theological development of music's power to make God present in praise. First, we trace the initial biblical argument of Praise-Presence theology within the Latter Rain. Second, we show how the primacy of music became a key outworking of this theology through the Tabernacle of David within

---

8. The use of the KJV is intentional here because it uses the particularly important term "inhabitest." This had the important connotation of God's residency in praise. Some later Pentecostals, influenced by modern translations like the NIV (which uses the word "enthroned"), accordingly read this verse with some significant variation. For a longer discussion of this, see Adam Perez, "Sounding God's Enthronement in Worship: The Early History and Theology of Integrity's Hosanna! Music," in *Essays on the History of Contemporary Praise and Worship*, ed. Lester Ruth (Eugene, OR: Pickwick Press, 2020): 86–108. For an example of this theology expressed in song, see Jeremy Riddle and Bethel Music, "Be Enthroned."

9. See, for example, Aimee Semple McPherson, *This Is That: Personal Experiences, Sermons and Writings of Aimee Semple McPherson* (Los Angeles: Bridal Call, 1919), 621.

10. For a theological exploration of this encounter for "renewalist" evangelicals, see Emily Snider Andrews, "Exploring Evangelical Sacramentality: Modern Worship Music and the Possibility of Divine-Human Encounter" (PhD diss., Fuller Theological Seminary, 2020).

Latter Rain–associated networks. Finally, we outline sources that show the mainstreaming of this theology into broader Pentecostal, evangelical, and Protestant contexts.

The (Re-)Discovery of Praise in the Early Latter Rain Movement

Psalm 22:3 and embryonic notions connecting praise and God's presence circulated in Pentecostalism in the first half of the twentieth century. The 1948 Latter Rain movement, however, was the first to cultivate and develop an entire worship theology around this idea.[11] This theological understanding would eventually result in the cultivation of a new way of worship.

Reg Layzell was chief among the early Latter Rain voices developing a theology and practice of worship based on Psalm 22:3. Layzell was a Pentecostal pastor in British Columbia, Canada, who became known for his emphasis on this verse with the nickname the "apostle of praise." Layzell first sensed the importance of Psalm 22:3 as he was praying in preparation for a revival meeting in 1946. Meditating on this verse, Layzell reasoned that if praise was the place where God dwelt, Layzell should fill the church space with praise. At the revival service that night, there was a new and powerful outbreak of the Holy Spirit's presence that seemed to be in response to Layzell's acts of praise. For Layzell, God had inhabited the praises of his people.

Several years later, the outbreak of the Latter Rain revival in 1948 (of which Layzell would be a critical leader) provided a broader platform for the dissemination of Layzell's praise revelation.[12] It is important to note

---

11. For a broader overview of the Latter Rain movement, see William Faupel, "The New Order of the Latter Rain: Restoration or Renewal?" in *Winds from the North: Canadian Contributions to the Pentecostal Movement*, ed. Michael Wilkinson and Peter Althouse (Leiden: Brill, 2010), 239–64; Richard Riss, "The Latter Rain Movement of 1948," *Pneuma* 4, no. 1 (1982): 32–45, https://doi.org/10.1163/157007482X00033;

12. For this history, see Lester Ruth and Lim Swee Hong, *A History of Contemporary Praise & Worship: Understanding the Ideas that Reshaped the Protestant Church* (Grand Rapids: Baker Academic, 2021).

that early on, praise was often spoken or shouted—rather than sung—acclamations about the splendor and worth of God.

Praise became the centerpiece of Layzell's teaching, so much so that he used the category of praise as the cornerstone on which to build his understanding of many passages and narratives in Scripture. For Layzell, when God moved in power, it was because he was responding to their act of praise. In this source, Layzell interprets the most iconic biblical scene in Pentecostal spirituality—the outpouring of the Spirit on the day of Pentecost as described in Acts 2—as a response to the disciples' act of praise. Note that the use of the word "experimental" in this source is antiquated and should be read as "experiential."

Source: Reg Layzell, *The Pastor's Pen: Early Revival Writings of Pastor Reg Layzell*, comp. B. Maureen Gaglardi (Vancouver: Glad Tidings Temple, 1965; edited by Marion Peterson and privately published, 1979), 159, 163.

On the last day [of the ten days the disciples waited in Jerusalem after the Ascension of Christ], all that were left were those that still remembered and believed in His Word to wait. (Praise waiteth for Thee, O God, in Sion.)[13] There was, I believe, excitement in heaven. At last God saw a beautiful sight, —120 brethren gathered together in unity. . . . Here was the fulfillment of Psalm 133, the unity was (as is only possible) around Jesus, worshipping Him.

God speaks? No—He does more than that—HE COMMANDS THE BLESSING. He even goes further, —He comes Himself as the God of fire and sits on each member in unity. They each one become the habitation of the God of fire. . . .

In Acts 2 we have a great secret yet to be learned by the present day church. It is not more doctrine, or more apostles or prophets that we need, but more of Jesus' manifest presence. Psalm 22:3—He inhabits the praises of Israel. They (i.e., the disciples at Pentecost) so believed it that they did not cease until it became a truth experimentally. Theologically we believe it—mentally we assent to it—experimentally more Christians are strangers to its truth. As the unsaved church-goer is to salvation—so most Christians are to this great secret of His presence.

---

13. Psalm 65:1 KJV.

The following source is from one of the earliest witnesses to Layzell's teaching on praise that was being spread through the Latter Rain revival movement. The author, George Warnock, testifies to his belief that there is a divine order of worship that is being restored to the church of which song and music are a central part. The reason for their centrality is not just the Psalm 22:3 connection. Instead, Warnock sees a connection between musical praise and prophecy.[14] Their recent experience of the outpouring of the Spirit was intricately connected to the restoration of a specific type of musical praise that was supposedly practiced in the Old Testament and had been revealed within the Latter Rain movement.

Source: George H. Warnock, *The Feast of Tabernacles* (Springfield, MO: Bill Britton, 1951), 91.

It is not without Divine purposes, therefore, that the ministry of spiritual song and music is being restored to the Church. Actually it is the voice of prophecy. We read therefore, "Moreover David and the captains of the host separated to the service of the sons of Asaph, and of Heman, and of Jeduthan, who should prophesy with harps, with psalteries, and with cymbals . . ." (1 Chron. 25:1). No doubt there was usually prophetic singing accompanied by the musical instruments; and together it formed this great prophetic orchestra and choir. And because it is the voice of prophecy, that is why there is a work of deliverance wrought when songs are sung in the Spirit, or when instruments of music are played in the Spirit. . . .

It is not difficult, then, for us to understand why the Choir of Praise has been restored to the Church. The Temple service is being restored. The saints are singing "by course,"—that is "alternately" in prophecy one to one another, because once again the Lord's Temple is being restored. . . .

The present work of the Holy Spirit in re-establishing the Temple of God and its spiritual order of worship, has really just started. But we can thank God, nevertheless, that the pattern has been revealed, and that the foundation has been laid.

---

14. This theme has become prominent again in recent years with diverse contexts practicing "prophetic worship." Such practices are especially prominent in contexts like Bethel Church but is evident elsewhere. For instance, see Busman's account of Passion conference: Joshua Kalin Busman, "'Yet to Come' or 'Still to Be Done'?: Evangelical Worship and the Power of 'Prophetic' Songs," in *Congregational Music-Making and Community in a Mediated Age*, ed. Anna Nekola and Tom Wagner (Routledge, 2015).

In the Latter Rain movement, foundational biblical ideas (such as Layzell's revelation on Psalm 22:3) often functioned as an interpretive "key" that could unlock the meaning of large and disparate passages of Scripture. Accordingly, Layzell's revelation that "God inhabits the praises of his people" became a framework through which the Bible's witness on the topic of praise was studied anew. In this source, we see this technique at work with another of Layzell's key praise passages—the sacrifice of praise (Hebrews 13:15). Layzell reads passages from Jeremiah, Jonah, Acts, and the Psalms through the key of the sacrifice of praise, arguing that it is this sacrifice that is the consistent turning point in redemptive history.

Source: Reg Layzell, *Unto Perfection: The Truth about the Present Restoration Revival* (Mountlake Terrace, WA: King's Temple, 1979), 13–14.

Before leaving the subject of the sacrifice of praise, I would like to discuss the following four Scriptures.

Jeremiah 33:11 states, "The voice of joy, and the voice of gladness, like the voice of the bridegroom and the voice of the bride, and the voice of them that shall say, Praise the LORD of hosts: for the LORD is good; for his mercy endureth for ever: and of them that shall bring the sacrifice of praise into the house of the LORD. For I will cause to return the captivity of the land as at the first, saith the LORD." This is an introduction to the great message of restoration about to be fulfilled. . . . The verse refers in particular to the voices that will be heard at that time. Specifically, the voice of them that bring the sacrifice of praise to the house of the Lord. This was restored with new force in 1946. What a privilege it is to be in the day Jeremiah prophesied about, and fulfilling that which was written by the weeping prophet. God moved sovereignly in restoring this verse. And like the Bereans of old we searched the Scriptures to see if these things were so. In spite of all the criticism in 1946, God revealed this verse to us and we experienced the anointing of the Lord upon it.

Jonah 2:5-10 illustrates the desperate situation of Jonah. He repented (promised to pay his vow), but was still in the fish. Verse nine especially, shows the act of faith producing the special presence of the delivering Lord. "But I will sacrifice unto thee with the voice of thanksgiving; I will pay that that I have vowed. Salvation is of the LORD." Because of this attitude, God ordered the fish to take him to Nineveh.

Acts 16:23-25 is an excellent illustration of the power that lies in the sacrifice of praise. Paul received a vision to go to Macedonia. Being sure it was God, Paul and Silas went. However, they ended up in prison, were beaten with many stripes, their feet placed in stocks, and cast into the inner prison. Verse 25 states, "And at midnight Paul and Silas prayed, and sang praises unto God: and the prisoners heard them." They filled the jail with God's presence and revival was on.

Finally, Psalms 50:23 states, "Whoso offereth praise glorifieth me: and to him that ordereth his conversation aright will I shew the salvation of God." I would like to note that we order our words, not wait for any feeling. Also by praising the Lord we glorify Him and see His deliverance. One time when I was in Denmark, a teacher quoted this verse to me this way: "Whosoever offereth the sacrifice of praise glorifies me and prepareth a way whereby I shall shew forth my victory." We prepare for the victory of Jesus to be seen in praise and worship.

Throughout much of the early Latter Rain material, there is often an understanding that right belief leads to right practice, which then leads to right experience. For instance, the Latter Rain started with a restored understanding of biblical praise (Psalm 22:3) that led to the sacrifice of praise being practiced. This was ultimately validated by the Latter Rain movement's experience of the manifest divine presence in their meetings. However, the following story from a church in Detroit that experienced one of the first manifestations of the Latter Rain revival beyond its geographic origins, demonstrates that there was fluidity to this logical sequence. In this case, the experience of God's immediate presence led to an outpouring of praise from which a new appreciation of Psalm 22:3 emerged. This demonstrates that in the Latter Rain movement, the practices, new biblical revelations, and an intoxicating experience of God's presence often flowed together as a seamless whole. This author, James Beall (1924–2013), ministered alongside his mother, Myrtle Beall (1896–1979) at Bethesda Missionary Temple in Detroit and was her successor leading that church.

Source: James Beall, *The Ministry of Worship and Praise* (Detroit: Bethesda Missionary Temple, n.d.), 18–19.

It was my place to open the service with prayer and to lead the congregation in song. I stepped to the pulpit and asked the people to stand for prayer.

Instead of quietly awaiting for someone to lead us to the throne of Grace, the congregation spontaneously, under the sovereign leading of the Holy Spirit, raised their hands and began to "sing praises to God," together and in harmony. It was the sound of a heavenly choir as wave after wave of praise swept over the congregation. It would subside to a faint whisper and then rise again in magnificent worship. We were spellbound. We laughed and cried as we experienced this tremendous new day in God. This praise continued for well over an hour. When finally the billows of praise ceased, an evangelist sat down at the piano and, in a moment of time, spiritual songs were born. . . .

We had experienced for the first time, the depth of Jesus' words, "They that worship God must worship Him in spirit and in truth." Now we knew what it meant to have Christ singing in the church, declaring the Name of the Father among His brethren. We discovered what it meant to be taught and admonished through the means of psalms, hymns and spiritual song. Through spiritual song we were taught that the visitation from God which we were then experiencing was the beginning of the promised "latter rain."

When we were asked what was happening and what this visitation was, we would declare, "This is the promise of the coming latter rain." Joel wrote about this when he said: "Be glad then, ye children of Zion, and rejoice in the Lord your God: for He hath given you the former rain moderately, and He will cause to come down for you the rain, THE FORMER RAIN, AND THE LATTER RAIN IN THE FIRST MONTH" (Joel 2:23). . . .

Now, in one service, our song was changed from a prayer request into praise. Since that time we have nurtured and endeavored to develop the ministry of praise and worship in this local church. We have learned the praises of His people provide a habitation for God. David said:

"But thou art holy, O thou thot INHABITEST THE PRAISES OF ISRAEL." (Ps. 22:3)

This is surely a divine principle. Praise MUST BE IN SPIRIT AND IN TRUTH. The reason: "God is a spirit." Now, because God is a spirit and inhabits that which is spirit, when His people praise Him in spirit and in truth they create for Him a habitation wherein He dwells among them.

Building the Tabernacle of Praise: Musicalizing the Praise-Presence Theology

By the 1960s, the Latter Rain movement had already spread globally. Though the movement was more than just a worship theology, it carried with it the Psalm 22:3 emphasis on extended periods of congregational praise and the experience of the presence of God. From the late 1960s onward, leaders who were directly influenced by the Latter Rain movement further developed their thinking on music and their worship theology, namely, the differentiation between *praise* and *worship*. Though the distinction between the two was not absolute, it became a helpful tool for articulating and teaching what these Pentecostals were experiencing and practicing. Thus, a standard pattern in congregational gatherings emerged: an extended period of singing *praise* (often upbeat) that manifested God's presence was then followed by loving songs of *worship* (often slower).

These developments also followed new emphases on the architectural plans for, and spatial journey into, the Old Testament tabernacle of David. Though these sources use the tabernacle of Moses as a foil for that of David, there are other sources not quoted here that focused on the theme of atonement in the tabernacle of Moses and its importance for understanding the work of Jesus, connecting both back to Praise & Worship. The fact that both models were used testifies to the way discrete articulations of the shared theology developed organically among these Pentecostals (see Cornwall below).

The following passage highlights one of the most significant developments of this second generation of Praise-Presence theologizing: making the Old Testament figure David the exemplary model for Praise & Worship, especially in his provisions for a new tabernacle for the Ark of the Covenant. By connecting David and the narrative of 1 Chronicles 15 to the Praise-Presence theology, teachers emphasized the apparent musical nature of biblical praise and worship. David's prominence also lent itself to renewed emphasis on the Psalms for restoring this Praise-Presence theology to the church, a "Davidic pattern of worship."[15]

---

15. For more on early Latter Rain theologies of the Tabernacle of David, see Jonathan M. Ottaway, "The Power of Tradition over Biblical Theology; Raising Up the Tabernacle of David: Pentecostal Memory in Praise and Worship Theology" in *Worship and Power: Liturgical Authority in Free Church Traditions*, ed. Sarah Johnson and Andrew Wymer (Eugene: Cascade, 2023), 114–31.

Source: Graham Truscott, *The Power of His Presence: The Restoration of the Tabernacle of David* (San Diego: Restoration Temple, 1969), 215–18.

David appointed singers and musicians to praise and worship God. And the keynote of their praise was joy. . . .

The Bible is insistent on this truth—the Good News of God's love, in both Old and New Testaments, is always accompanied by joy. . . . It is obvious from Scripture, that this joy is expressed with noise—"by lifting up the voice with joy," as they did when they went down to Obededom's house to bring back the Art of God to Zion. This was not the morbid formality so often seen in much of Christian worship today. This was a joyful expression of the Life of Him who was anointed with the Oil of gladness above His fellows. . . .

One other important point should be noted here. This rejoicing, and audible praise and worship, commenced before the Restoration of the Ark of the Covenant to its proper place in the Tabernacle of David. As soon as the place and people were prepared, and the biblical pattern and order restored, the people began to enter into an altogether new experience of demonstrative praise and worship to their God.

The worship in the tabernacle of Moses, as we have seen, was mostly silent. Only the gentle tinkling of the bells on the borders of the priest's garments could be heard. But here was something new. David longed after God. God had revealed to him his need for the Presence of the Ark of the Covenant. As soon as the people began to move with God, even before the Ark of God was restored in all its fullness, they began to show their gratitude to God for the blessing of His presence by doing a new thing—loudly praising and worshiping Him.

This teaching runs right through the Old and New Testament. . . .

In the Latter Rain Praise-Presence theologizing, the emerging emphasis on David's Tabernacle as the key example of ideal biblical worship was sometimes in tension with a concurrent emphasis from others—like Judson Cornwall—on Moses's Tabernacle.[16] The following passage is clearly aware of this tension but argues that the tabernacle of Moses primarily functions as a foreshadowing of

---

16. See chapter 4 especially but also the source from Judson Cornwall below. For earlier Latter Rain reflections on the importance of the Tabernacle of Moses, see Maureen Gaglardi, *The Path of the Just: The Tabernacle of Moses* (Vancouver: New West, 1963); Kevin J. Conner, *The Tabernacle of Moses: The Riches of Redemption's Story as Revealed in the Tabernacle* (Portland, OR: City Bible, 1975).

the person and ministry of Jesus Christ, particularly in his atoning sacrifice for sin. The principle of Moses's tabernacle remain but the worship patterns are down away with. The tabernacle of David functions as a different kind of pattern. For Blomgren, the tabernacle is a picture of how Christians participate in the covenant of grace that has been ushered in by Christ. Whereas the tabernacle of Moses reserved the Holy of Holies for the high priest, in the tabernacle of David, all the priests who were ministering could enter. This had important implications for worship. The tabernacle of David with its emphasis on music and joyful exuberance in the presence of God was the picture of what they believed God intended the New Testament church to practice.

> **Source:** David K. Blomgren, *Restoring God's Glory: The Present Day Rise of David's Tabernacle* (Regina, Saskatchewan: Maranatha Christian Centre, 1985), 30–32.

The sacrifices of Moses' Tabernacle were of animals, to atone for sin. Those ministering in David's Tabernacle offered spiritual sacrifices only—sacrifices of joy and of praise and worship.

Among those who ministered in David's Tabernacle were those who were appointed as singers. Singers ministered before the Lord 24 hours a day, in shifts, and it was from the songs they sang that we get many of the Psalms. . . .

Songs were an integral part of the worship in David's Tabernacle but they played no role in the Tabernacle of Moses Why is this? We know from Psalm 90, which was written by Moses, that he had the ability to sing songs of praise unto God, and Josephus records that Moses was gifted in music. Moses therefore had an ability in music, but that ability never saw fruition in the worship of the Mosaic Tabernacle because it was not yet in God's timing. The Tabernacle of David fulfilled all that was necessary for this vital ministry to become a part of the worship of God's people.

There were also instruments played in David's Tabernacle, while there were no instruments in the Tabernacle of Moses. Recorders were appointed in David's Tabernacle to record the new songs and psalms of the Lord. None were needed in Moses's Tabernacle. . . .

There was no dancing before the Lord in Moses's Tabernacle, nor any clapping. In the Psalms, both were commanded (Psalm 149, 150, 47:1).

Finally, in David's Tabernacle, "Amen" was said to blessing. In Moses' day, "Amen" was said only to curses (Deuteronomy 27).

These are exciting days for the church! We are coming to Mount Zion, which was the place where David's Tabernacle was pitched, and we are worshiping according to David's pattern.

This source explains the core teaching that provided the foundation for the link between the act of praise and the presence of God. There is a promise that when the saints offer the joyful act of praise, they will walk in the light of God's countenance. Notice how this Seattle-based pastor presents the Psalm 22:3-based theology not only in a general way as truth but as a specific affirmation that God is heard to say. Such theological confidence reflects how critical the theology had become. Charlotte Baker was also known for her role in coordinating teams of dancers that participated, alongside music, in enacting their vision of the fully restored tabernacle.

Source: E. Charlotte Baker, *On Eagles Wings: A Book on Praise and Worship* (1979; Shippensburg, PA: Destiny Image, 1990), 6–7.

Psalm 22:3 states, "But thou art holy, O thou that inhabitest the praises of Israel." Throughout the ages God has visited many people, but there is only one people with whom He will make His habitation, that is the people who will praise Him. God is saying, "I am holy, but I will have a dwelling place on earth. The place which I will inhabit is where My saints are praising Me."

"Blessed is the people that know the joyful sound: they shall walk, O LORD, in the light of thy countenance. In thy name shall they rejoice all the day: and in thy righteousness shall they be exalted" (Ps. 89:15, 16). Some people feel that praise is meaningless noise; others, in tune with heaven, identify praise as a joyful sound which pleases the heart of God. God says the people to whom praise is a joyful sound are blessed, and shall walk in the light of His countenance. The ability to walk in the light of God's countenance is given to us when we learn and practice praise.

Breaking Through to Victory: The Praise-Presence Theology Spreads

Starting in the 1970s, the Psalm 22:3-based Praise-Presence theology began to spread broadly, far beyond the Latter Rain movement. To connect praise—especially as done musically—and the presence of God became commonplace among other Pentecostal and charismatic movements and a large swathe of Protestant evangelicalism. This was accomplished through itinerant teaching ministry, conferences, published literature, and non-denominational networks of churches (among other ways). By the twenty-first century, it is difficult to imagine discussions of Protestant worship without addressing the impact of the theology of praise and presence and the central place of musical power and the experience of God. The musicalization of Praise & Worship became so complete that it was all-but-assumed when discussing worship. The connection between these terms became so complete that some authors began writing about how Praise & Worship is more than just music.

Judson Cornwall, a former Assemblies of God pastor who eventually became a full-time speaker and author, was perhaps in the last quarter of the twentieth century the most widely read and heard promoter of the Praise-Presence theology. With a non-Latter Rain background, he was able to make the theology more palatable across many denominations. (The Latter Rain movement was held in low regard by many.) In the following passage, Cornwall describes how he introduced the practice of an extended period of praising God to his congregation and how they experienced the manifest presence of God. Starting from extended times of mainly vocal praising, it was a short step to introducing extended times of congregational singing, thanks, praise, and worship. Note the emphasis upon Psalm 100:4 and the tabernacle of Moses.[17] In contrast to many in the Latter Rain movement who emphasized the tabernacle of David, Moses remained the important touchstone in Cornwall's teaching.

Source: Judson Cornwall, *Let Us Praise* (Plainfield, NJ: Logos International, 1973), 24–26.

"Look," I said, "let's all gather together at the front of the auditorium. Choir, come off the platform and join the congregation. God's Word declares in Psalm 100, verse 4, 'Enter into His gates with thanksgiving, and into His courts with praise.'" As they came forward, I went on to explain,

---

17. Also see the quotation from Judson Cornwall in chapter 3, which also refers to Psalm 100:4 and the tabernacle of Moses.

"In the tabernacle in the wilderness, God's place of habitation was the holy of Holies. It sat in a courtyard surrounded by a linen fence which had only one gate. Anyone approaching God came through that gate and walked through the courtyard to get to the tabernacle in which God dwelt. The gate is called 'thanksgiving' and the court is called 'praise.' That is why Psalm 22:3 declares that God inhabits the praises of His people. . . .

"All right," I said, looking around at all of us sheepishly gathered up front, "now that we're united physically, let's get united in the activity of praise. So no one will feel he is being looked at, let's all close our eyes and focus our attention on our lovely Lord Jesus. Now, even if it takes all the will-power you've got, lift your hands and faces Godward and tell Him that you love Him. . . ."

A pair of half-raised arms reached to a full stretch. A bowed head became a lifted head. Whispered words became exclamations of praise. Some wept, some shouted, some sang softly, and a few gently clapped their hands. Bit by bit, we seemed to be tuning one another out and tuning God in.

It was obvious, from facial expressions and the changing level and pitch of the vocal praise, that as some broke through to victory, others were coming under the dealings of God. What had started as a simple praise session had, for some, become a time of direct confrontation.

As the level of praise subsided, I led them in a chorus of praise that sparked them to a renewed outpouring of worship to God. Gently, but very pronouncedly, we became conscious of a sense of the Divine Presence of God greater than we had ever known before. It was as though we had bridged the gap between His world and ours, and we were on the outskirts of His glorious realm.

Eventually within Pentecostalism, the theology connecting praise and God's presence was ubiquitous. The following are two short passages from a Study Bible aimed for broad consumption within Pentecostalism. The first is from the introduction to the entire Bible and the second from an introduction to Psalm 22:3-4. The passages show how the Praise-Presence theology was not limited to an understanding of worship but could undergird fundamental aspects of a basic spirituality, including the question of how we as humans can have relationship with God. The author originally came from a United Pentecostal Church denominational background but migrated into a more independent ministry with connections throughout global Pentecostalism. The editor was an important Foursquare Gospel denominational figure and became a main-

stream figure in American evangelical worship through the Promise Keeper's men's ministry.

Source: Charles Green, "The Pathway of Praise," in *Spirit-Filled Life Bible*, ed. Jack W. Hayford (Nashville: Thomas Nelson, 1991), xxix, 770.

[In an introduction to the whole Bible]
Man was created to live and breathe in an atmosphere of praise-filled worship to His Creator. The avenue of sustained inflow of divine power was to be kept by the sustained outflow of joyous and humble praise to his Maker. The severance of the bond of blessing-through-obedience that sin brought silenced man's praised-filled fellowship with God. . . .

But now has come salvation and life in Christ, and now upon receiving Jesus Christ as Savior, daily living calls us to prayer and the Word for fellowship and wisdom in living. But our daily approach to God in that communion is to be paved with praise: "Enter into His gates with thanksgiving, and into His courts with praise" (Ps 100:4). Such a walk of praise-filled openness to Him will cultivate deep devotion, faithful obedience, and constant joy.

[In the commentary on Psalm 22:3, 4]
Unquestionably, one of the most remarkable and exciting things about honest and sincere praise is taught here: Praise will bring the presence of God. Although God is everywhere present, there is a distinct manifestation of His rule, which enters the environment of praise. Here is the remedy for times when you feel alone, deserted, or depressed. Praise! However simply, compose your song and testimony of God's goodness in your life. The result: God enters! His presence will live (take up residence) in our lives. The word "inhabit" (Hebrew *yawshab*) means "to sit down, to remain, to settle, or marry." In other words. God does not merely visit us when we praise Him. But His presence abides with us and we partner with Him in a growing relationship. Let this truth create faith and trust, and lead to deliverance from satanic harassments, torment, or bondage. Notice how this text ties three words together: "praises," "trusted," and "delivered"!

An African American pastor, who also had extensive experience in worship leading, showcases the Praise-Presence theology as not only the foundation for what it meant to approach God in worship but also for people's basic relationship with God. Such passages show how the expectation of encountering God through praise was at the center of worship-related Pentecostal spirituality at the end of the twentieth century, including discrete acts of musical praise and extended into an empowered "lifestyle" of praise.

Source: Joseph L. Garlington, *Worship: The Pattern of Things in Heaven* (Shippensburg: Destiny Image Publishers, 1997), 19–20.

We build a throne for our First Love with our praises. Psalm 22:3 says, "Yet Thou art holy, O Thou who art enthroned upon the praises of Israel." God's throne is as significant as we want to make it through our praises. Now if He dwells in the midst of your praises, how much of a throne do you want Him to have?

As you praise Him, you are shaping a throne for God Almighty, Himself, in your life or in the corporate body seeking His face. As you worship Him, you are sacrificing your life and body on an altar of surrender as a living sacrifice. This says to God, "I have confidence that You are the sovereign God of the universe. My whole being leans upon You for life and fullness. . . ."

Anytime you choose, you can build a throne for the Lord through your praises, and you can worship your all powerful God by offering your life on the altar of submission. Your acts of selfless worship to God can create an atmosphere in which He can say, "I want to spend some time with you! I like the throne you have built for Me. I like the way you lavishly put this thing together, and I especially appreciate the living sacrifice you are offering to Me on the altar of sacrifice." True spiritual worship will cause God Almighty to come and sit with you, for He is enthroned in the midst of your praises.

The Praise-Presence theology had an impact on how worship leaders began to think of their role. Spatial images abound, especially in terms like "leading," "ushering," or, as in the example below, "bringing" people into the presence of God. Since several of the biblical images used to explain the Praise-Presence theology involved buildings and spaces (e.g., the tabernacle of Moses) perhaps it is not surprising that such terms began to be used. That this expectation—and even the term "worship leader" itself—rested upon musicians showed how widely the musicalization of the Praise-Presence theology had spread by the 1980s and 1990s. Notice how the presence of God through worship leads to the Spirit acting powerfully in the worshiper's life.

Source: Ron Kenoly and Dick Bernal, *Lifting Him Up* (Orlando, FL: Creation House, 1995), 23–26.

The function of a worship leader is to bring other people into God's presence. I'm often asked how I know when I have accomplished my job. The truth is that it's not something I see with the natural eye. I do not have a written formula. Sometimes I know I'm finished when I can feel the presence of the Lord in the room so strong that I know the only thing left for me to do is to get out of God's way. Many times it is not appropriate for me to say or do anything.

When I get to the place where I know that it's no longer me leading the people, but the Spirit of the Lord, I know they are there....

Once that happens the Spirit can do things like healing, deliverance, revelation and more. Everything that He does is going to be good. At that point the worship leader has become a facilitator.

Perhaps the greatest evidence of the pervasiveness and centrality of the Praise-Presence theology by the end of the twentieth century was that proponents placed the theology on the lips of God himself. The following piece from the first important worship leader–oriented trade magazine does exactly that. In it the divine Voice explains how singing brings about the divine presence in corporate worship.

Source: Bob Mason, "I Inhabit Your Praises," *Psalmist* 2, no. 3 (April/May 1987): 20.

As a trained musician in college the Lord spoke very clearly to my heart and said, "Do you believe that Psalm 22:3 really happens, that I inhabit the praises of My people?"

I said, "Sure Lord, it's in Your word. I believe it."

He asked again, "No, no, do you REALLY BELIEVE it?"

I replied, "Yes, Lord."

"Do you really believe that I actually inhabit your praise?"

Finally I said, "Lord, to be perfectly honest, I need a revelation on that."

He said, "Okay, I want you to start with the concept of singing. Where does singing begin?"

I responded, "It starts with my diaphragm and abdominal muscles and lungs."

He said, "That's right. Now I want you to see in the Spirit and see Me as the cloud of the Old Testament. And so you will see it clearly, I am going to be as a mist." And in my spirit I saw this.

God spoke again, "If I am like a mist and you really believe that I inhabit your praise, what would happen if you began to praise and worship Me right now? What would be the initial act?"

"Well Lord, I guess my lungs would be filled with this mist," I replied.

"That's right. Then what would happen?"

I said, "Then it would come out through my vocal chords, all the way through my throat and out my mouth."

And God said, "Wherever your voice would go, wherever your praise would go, the mist would go also. The mist would fill the entire room, even the cracks and crevices because I inhabit your praises. It would go out through the doors and windows, wherever the sound of your voice could be heard. . . ."

One of the reasons why musicians are often seen as the leaders of worship is the theological belief that the power of God is released when God's people praise him, especially by singing. In the following passage, a Nigerian pastor (who is the pastor of the church attended by Sinach, the worship leader who composed the award-winning song "Way Maker") uses biblical examples to make that point. Stressing the importance of sung praise in this way makes it a small step to see the musicians as the critical leaders of worship. Notice, too, how the author highlights the dependability of praise to produce or manifest God's power over a negative situation.

Source: Chris Oyakhilome, *Rhapsody of Realities: A Topical Compendium*, vol. 5 (Lagos, Nigeria: LoveWorld Publishing, 2018), 98.

As Christians, God hears and answers when we pray, but how to make His power that is released on our behalf work for us is what many don't know. One of the ways to activate that power is through praise! Throughout the Scriptures, we find amazing and inspiring accounts of how God delivered His people from imminent destruction and dire circumstances, when they activated His power through praise.

Three nations—Ammon, Moab, and Mount Seir—came out against Judah and made ready to attack her. However, King Jehoshaphat was wise. He gathered all Judah together to seek the Lord in prayer and fasting. When they prayed, God revealed to them the exact location of their enemies' camp, and gave them the strategy to defeat them (2 Chronicles 20:22). When trouble strikes, like Jehoshaphat, "put the singers in front" and you'll have the same result.

Don't wait until you feel like singing before you make a melody in your heart and sing praises unto the Lord. Whether you feel like it or not, whether you're happy or not, praise Him all the same. Paul and Silas experienced a supernatural jailbreak by offering this kind of unusual praise....

You may be faced with a difficult situation today for which you've prayed and confessed that it's all working out for your good, yet, nothing seems to have changed. Don't give up! It's time you offered to God the unusual praise. Speak and sing joyous tongues of praise and thanksgiving, and as you do, the power of God will move on your behalf, and you'll have a great Miracle.

A longtime worship leader at Willow Creek Community Church—the best-known American megachurch at the end of the twentieth century—expresses the view that fundamentally, contemporary worship is not about styles of worship music but about adopting new music that would enable worshipers to enter more deeply into personal relationship with God. This is the mature synthetic view of Contemporary Praise & Worship that joins together the earlier notions of an evangelical view that stresses music's ability to work upon emotions and the Pentecostal view that stresses praise as the site of God's presence. Here the power of music both moves the emotions and manifests the presence of God.

Source: Joe Horness, "Contemporary Music-Driven Worship," in *Exploring the Worship Spectrum: 6 Views*, ed. Paul A. Basden (Grand Rapids, MI: Zondervan, 2010), 103–4.

But just as traditional worship is more than a hymnbook and liturgy far more than the reciting of the Apostles' Creed, the first step to understanding contemporary worship is to understand the goal of the changes that are being made. More of the struggles and boardroom discussions taking place in churches seem to revolve primarily around issues of instrumentation, volume, traditional versus contemporary song selection, and how our constituency will react. On the negative side, decisions are made to "keep worship the way it is" simply so that no one will be offended. Conversely, changes are often made not because of the joy it would bring our Savior but because someone thinks it would increase attendance. "How quickly we forget what it's all about," says Tommy Walker, a good friend of mine and a well-known contemporary worship leader. "We can get so strategic that we worship so our church will grow, not because He is worthy. But we're doing all this because God is worthy and we want to worship Him."

If you were to take away only one insight into contemporary worship . . . let it be this: People of this generation are longing to experience the genuine presence of God. And God is longing to move in and among the hearts of his people. If we will learn to worship from hearts that are fully engaged, God will be glorified and set free to move in us and among us. . . .

Worship, as it is described so vividly in Scripture, was meant to be a dialogue, flowing from the outpouring of a relationship with God.

Discussion Questions

- Many of the sources we encountered in part 1 believed that there is an important correlation between the emotional response that music produces and the spiritual encounter it facilitates. Should this be a normative way of understanding spiritual experience? Do all spiritual encounters need to be accompanied by emotional experiences?

- What roles do you see music playing in shaping the affections and beliefs of worshipers in your worshiping community? What roles do you think it should play?

- Can you think of specific instances where music was used in worship in ways that you felt were manipulative or inauthentic? What distinguished that experience from positive ones? Was it something within the music itself, the leadership, the content of the service, the context?

- Where have you seen the theology of Psalm 22:3 in recent books, social media, or other worship content? Do you see the influence of Praise–Presence theology in how you plan and lead worship?

- Is the idea of music creating a dwelling place for God's presence a compelling one for you? What biblical or theological grounds support that idea for you?

- What understanding of music's power in worship from this chapter do you relate to most easily?

CHAPTER 4
FLOW: STRUCTURING TIMES OF MUSICAL WORSHIP

For modern worship leaders, the song set has become one of the basic structural units of the worship service. In a normal Contemporary Praise & Worship service, three or four songs open the gathering and occupy much of the first half of the service. In the history of Christian worship, this fact alone is worthy of note. However, this is not the only notable feature of how songs are grouped and structured in Contemporary Praise & Worship. Not only is the song set its own structural unit, but worshipers today expect that the song set should follow a predetermined progression or narrative arc. Worship leaders and planners do not just lead *any* three or four songs, but three or four songs that lead worshipers *somewhere*. While there is variation in the specifics of the destination that worship leads to, there is a general sense in much worship today that worship should lead deeper into God's presence.

Because the order of the songs facilitates a spiritual journey, it has become critical for many leaders that the songs progress *seamlessly* from one to another. Worship songs should form a unified whole. Individual worshipers may or may not be able to clearly identify the unity, but they should sense it as they are drawn into the progression of worship. This seamless progression of worship is often called *flow*.

Multiple explanations can help make sense of the historical development of the song set. There is a simple, functional explanation: modern music-making is so technically complex (involving instruments, sound technicians, lights, cameras, etc.) that it is more efficient to group the songs together than to spread them out between other activities. Another explanation is the development of the secular pop music concert and its conventions that have shaped mainstream expectations for live music. In this, Christian worship is possibly informed by a cultural desire for longer, uninterrupted musical performances. A third explanation can be found in the legacy of revivalistic Christianity in the nineteenth century. One of the innovative practices of the new revival and camp meetings of the nineteenth century was a greatly expanded amount of singing in worship as hymns and songs were interspersed between spiritual exercises. Sometimes the singing could go on all night![1] Later Christians continued these practices, often with their own distinctive flavor. For instance, early Pentecostals embraced both the singing of spontaneously led hymns and songs as well as extended times of what they called "singing in the Spirit."[2] Meanwhile, evangelicals began to experiment with the public song service as an extended time of singing that was an aid to evangelistic services.

In this chapter, our aim is not to understand the history of extended times of singing in modern worship services but to understand the sense of progression and flow that is integral to the Contemporary Praise & Worship song set. At the headwaters of this progression was the sense, derived from the Latter Rain movement, that through the activity of praise, worshipers encountered the presence of God. (This has been described in chapter 3.) Accordingly, musical praise was the primary means of facilitating that progression.

Out of this fundamental conviction, multiple different streams have emerged, which we will encounter in this chapter. Many of the sources in this chapter are broadly contemporaneous with each other, demonstrating that different avenues to musical flow have existed simultaneously. Each

---

1. For instance, see the description of camp meetings in the early nineteenth century in Bruce Dickson, *And They All Sang Hallelujah: Plain-Folk Camp-Meeting Religion, 1800–1845* (Knoxville: University of Tennessee Press, 1974), 61–122.

2. Sometimes, singing in the Spirit could last as long as half an hour. Cecil Robeck, *The Azusa Street Mission and Revival: The Birth of the Global Pentecostal Movement* (Nashville: Thomas Nelson, 2006), 144–53.

of these sources are underpinned by the shared conviction that musical worship must prepare and invite the worshiper into the deep places of worship. There may be one mountaintop that worship music reaches, but there are multiple paths toward it.

For figures closely associated with the Latter Rain movement, the heavier emphasis was on musical worship preparing the ground for the outbreak of the "Song of the Lord." Much like their earlier Pentecostal forebears who had reveled in times of extended spiritual singing, Latter Rain Pentecostals saw the end goal of musical praise as a time of prophetic musical expression (either vocally or instrumentally).

In the broader Praise & Worship movement that emerged out of the Latter Rain, the focus was not as rigidly on the Song of the Lord. Instead, many of these figures taught about the progression that happens in music from "praise" into "worship"—the site of intimate encounter with God. Old Testament patterns and institutions (especially the tabernacles of David and Moses) were critical in narrating what this progression should look like and be for the modern worshiper. Through the progression of songs, worshipers were entering into the Holy of Holies.

Finally, this chapter also includes a cross-section of voices that emphasizes neither the prophetic nor the ecstatic. Instead, they highlight the utility of the song set to close the gap between contemporary people and their expectations for worship. The IMPACT model at Saddleback Church under pastor Rick Warren (a leading Church Growth movement site) demonstrates the function and purpose of musical flow: it can loosen people up, turn them inward to worship God and make deeper commitments to Christian life, and then pick up the tempo to conclude the song set and get them ready to hear an inspiring sermon. In this and other similar sources, the rationale for the flow of worship music highlights theological concerns for evangelism rather than God's manifest presence (not that the two cannot coexist!).

The Song of the Lord: Progressing into the Prophetic

Some leaders and teachers within the Latter Rain movement emphasized the particular role musical worship had in facilitating the outbreak of the Song of the Lord. During the Song of the Lord, Latter Rain leaders expected that new songs would be given by the Holy Spirit, either in the form of a sung prophecy or prophetic musicalization from an instrument. As you will see in the upcoming sources, the role of the lead musician was to create extended periods of congregational singing that would make space for both God's presence and that would prepare the congregation to enter into the Song of the Lord. (This high status of the role of the lead musician is explored further in chapter 5.) To facilitate the Song of the Lord, musicians had to be spiritually attuned, skillful, and able to improvise as the Holy Spirit poured forth new songs into the hearts of worshipers and leaders alike.

As one of the faculty members at the Bible College associated with Bible Temple in Portland, Oregon (pastored by Dick Iverson), David Blomgren is a helpful representative of the Praise-Presence theology that developed in the Latter Rain movement. (Bible Temple was a key school associated with the Latter Rain revival where this book was developed as a textbook for use within their programs.) For Blomgren, the restoration of the church that he was witnessing was particularly marked by the restoration of spiritual singing. It is through this medium that singers could channel the prophetic voice of the Holy Spirit within the congregation.[3] Blomgren's argument about the importance of the Song of the Lord established an ultimate goal for musical worship. Other Latter Rain figures would build upon this foundation.

---

3. The source from George Warnock in chapter 3 provides further historical context for how the Latter Rain movement understood the restoration of prophetic, spiritual music in their day.

Source: David K. Blomgren, *Song of the Lord* (Portland, OR: Bible Press, 1978), 43.

The Song of the Lord is a spiritual song directed primarily to God's people as the singer becomes a channel for the Lord to convey a message in song. As with a Song of Praise, the "new" Song of the Lord might be sung with a melody spontaneously composed or it may be non-melodic (chordal intervals); it may be with a rhythm or non-rhythmic. The style of the song is not the essential element but rather the message is the significant factor as the Bridegroom, Christ, sings to His bride, the church.

1. The Nature of the Song of the Lord.

    a. A Word of Prophecy in Song.
    The Song of the Lord is often a prophetic song which may warn, instruct in the Spirit, or even sometimes give direction to the local body of Christ. . . .

    b. A Word of Encouragement in Song.
    There are times when we all need to be encouraged in the ways of God. Many times the Song of the Lord serves to lift our spirits unto God and encourages us in Him.

    c. A Word of Exhortation in Song.
    The Song of the Lord comes to exhort us in the area that God would have us to be stirred. It may be in specific areas of our Christian walk or response to Him in worship. The Song of the Lord will function to shake us to action and to do His bidding.

    d. A Word of Comfort in Song.
    The Song of the Lord also serves to bring comfort to those that are bereaved or in times of great troubling in their lives. The Comforter, the Holy Spirit, stirs a Song of the Lord in the human vessel to sing the soothing, comforting word which is as a healing balm to those who are suffering.

2. The Function of the Song of the Lord
    Everyone should exercise faith that the Lord will use him to bear a message in song to God's people. Although not everyone will have a "ministry" in singing the Song of the Lord, yet everyone may minister such a song at different times. One who has never ministered in spiritual songs might first begin with singing a Song of Praise before attempting the Song of the Lord. It usually takes more faith to sing the Song of the Lord.

Latter Rain leaders developed highly systematized ways of progressing through worship toward the release of the Song of the Lord. This required skillful participation of the musicians—typically in this context, an orchestra—so that they could follow, playing by ear. Encouraging this kind of practice required preparation and a clear sense of organization. This source from Mike Herron, the music minister at Bible Temple during the 1970s to 1980s, demonstrates the kind of preparation necessary to enable musicians to flow together. Herron's notes suggest that musicians waited for direction from the Chief Musician who, in turn, was following the Song of the Lord being received from God and which was being led by a singer or instrumentalist.

Source: Mike Herron, "The Song of the Lord" (unpublished teaching materials, n.d.).

When the Song of the Lord begins
1. Musicians come expecting to move in this area
2. Back up the flow of worship while waiting, the spirit of the Lord brooded over the waters until the creative word came. Soft humming creates a "seed bed" of song.
    a. Flow in worship progressions led by the piano or organ
    b. Harmonized by the choir in four part harmony
    c. Instruments provide harmony and perhaps melodies improvised in this setting.
    d. Solo singers develop melodies, praises and thanksgiving.
3. When singer or instrument begins, everyone else hold back until the song is established.
    a. 1st to join should be the harmony instruments. One should clearly be the leader on the piano or the organ and should not fight each other harmonically.
    b. Rhythm should express the characteristic of the song, the danger in this area is to impose your standard style in the song when it does not match the rhythm and harmony that the singer or instrument is portraying. Each melody naturally creates its own rhythm and harmony.
    c. Instruments should enter under the direction of the chief musicians.
        i. Example—strong bass solo—add the brass, strong sound
        ii. Example—soft high soprano melody—add the flutes, violins, guitars, vibes.

   d. Instruments must follow basic principles
     i. Be attentive, you must watch during this time.
     ii. Don't join until you are directed or unless you feel what you have is going to enhance the melody.
     iii. Watch your action leader for directions.

The International Worship Symposium was another key hub for teaching the theology and practice of Latter Rain ideas about Praise & Worship. In the larger teaching from which this section is excerpted, Glaeser is teaching on how to use various predetermined chord progressions to help facilitate times of spontaneous musical worship. Glaeser is using biblical quotes to show how the spirit of prophecy might descend on an instrumentalist to either accompany the singing of prophetic words or simply lead it non-verbally. For both Herron (above) and Glaeser, a period of open-ended instrumentation created the opportunity for encounter with God. This is, perhaps, not unlike the expectations around the use of an extended bridge in modern worship music since the mid-2010s.

 Source: Joannah Glaeser, "The Use of Chord Progressions in Spontaneous Worship," *Symposium 85: 8th Annual International Symposium* (August 1985).

 I. *Instrumental Accompaniment* Provides Foundation Worship.
   a. By definition, accompaniment provides a *richer effect* to the overall expression.
   b. The scriptures link the prophetic flow with the use of instruments.
     i. Elisha asked for a minstrel. (II Kings 3:15)
     ii. Saul's encounter with prophets describes them carrying instruments. (1 Samuel 10:5)
     iii. The sons of Asaph, Heman and Juduthan *prophesied* with harps, psalteries and cymbals. (I Chronicles 25:1)
     iv. Some Psalms are written for specific instruments, as implied in the title of the Psalm:
       1. Neginoth: Implies a "stringed instrument" (title of Psalm 4)
       2. Nehiloth: Means a "flute" (title of Psalm 5)
       3. Gittith: Implies a "harp" (title of Psalm 8)
       4. *Shoshannim*: Can mean a "straight trumpet" (title of Psalm 45)

        5. *Shushan eduth*: Implies a "trumpet of assemblage" (title of Psalm 60)
   v. Use of chord progressions provides an arena for instruments to prophesy.
  vi. The instrumental lead helps alleviate fear and intimidation and creates the atmosphere for the prophetic singing.

II. There is Only One "Formula" for *Ascending* Into His Presence
  a. Psalm 24 emphasizes the condition of our *hands* and our *heart*.
  b. *Ascent* is effectively communicated by a progression rather than a plan.

Vivien Hibbert was a prominent teacher at the International Worship Symposium in the 1980s (like Joannah Glaeser above). In this source, Vivien Hibbert with her husband Mike express a core component of a more developed Latter Rain praise teaching: each service has a divine telos that God is leading his attentive people toward. This requires worship leaders to be adaptable but also be able to sequence and lead people deeper into worship so that they are attentive to what God is saying. Repetition of songs and biblical truths is key to this "clear unfolding of revelation" of meaning.

Source: Mike and Vivien Hibbert, *Music Ministry* (Christchurch, New Zealand: Self-Published, 1982), 43.

The worship service needs to be free enough to "flow" into the specific revelation that God desires for each time we approach Him. This is not necessarily a "deep" and "heavy" thing, but an enlightening of the word of God to our spirit. (For years this truth may have been an intellectual understanding only). It is normal and natural that each Christian should live in a constant stream of revelation knowledge of God as a natural outflow of our worship relationship with Him. Because God is infinite, we will continue for eternity and still not have begun to realize the extent of any one aspect of His character or person.

    God has a plan and purpose for every service, so as the musicians, singers, dancers and worship leaders seek God throughout the week, then they can come, and flow in the same Holy Spirit. As we move into praise and worship God will develop *His* service, and there will be a clear unfolding of revelation in the midst of the people. There are so many directions that the Spirit may take within worship, and we can prepare our service and our hearts without leaving the congregation with the feeling that we have pre-arranged the whole service. Often one theme, or continuous stream of revelation may flow through an individual or congregation for weeks or even months. . . .

We need to be able to explore the depths of what God is saying in the midst of the church—we need to be able to explore the depths of who God is—we need to be able to explore the depths of the kingdom of God in the midst of the church. It will take eternity before we have even begun to understand one small aspect of God, and His character. . . . Don't allow yourself to sing the words without expecting the truth and the depths of meaning of those words to be demonstrated in your life, and understood, in part deep in your spirit. You may have to sing a song over and over many times because each time you sing it the Spirit of God takes you beyond the words and adds layer upon layer of powerful truth and revelation within your spirit.

Entering Past the Veil: Biblical Models for Flowing in Praise and Worship

As well as encouraging a more general movement through musical worship towards the release of the Song of the Lord, the Latter Rain movement also precipitated an even broader reflection about the biblical progression of worship. Common among teachers and leaders influenced by Latter Rain Praise-Presence theology, was an understanding that congregational singing progresses from exciting and upbeat times of praise into slower and more reflective times of worship (marked by intimate encounter with the presence of God). In this section, we will encounter several different theological models of musical worship that were becoming popular, especially during the 1980s. Many of these teachings focused heavily on patterns of worship found in the Old Testament. Institutions like the Tabernacle of Moses proved to be rich sites of biblical reflection that could provide a form and structure for Christian worship today. While tabernacle and temple models don't always mention music, the broader understandings of Old Testament worship practices presumed that the Levitical priesthood was inherently musical in its practices.

Judson Cornwall was one of the most well-travelled and well-published teachers in Pentecostal and charismatic circles in the 1970s and 1980s. (Some of his books on Praise and Worship sold over half a million copies, demonstrating his popularity in this period.) In this source, an excerpt from one of Cornwall's most popular books, Cornwall develops a model for times of congregational song modelled around the Tabernacle of Moses. This gave a clear developmental and thematic path that worship was to follow so that the congregation was invited into a deep spiritual fellowship with God through the music. In line with this progression, Cornwall highlights that the closer we get to the presence of the Holy of Holies, the more that the content of the songs should express something about the character and nature of God.

Source: Judson Cornwall, *Let Us Worship* (So. Plainfield, NJ: Bridge Publishing, 1983), 154–57.

Leading people always requires beginning where the people are. The song leader must locate their present spiritual position or he will miss them entirely, for few people will run to catch up once the march has begun. In most church services, locating the level of the people will generally be easy, for people have come to church from the activities of normal life and have a very minimum of God-consciousness. Their minds are concerned with people, places, things, and personal needs. They are very self-conscious.

The song leader might well start with a song or chorus of personal experience or testimony—one of the many "I am" or "I have" musical testimonies. This meets the people where they are and gives them something with which to identify early in the service.

In the typology of the Tabernacle in the wilderness, to which this hundreth Psalm alludes, this would be the encampment immediately outside the fence that surrounded the Tabernacle. It was the home of the priests, who, although encamped close to the Tabernacle, could not worship until they had entered the Tabernacle itself. And neither can we. If the song leader will bear in mind that songs about personal condition or experience are songs to be sung when the people are outside the Tabernacle enclosure, he can make excellent use of them to gently get the attention of the singers.

Since the Scripturally-declared purpose of gathering together is to worship, the goal of every song service should be to bring people into a worship experience. That would occur in the holy place, where the illumination of the Holy Spirit (the candlestick) makes fellowship with God (the table of shewbread) and worship of God (the altar of incense) possible, pleasurable, and profitable. We want to bring the singers into the holy place where they are conscious of this; but as it is more than one step from outside the court to inside the holy place, songs of experience should not be immediately followed by songs of God's greatness.

"Enter into his gates with thanksgiving . . ." (Psalm 100:4), the Psalmist instructs. Don't leave the people in the priestly encampment all the time; take gentle, progressive steps to move them closer to God's presence. This psalm lists three or four such steps, and thanksgiving is the first. Let the congregation enjoy singing songs of testimony until they are sufficiently united to begin moving closer to God. Use such songs to move the people through the gate that will separate them from the profane into the sacred, and then introduce songs and choruses of thanksgiving.

It is a matter of bringing them from a consciousness of what has been done in and for them (testimony) to Who did it in and for them (thanksgiving). The procession through the eastern gate into the outer court should be a joyful march, for thanks should never be expressed mournfully or negatively. While the people are singing choruses of thanksgiving, they will be thinking both of themselves and of their God, but by putting the emphasis upon the giving of thanks, the majority of the thought patterns should be on their God. Singing at this level will often invoke a beginning level of praise, but it will not produce worship, for the singers are not yet close enough to God's presence to express a worship response.

Step number two is "enter . . . into his courts with praise" (Psalm 100:4). Once the heart has been lifted in thanksgiving, it is natural for it to take the progressive steps into praise. To thank God for what He has done evokes praise for Who he is, so move the songs from thanksgiving for past favors to praises for His present mercy. The outer court is a fairly large place, so it may require more time singing choruses and songs of praise to move the people toward the holy place than it required to get them through the gates with music of thanksgiving.

The closer we get to the presence of God in the Holy of Holies, the more the songs will be concerned with God Himself. "Be thankful unto him, and bless his name," the Psalmist says (Psalm 100:4). Whereas we started singing about ourselves outside the walls, we will end up singing about God inside the holy place, for nothing in there speaks of man; it is in its every aspect a revelation of God. Here is where some of the majestic hymns give expression of higher concepts of God than do some of the simple choruses, but if it is a chorus-oriented congregation, let the choruses be those which direct all of the attention to God, Jesus, or the Holy Spirit.

If the leader has been successful in bringing the people step by step into the outer court and on through it into the holy place, there will be a rise in the spiritual response of the people. Instead of mere soulish, emotional responses, there will be responses from the human spirit that have depth and devotion in them. The emotional clapping will likely be replaced with devotional responses of upturned faces, raised hands, tears, and even a subtle change in the timbre of the voices. When there is an awareness that we have come into the presence of God, we step out of lightness into sobriety.

In this source, prominent British worship leader and composer, Graham Kendrick (one of the founders of the global March for Jesus movement) articulated his understanding of the progression of worship. Kendrick's teaching echoes many of the themes that were not only extant in Praise & Worship contexts but also in global Pentecostalism more broadly.[4] While Cornwall (above) and Kendrick both describe a similar progression of worship rooted in Psalm 100:4 and the Mosaic Tabernacle, Kendrick's description maps worship more closely onto the furnishings of the tabernacle. By contrast, Cornwall describes a more general move from outer courts into the Holy of Holies. While Kendrick doesn't explicitly mention a song set, this is implicit—the progression of Praise and Worship occurred through the songs that gave voice to the dispositions and attitudes fitting to each stage of the progression.

Source: Graham Kendrick, *Learning to Worship as a Way of Life* (Minneapolis: Bethany House Publishers, 1984), 144–51.

Our first step is to bring ourselves, setting our faces in God's direction, stepping for a moment out of the distractions of everyday life in order to

---

4. For instance, in 1993 the popular Korean pastor David Yonggi Cho published his own teaching on the progression of Christian worship also structured around the furnishings of the Tabernacle of Moses. See David Yonggi Cho, *Dr. Cho's Patterns of Prayer* (Seoul: Seoul Book Center, 1993).

give our attention entirely to worship. It is a choice we make, an entrance we deliberately step through. In Psalm 100:4 we read the exhortation: "Enter his gates with thanksgiving and his courts with praise." ... It could be argued that strong thanks and praise is the best way of preparing us to draw close to God, enabling us to break free from the burdens of life, and an overconcern with ourselves. ... A worshiper would not enter the tabernacle empty-handed but would bring an offering for sacrifice. While our offering is first and foremost ourselves, as a "living sacrifice" (Rom 12:1), we do not come empty-handed, and as a token of the fact that we are continually offered up to God, we bring the sacrifices described in Hebrews 13:15 [i.e., a "sacrifice of praise"]...Psalms of thanks and praise usually focus upon particular reasons for praising God, and the deeds he has done, his unchanging character and so on, and this is very practical because our hearts often need to be stirred to an awareness of him, and our minds reminded of the marvelous truths about him before we can even begin to expect a "face to face" encounter! We cannot expect to be intimate with somebody before we have become aware of the facts about them, and their qualities of character.

In the tabernacle worship there is much that speaks about the need to prepare ourselves for God's presence. The altar of burnt offering where the sacrifice in its entirety went up in smoke to heaven, illustrates the need for total consecration of ourselves to God, as Jesus gave himself totally for us. The brass laver, where priests would wash themselves before offering service to God, speaks of our need for cleansing. ...

The only light in this enclosed space comes from the golden candlestick, signifying the spiritual light which the Holy Spirit sheds on the word of God. ... Our worship needs to be enlightened, informed and beautified by the word of God, which is spiritually discerned and not by the natural light of human understanding.

In front of the veil of the holy of holies (now torn in two and wide open!) is the altar of incense, a symbol of prayer. It signifies the intercession of the risen ascended Christ before the throne of God on our behalf, and caught up as one with his prayers are the prayers of the people rising like a fragrant perfume to the Lord.

Now we approach our destination, through the torn veil, the way opened to us by Christ's broken body on the cross. After the noise of joyful singing, thanksgiving and praise, we begin to sense the majesty of God and our activity quietens down to be replaced by reverence and awe. ... Our praise turns to worship and adoration as we ponder on his [Christ's] great mercy. ...

It may seem strange to apply these last three "types" [i.e., the tablets of stone speaking to the righteousness of God; the pot of manna pointing to God's provision; and Aaron's rod revealing Jesus' eternal priesthood] to our worship today, but I believe that there is a vital significance here for application in our current understanding of where worship should lead us. Too often our approach to God stops short of entering the "inner sanctuary," and we hover around aimlessly wondering what to do after we have praised, thanked, prayed, sung and so on. These pictures show us that the place of communion with God is a place of rest. The 'rest' is there because in Jesus God has done everything necessary for our salvation and for the supply and sustenance of our lives.

I have no desire to create out of the lessons of the tabernacle a "formula" for worship, a strict sequence of events, or a standard "checklist" against which to measure what we do. . . . However, the principles embodied in it are put there by God for our instruction, and should serve to increase our vision of where we are going and how we get there when we are given the responsibility of leading people into the presence of God.

The Tabernacle of Moses was not the only model that Praise & Worship teachers relied upon in this period. In this source, John Wimber defines the progression that he encouraged leaders to follow in the Vineyard movement. For Wimber, worship was fundamentally about the outpouring of love from the human heart to God. Accordingly, the role of leaders was to lead the congregation to a place where they could express their love towards God and know God's love in return. While Wimber's teaching here is not rooted explicitly in an Old Testament model of worship (like the Tabernacle of Moses), his sense of the overall progression of musical worship sounds familiar in the broader Praise & Worship context.[5]

Source: John Wimber, "Worship: Intimacy with God," *Worship Conference* (Mercy Publishing, 1989).

In the Vineyard we see five basic phases of worship, phases through which leaders attempt to lead the congregation. Understanding these phases is helpful in our experience of God. Keep in mind that as we pass through

---

5. For a thicker description of worship at the flagship church of the Vineyard network under John Wimber, see Andy Park, Lester Ruth, and Cindy Rethmeier, *Worshiping with the Anaheim Vineyard: The Emergence of Contemporary Worship* (Grand Rapids: Eerdmans, 2016).

these phases we are headed toward one goal: intimacy with God. I define intimacy as belonging to or revealing one's deepest nature to another (in this case to God), and it is marked by close association, presence, and contact.

The first phase is the call to worship, which is a message directed toward the people. It is an invitation to worship. . . . The underlying thought of the call to worship is "Let's do it, let's worship now." . . .

The second phase is the engagement, which is the electrifying dynamic of connection to God and to each other. Expressions of love, adoration, praise, jubilation, intercession, petition—all of the dynamics of prayer are interlocked with worship—come forth from one's heart. In the engagement phase we praise God for who he is through music as well as prayer. . . .

As we move further in the engagement phase, we move more and more into loving and intimate language. Being in God's presence excites our hearts and minds and we want to praise him for the deeds he has done, for how he has moved in history, for his character and attributes. Jubilation is that heart swell within us which we want to exalt him. . . .

Expression then moves into a zenith, a climactic point, not unlike physical lovemaking (doesn't Solomon use the same analogy in the Song of Songs?). We have expressed what is in our hearts and minds and bodies, and now it is time to wait for God to respond. Stop talking and wait for him to speak, to move. I call this, the fourth phase, visitation: the almighty God visits his people.

His visitation is a by product of worship. We don't worship in order to gain his presence. He is worthy to be worshiped whether or not he visits us. But God "dwells in the praises of his people." So we should always come to worship prepared for an audience with the King. . . .

The fifth phase of worship is the giving of substance. The church knows so little about giving, yet the Bible exhorts us to give to God.

In contrast to the theological progressions of worship described above, this source uses the story of the dedication of the Solomon's Temple in 2 Chronicles 5 as a foundation for the progression of worship. However, the author cautions leaders and congregations against seeing this progression as a mechanism that will guarantee the presence of God. Praise in the temple is connected to—but does not guarantee—God's presence with his people. While praise was a necessary precondition of God's presence, God is still sovereign over the timing and nature of how he shows forth his glory. Though a decade or more later than some other writers on the topic, Teal's work on this topic was among the first published by an African American author.[6]

Source: Rodney A. Teal, *Reflections on Praise & Worship from a Biblical Perspective* (privately published, 1999), 19–21.

When looking for models of corporate praise & worship, we often focus on the Chronicler's account of the dedication of Solomon's Temple. See II Chronicles 5:12-14. While that passage is a powerful account of what can happen when the people of God come together "as one" in praise & worship, that account is often a fountain of frustration for the New Testament Church because we think that unless we have the "Cloud Experience" every Sunday, we have not worshiped.

A proper understanding of II Chronicles 5 can help [a] ease our anxiety over trying to re-create the "Cloud Experience" and [b] foster the "atmospheric conditions" conducive to the formation The Cloud. In worship, God is in the driver's seat, and, whatever He does, we flow right along with Him, instead of trying to direct Him. . . .

Before we leave our study of II Chronicles 5, take note of the "when" factor in the passage: God's Presence filled the Temple when the singers and musicians (the musical Levites) lifted up praises unto God by singing and playing "as one." The importance of "praise" cannot be understated. If God decides to show up in an unusual way, He will do so in the midst of praise. See Psalm 22:3. Compare II Chronicles 20. LET THERE BE PRAISE!!!

Just praise Him and let Him take care of filling the temple, if that is what He wants to do at that time. Often, instead of praising/worshiping God, we praise/worship a "feeling"—the feeling we had three Sundays ago when "the Spirit was high." Don't worship worship. Worship God! The truth of the matter is that God manifests His Presence in His Way at His Time.

Myles Munroe, a prominent speaker on Praise & Worship from the Bahamas and a graduate of Oral Roberts University, utilizes a well-known key for interpreting Scripture's witness on Praise & Worship. Like many authors

---

6. See broader descriptions of Praise & Worship and its place in the flow of service in Birgitta Joelisa Johnson, "'Oh, For a Thousand Tongues to Sing': Music and Worship in African American Megachurches of Los Angeles, California" (PhD diss., University of California, Los Angeles, 2008).

and speakers in the previous two decades, Munroe looked to the Hebrew words in the Old Testament that stand behind the translation into English as "praise."[7] The distinctive feature of Munroe's teaching though is that he suggests that not only are these words cumulative (i.e., all facets of praise are necessary) but that they should occur in a certain sequence. For God to become enthroned upon the praises of his people—and the release of the Song of the Lord to occur—the church must practice the pattern of praise that God established in Scripture.

Source: Myles Munroe, *The Purpose and Power of Praise & Worship* (Shippensburg, PA: Destiny Image Publishers, 2000), 120–26.

Although they [i.e., the seven dimensions or portraits of praise] do not occur in the Scriptures in a strict order, or even all in the same praise experience, there is a sense in which one builds upon the other as the worshiper is caught up into seeking the presence of God. At first, there is the verbal thanksgiving for what God has done (*todah*). This usually recounts specific ways the Lord has protected or blessed the worshiper. Then, as the praise becomes more spontaneous, outburst of thanksgiving combined with the extension of the hands to God in adoration may occur (*yadah*). As the worshiper continues to thank God for personal blessings, a more general honoring and adoring of God may follow (*halal*). This in turn may progress into the making of music (*zamar*) and into expressions of victory and celebration, often with dance. This heightened exhilaration may lessen at times as the worshiper waits with expectancy for God to lead in a new direction or to reveal Himself in some manner (*barak*). Thus, as the intensity of praise ebbs and flows, the worshiper may slip back and forth among the various dimensions of praise. . . . A good example of progression through the dimensions of praise is found in First Chronicles chapter 16 when King David takes the Ark of the Covenant to Jerusalem. . . . This pattern in praise has not changed. God still requires that we approach Him with sacrifices before we seek His favor and blessing. This is why *tehillah* is the last dimension of praise, not the first. God is not willing to be enthroned among us until He sees that we want *Him*, not just the things He can give us. . . . In essence, not just any praise brings God's

---

7. For more background on this theology of worship, see Jonathan Ottaway, "The Seven Hebrew Words for Praise: Pentecostal Interpretation of Scripture in Liturgical Theology," *Worship* 97, no. 1 (2023): 10–30.

presence to us. Only praise that follows His pattern, starting with the sacrifices of a willing heart and a contrite spirit and continuing as we quiet ourselves before Him until we yield ourselves completely to Him, will do. Our hearts must be totally consumed with Him, and only Him, as His Spirit reigns supreme in our spirit. This is when God becomes enthroned in our praise and the songs of the spirit begin.

While many of the sources we have considered in this section have embraced specific biblical passages as the foundational shape for worship, there has been a growing movement among evangelical theologians and teachers to embrace a more wide-ranging "gospel-centered" shape for worship.[8] *In gospel-centered worship, the entirety of the service narrates the broad scope of the Christian gospel so that worshipers hear its message, receive its grace, and are sent to live in its light. As one representative example of this movement,*[9] *this source—a highly influential worship textbook in the past two decades—explains how the gospel story that worship does should affect the selection and structuring of songs within the service. Fundamentally, Cherry argues that songs serve the storyline.*

Source: Constance M. Cherry, *The Worship Architect: A Blueprint for Designing Culturally Relevant and Biblically Faithful Services* (Grand Rapids: Baker Academic, 2010), 193–96.

[The worship service] begins with the general part of the story by introducing the Triune God as the main character—singing of God's attributes and rehearsing the marvelous ways he has acted for all people (gathering). As the service progresses, the story becomes more particular as worshipers learn more and more about their relationship with God (Word). Worshipers are increasingly invested as the storyline becomes more specific. . . . Eventually the pathos of the story reaches a climax of willful surrender (Table or alter-

---

8. For a description of how this gospel-centered movement allies with a corollary aim to practice "biblical worship," see Emily Snider Andrews, "The Power of Claiming Biblical Authority; We Practice Biblical Worship: A Southern Baptist Vision of Liturgical Authority" in *Worship and Power: Liturgical Authority in Free Church Traditions*, ed. Sarah Kathleen Johnson and Andrew Wymer (Eugene: Cascade Books, 2023), 132–50.

9. For a broader discussion of recent evangelicals who have promoted a gospel-centered structure for worship, see Jonathan Ottaway, "Dipping a Ladle in the Cauldron of Story: Assessing Worship Leadership as Gospel Narration," *Proceedings of the North American Academy of Liturgy* (2025), https://doi.org/10.70927/f9ynah46.

native response), and then the story winds its way to the resolution (sending). Essentially, the progression of worship is a journey in which the truth of God's story forms the substance of the journey. . . .

The pastoral musician is cognizant of the development of the storyline, of the movement from general to specific, and of this journey we call worship. He or she is interested in selecting songs that convey the story of God. Music is a vehicle for the content of worship. It is a primary way that the story is told. . . .

Music is an appropriate medium for telling all aspects of the story. Songs convey general truths about God, narrate the story of the life of Christ, celebrate the Christian year, and interpret a specific Scripture text while also allowing the worshiper to respond to that text. All parts of the story are sung. . . .

As the story of God moves from the general to the specific, so the musical selections will likely progress from the general celebration and acknowledgment of the attributes and actions of God towards consideration of more specific aspects of the story. . . .

One important role the pastoral musicians play, then, is that of storyteller. They tell the story of God by helping God's people sing the story of God.

Making an IMPACT: Structuring Worship for Maximal Effect

This last section of the chapter—named for Rick Warren's structure for worship that was developed at Saddleback Church—describes a broader set of liturgical sensibilities about how musical worship needs to flow. Unlike the sources in the previous sections, which formed elaborate progressions of worship out of biblical practices or institutions, the sources in this section are more pragmatically oriented. These sources describe the necessity for worship to flow musically and thematically because they are more highly attuned to the participation of the congregation. By making the music flow, worship leaders are better able to plan and lead times of worship that will gain the buy-in of worshipers.

In this source, Tom Brooks, a producer for Integrity's Hosanna! Music (one of the largest recording companies focused on Praise & Worship), provides general guidance for how worship should spontaneously progress in ways that seem natural to the congregation. For Brooks, selecting songs so that the congregation could perceive the service as a continuous whole was critical for maintaining the congregation's deep participation in worship.

Source: Tom Brooks, "Spontaneity in Worship," *Worship Times* (Summer 1986), 4.

Choose songs that flow together *conceptually*. Music is a vehicle by which we express Scriptures, thoughts, and ideas about the Lord. Imagine each song as a paragraph in a letter. If you change subjects every paragraph, your letter won't make sense. If you start off your set of songs with one that speaks of God's love, stay on that theme for a while. Select other songs which explore which subject further.

Choose songs that flow together *musically*. Don't change the tone abruptly when you start a new song. If you are singing about the love of God and switch to "Onward Christian Solders," your congregation may be more apt to think about Mrs. Jones' silly new hat. Be sure to select songs with similar rhythms, keys, and moods so that the movement from one song to another is smooth and conducive to worship.

Don't be afraid to linger in God's presence. When you come to a place in worship where people are "tuned in," sometimes the best thing to do is nothing. Let your people enjoy God's presence.

Although this source from Jack Hayford employs Psalm 100:4 as the starting place for his description of worship—a verse that was critical for both Judson Cornwall and Graham Kendrick—Hayford demonstrates a different approach to reflecting on flow. Rather than describing worship as a progression into the Holy of Holies (like in the tabernacle of Moses), Hayford speaks more generally here about the flow of the service. Good flow means that the entire service is clearly oriented towards the truth that the service proclaims—unlike what he sees in other congregations that select songs "arbitrarily." Coherent thematic flow, for Hayford, is a sign that the worship is led by the Holy Spirit.

Source: Jack W. Hayford, *The Church on the Way: Learning to Live in the Promise of Biblical Congregational Life* (Old Tappan, NJ: Chosen Books by Fleming Revell Co., 1983), 102–3.

On Sunday morning we gather to carry out the three-fold ministry which characterizes our mission as a congregation. We exalt the Name of Jesus Christ and summon every person to "enter into His gates with thanksgiving and into His courts with praise" (Psalm 100:4). From the platform, we direct prayer, praise and other expressions of worship, but at the same time we try to give simple guidelines to encourage each person to express his own sensitive and thoughtful worship. . . .

We use songs to emphasize each truth involved in the flow of the service. Music helps sustain a unified focus on the truth being emphasized. We reject the arbitrary selection of choruses as being fundamentally dishonest with God and the congregation. What we speak and what we sing must constantly move toward the goal of the gathering. This direction is at the heart of *order* in a service.

Many people mistakenly consider themselves led of the Holy Spirit, even though the "leading" may cause a service to drift from theme to theme with no coherence. This is not motivated by the Holy Spirit, but by human subjectivity, and is the cause for many pointless gatherings.

Rick Warren and his congregation, Saddleback Church, are two of the most famous names in the seeker-sensitive model of worship informed by the Church Growth movement.[10] In addition to Warren's writing and itinerant speaking on the topic of church growth, the church was a hub for prominent worship conferences in the 1990s. In this excerpt, Warren is describing how an approach to worship might follow from a broader philosophy of growth. The IMPACT model was developed at Saddleback, a Baptist congregation, by their worship leader Rick Muchow after visiting Pentecostal churches. Note how the gap between church practices and modern culture are the basis for commending this model, especially the elimination of "dead time" and improving flow. Knowing the model was derived from a visit to Pentecostal churches, the goal of leading people into an intimate time with God is perhaps unsurprising— sharing more with Cornwall (above) than might be expected.

Source: Rick Warren, *The Purpose-Driven Church: Growth Without Compromising Your Message & Mission* (Grand Rapids, MI: Zondervan, 1995), 255–56.

---

10. For a broader study of this movement, see Kimon Howland Sargeant, *Seeker Churches: Promoting Traditional Religion in a Nontraditional Way* (Rutgers University Press, 2000).

Almost all churches need to pick up the pace of their services. Television has permanently shortened the attention span of Americans. In one time-out during Monday night football you'll see a replay, three commercials, and a network news brief—they don't want you to get bored! MTV has shortened the attention span for baby busters even more. In one three-minute video alone you may be bombarded with several thousand images.

In contrast, most church services move at a snail's pace. There is a lot of "dead time" between different elements....

In addition to speeding up your service, work on improving its flow. The difference between an average service and an outstanding service is flow.

At Saddleback, we use the word IMPACT as an acronym to remind us of the flow we desire to create with our music:

Inspire Movement: This is what we want to do with the opening song. We use a bright, upbeat number that makes you want to tap your foot, clap, or at least smile. We want to loosen up the tense muscles of uptight visitors. When your body is relaxed, your attitude is less defensive....

Praise: We then move to joyful songs about God.

Adoration: We move to a more meditative, intimate song to God. The pace is slowed here.

Commitment: This song gives people an opportunity to affirm or reaffirm a commitment to God. It is usually a first person singular song like "I Want to Be More Like You."

Tie it all together: The very last thing we do is end the service on another short, upbeat song.

Sally Morgenthaler was one of the most prominent writers in the conversation around attractional worship for the seeker-sensitive movement of Church Growth.[11] In this setting, worship was seen as an opportunity for, as the title suggests, evangelizing unbelievers by inviting them to encounter the presence of God (rather than just attracting them with contemporary "secular" songs). This excerpt is from one of the best-selling books on the topic. Here, she describes generationally targeted worship services for "Boomerangs"—members of the Boomer generation who were returning to church. Morgenthaler ar-

---

11. One of the most prominent pastoral and theological critics of this movement and its impact on worship in the 1990s was Marva Dawn. See Marva J. Dawn, *Reaching Out Without Dumbing Down: A Theology of Worship for the Turn-of-the-Century Culture* (Grand Rapids: Eerdmans, 1995); Marva J. Dawn, *A Royal "Waste" of Time: The Splendor of Worshiping God and Being Church for the World* (Grand Rapids: Eerdmans, 1999).

gues that continuous, flowing worship helps the boomerang worshiper engaged more deeply with God.

Source: Sally Morgenthaler, *Worship Evangelism: Inviting Unbelievers into the Presence of God* (Grand Rapids, MI: Zondervan, 1995), 157.

Boomerangs expect public events to progress toward a "defining moment" or experience. In a worship setting, that translates into greater intimacy with God. Consequently, in worship planning for boomerangs, take care that each worship response or event builds on the one before, producing a sense of constant momentum, of moving forward toward closeness with God through Christ (Heb. 10:22). . . .

Large blocks of similar or related events allow the boomerang to experience the worship process more deeply. Whereas the startstop effect of many individual, unrelated events tends to short-circuit the boomerang's ability to invest wholeheartedly in a service, unified blocks of activity allow for uninterrupted, advancing engagement with God. They give the boomerang the sense of being led gently into a worship experience rather than being jerked along or force-fed.

This source from a worship leader at Hillsong Church[12] encourages worship leaders to be sensitive to the needs and expectations of the congregation in how they lead worship. There is an implicit critique here of earlier Praise & Worship models of progression that lasted so long they became ineffective. Instead, Zschech argues that worship needs to be sensitive to the leading of the Holy Spirit but also economical with time by being sensitive to how the congregation is responding.

Source: Darlene Zschech, *Extravagant Worship* (Minneapolis: Bethany House, 2001), 172–73.

---

12. More has been written about Hillsong Church and its music than any other contributor to Contemporary Praise & Worship. In addition to numerous individual articles, see also the edited collection by two of the most-published authors on Hillsong, Tanya Riches (a former Hillsong College faculty member) and Tom Wagner, eds., *The Hillsong Movement Examined: You Call Me Out Upon the Waters* (Palgrave Macmillan, 2017). See also Nelson Cowan, "Liturgical Biography as Liturgical Theology: Co-Constructing Theology at Hillsong, New York City" (PhD diss., Boston University School of Theology, 2019).

When the Holy Spirit leads people and worship, there is a natural ebb and flow to the times of high praise and deep worship that builds up the spirits of those who participate.

If you have the privilege of leading worship, be considerate of the time. "Free worship" doesn't need to go on for two hours. How awesome the service is and how long it lasts are totally irrelevant. Sovereign visitations from the Lord do happen, but don't try to manufacture them. It does not help to build the church if the worship team is having a great time and totally misses the fact that everyone else in the church has fallen asleep or left for a cup of coffee!

At Hillsong Church, we have extreme moments of praise, and then we will often pull back so that people can hear the voice of God speak to them in the stillness of his presence. Sometimes worshipers run right over what God is trying to say to them! But with that ebb and flow of worship, we are aiming to keep everyone together, because we want to see everyone engage in bringing their worship before the King.

Discussion Questions

- Think about the last worship service you attended or led. Was there a particular shape to the time of musical worship? Were you aware of a goal that the time of worship was trying to move toward? Would a worshiper "in the pews" be able to discern what that shape was?

- Many of the Latter Rain–influenced leaders encouraged musicians to be prepared for times of spontaneous worship. Is spontaneous worship something that is valued in your worshiping community? If so, how do musicians prepare themselves to help lead that time? How are such times managed practically? Who leads?

- What role should spontaneity and improvisation play in worship services? Is it something that we should plan to incorporate into worship or instead, merely welcome when the Spirit moves? Are there any dangers to be aware of in prioritizing spontaneity over structure, or vice versa?

- How should worship be attentive to the needs and expectations of seekers in how the worship service is structured? Should it be?

- What does the concept of "flow" mean in your worship context and how do you cultivate that?

CHAPTER 5
PROFESSIONALS: MUSICIANS AS LEADERS OF WORSHIP

The leadership of Contemporary Praise & Worship services is one of the most visible features of the practice. In contrast with "traditional worship" where the organist or accompanist is located off to the side, in Contemporary Praise & Worship, the worship leader usually stands front and center.

This is more than merely a shift in visibility. It signifies a much deeper evolution in the role of the church musician. Consider the name of the chief musician's role: a worship leader. This is a term that was not commonly used before the 1970s, especially to describe musicians. Calling a musician a worship leader suggests that the musician's function has much more significance than merely playing notes or leading songs. This change in title is underscored by the worship leader's physical position, directly facing the congregation. This position implies that not only does the congregation need to see the worship leader but the worship leader needs to see and engage the congregation. This illustrates the way the worship leader's role has developed into a dynamic and relational act of liturgical leadership. Worship leaders are not just facilitators of music. They are musical priests, leading the congregation into (as we saw in the last chapter) the Holy of Holies.

Undoubtedly, the most significant influence on this new role of leadership was the Praise and Worship movement that emerged from the Latter Rain revival. Because the idea that God inhabits the praises of his people—citing Psalm 22:3—was commonplace within this movement (see chapter 2), it naturally followed that those who led the church's praise were undertaking a significant priestly ministry. Not only was their musical ministry important but so was their spiritual leadership of the congregation. As leaders of praise, worship leaders helped to usher the congregation into the Holy of Holies.

At the same time, the emergence of the worship leader in the Praise and Worship movement occurred within a broader historical context. Throughout the twentieth century, musicians were starting to acquire more recognition for the significance of their role within the church's broader ministry. Many churches increasingly recognized that lively congregational singing or relevant musical performances that would appeal to outsiders necessitated professionals trained in new ways. Musicians increasingly became an indispensable feature of the ecclesial organizational chart. Although musicians were not exactly pastors, their roles within the church started to assume pastoral functions; many were ordained in their churches. Supporting this development was a rise in programs, resources, and conferences to support these new musician-pastors. This new class of professionals not only needed regular employment but support and encouragement as well!

In the 1990s and beyond, as the Praise and Worship movement and the Contemporary Worship movement increasingly began to influence and shape each other, a shared vision of the worship leader emerged. This new role combined the spiritually attuned musician who leads the congregation into God's presence, the professional musician responsible for the organization and administration of the church's music ministry, and the ability to communicate the gospel in evangelistic ways. In this period, another development—the emergence of the worship artist—further cemented the ubiquity and centrality of worship leaders as Christian leaders.

"The Ministry of Song Is a Priestly Ministry": The Praise and Worship Movement and the Worship Leader

In the Praise and Worship movement that arose out of the Latter Rain revival, the dominant emphasis on the presence of God within praise and the telos of worship as the Song of the Lord (see chapter 2) gave new significance to the music or song leader. Such leaders did not just facilitate the congregation's singing. Through leading praise, these leaders ushered their churches into the very presence of God. They were "worship leaders." In the sources below, we will see that responsibility reflected within the music leader's task. In typical Latter Rain fashion, many of these sources will draw an equivalence between the musicians of the Old Testament tabernacles and temple and the modern-day song leader. Drawing this parallel greatly heightened the importance of the music leader's role.

One of the most important early leaders within the Latter Rain network of churches, Charlotte Baker, makes a typical Latter Rain argument for the significance of musical praise. Notice how Baker draws an equivalence between the Levitical priests and the musicians of the Old Testament. For Baker, the fact that priests and musicians were provided for financially in similar ways indicated that their roles were equivalent. Accordingly, the church of her day needed to re-discover the significance of these musical priests who can lead the congregation in the new song of praise.
Note: Although we have quoted from the 1990 edition, this source was originally published in 1979.

Source: E. Charlotte Baker, *On Eagles Wings: A Book on Praise and Worship* (1979; Shippensburg, PA: Destiny Image, 1990), 93–94.

One thing God requires of His people is that they come before His presence with singing (Ps. 100:2). A large number of attending church members do not know the true function of singing in a worship service or why they sing in church. They only know that singing is incorporated into most worship services. Singing was such an important part of the worship in the house of God, that David systematically appointed those who were to minister in music and in song. A distinct charge was laid upon them for this ministry (1 Chron. 9:33). Today, there are those in the house of God whose ministry is to enter into spiritual song during times of worship.

Nehemiah 13:5 notes that the portion to the singers was given along with the portion to the priests. Today the ministry of song is a priestly ministry, and plays an essential part in our worship. We need a new song each day as we come into the presence of the Lord (Ps. 98:1); a song which has never been sung before, a fresh response to the Lord. That new song brings refreshing to us, builds and draws us closer to Him. At a time when Israel needed water the people sang to the well, "Spring up, O well." At times we should sing to the well with our hearts. During dry seasons we can sing to that well, and the song of the Lord and the Word of God will begin to flow, watering our desert lands.

This source is from David Blomgren, another key figure in the early Latter Rain movement. Here, Blomgren provides a different angle upon the significance of the worship leader, again drawing upon Old Testament institutions. The musicians in David's service were trusted stewards who had an important function in the worshiping life of Israel. Their work of singing was strenuous and difficult—not something to be taken lightly but a position of great importance. So, too, was the position of the worship leader.

Source: David K. Blomgren, *Song of the Lord* (Portland, OR: Bible Press, 1978), 3.

1 Chronicles 25:1 tells us that those who were appointed to be singers in the Temple were separated by David "to the service" (Hebrew, *Abodah*). This word in the original Hebrew had the idea to serve in the sense of acting as a slave for the owner. It was used not only of the household slave but to important persons such as vassel [sic] kings who were under an overlord.

The emphasis of this word was not so much on the servile status of the servant as on his function to carry out the will of his lord. The word suggested rather a relationship as a trusted steward of some particular obligation, especially in the sense of faithfully discharging the work given to him. This concept of the word should be central in our thinking when we realize that this same word *"Abodah"* was one of the regular Hebrew words for worship in the Old Testament.

Thus inherent in the Scripture concept of worship is something active and strenuous. To the Levitical singers in the Temple, worship was some action they performed, namely singing unto the Lord. They were entrusted with the Levitical obligation to faithfully worship in their "service" of singing.

If the congregation enters God's presence through musical praise, is that solely dependent of the worship leader? What role did the congregation play in their own spiritual experience? These were questions that leaders within the Latter Rain Praise & Worship movement had to wrestle with. In a key newsletter produced by Latter Rain leaders, the author argues that trained musicians are particularly crucial because they lead the congregation into the song of the Lord—a time of ecstatic spiritual singing, often in tongues. These trained musicians needed to be prepared both spiritually and musically to lead the congregation into worship. (Note again the heavy emphasis placed on Old Testament institutions.)

Source: [Barry Griffing], "Catechism Corner," *Music Notes* 2, no. 4 (1980), 4 [emphasis original].

Q. Is the Song of the Lord to be sung by the appointed worshippers or by congregational worshippers?
A. Both. Usually, the appointed worshippers (worship leader, choir, orchestra) initiate the song of the Lord, then congregational worshippers respond. In II Chr. 29, the Levite-musicians initiated the song of the Lord because that was their appointed ministry in the temple, according to verses 25 and 26: "And he (King Hezekiah) *set* the Levites in the house of the Lord with cymbals, with psaltries, and with harps . . . and the Levites stood with the instruments of David." Subsequently, we see in verse 28, that "all the congregation worshipped. . . ."

Q. Is the Song of the Lord improvised music or prepared music?
A. It can be either. In I Chr. 25, we saw that the Levite musicians "were *instructed* in the *songs of the Lord*," from which we can conclude that there were specific songs they were taught. And yet in the same chapter, we see that they "prophecied with harps, psaltries, and cymbals . . ." from which we conclude that there was also an inspirational spontaneity to their music ministry.

Q. What are the main prerequisites to the Song of the Lord flowing in a church's worship experience?

A. According to II Chr. 29, there are three:

1) Church leadership (typified by King Hezekiah) must not only believe that Jesus is restoring His singing voice to the church, but, they must actively promote the restoration of this experience in their particular assembly. Notice that Hezekiah, between v.2-25, prepared the *Temple*, the *elders*, the *musicians*, and the *congregation* for this worship experience.

2) The *appointed worshipper* (typified by the priest and Levites) must be prepared spirit, soul, and body to respond musically to the prophetic atmosphere of the Spirit of Christ in the worship service.

3) The congregation must bring the *sacrifice of praise* (typified by the *burnt offering*) into the House of the Lord (Jer. 33:11).

By the early 1980s, the concept of the "worship leader" was starting to filter into popular use.[1] This source tries to encourage churches to gain a fuller vision of what this role entails. Leading worship is more than hosting the meeting but a ministry of both prophetically releasing the Holy Spirit's presence in the congregation and attuning the congregation to the Holy Spirit's leadership.

Source: Mike and Vivien Hibbert, *Music Ministry* (Christchurch, New Zealand: Self-Published, 1982), 72–73.

Probably of all the worship ministries, the role of the worship leader is the hardest. It is an often misunderstood ministry. Many people only see this role as a person who waves their arms around and leads a few songs. Sometimes that is all that is required in a service—a few songs, neatly strung together with a scripture verse or comment here and there. However, if we are really going to see congregations led into, and established in worship, then the whole concept of worship leading has to be developed.

. . . If, as a worship leader, you are not particularly musical, then learn how to stand back at times, and release the singers and musicians to lead

---

1. Cowan documents the emergence of and transformation of the role of the worship leader in recent years among evangelicals and Pentecostal-charismatics. See Nelson Cowan, "Lay-Prophet-Priest: The Not-So-Fledgling 'Office' of the Worship Leader," *Liturgy* 32, no. 1 (2017): 24–31.

and minister. How submitted to the Holy Spirit a worship leader has to be. We try to do everything for Him, and organize Him out of His role.

There is a need during worship, for a prophetic anointing to flow in the meeting. I don't mean for this to sound like some Pentecostal cliché—there is a reality to this that can only be known through prayer and seeking God for your situation. There is a lot said to worship leaders about talking too much. However, I see a need for a new prophetic voice to come in the midst of the worship, and often that can come through a worship leader prophetically exhorting the congregation. . . . It takes a prophetic voice and anointed leadership for the congregation to be led into a new place of encounter with the Lord in worship.

The Latter Rain vision of the worship leader has continued to be deeply influential into the present. This source from 2014 makes a robust case for the deep spiritual significance of the worship leader's role. Their ministry delves into the deep mysteries of the heart of God and releases that into the congregation, bringing about healing and deliverance. Thus, a high moral standard is set for them. Notice, too, in the title, the reference to the key and pattern of the tabernacle of David.

Source: Rodney Williams, Sr. (Prophet), *The Key of David: Davidic Patterns and Blueprints for Worship Leaders* (Zion Muzik, 2014), 30–31.

We need healthy, sober and anointed musicians in our midst; the kind that carries the skill and keys needed to unlock greater dimensions in the spirit. Music activates, it stirs, it announces, it reveals, it breaks open and it establishes. But we must have willing vessels in place ready to labor before the Lord. . . . There is a sound that comes from the minstrel's instrument that brings deliverance but that sound is only an interpretation of the knowledge, relationship and love of God hidden in the heart. Minstrels have the ability to loose a sound that like a surgeon cuts open and removes unwanted pain. A familiar story in the Bible talks about a tormented king named Saul and how miserable he was because the presence of God had left him. King Saul requested a minstrel and one of the servants suggested David saying "Behold, I have seen a son of Jesse the Bethlehemite, that is cunning in playing, and a mighty valiant man, and a man of war, and prudent in matters, and a comely person, and the Lord is with him" (1 Samuel 16:18 KJV).

A Developing Guild: The Rise of the Professional Musician in Evangelical Churches

The Latter Rain discussion of the significance of the worship leader's role did not take place in a historical vacuum. In the late nineteenth century into the twentieth century more broadly, musicians started to take a more prominent role in evangelical church and parachurch ministries. With this enhanced role, there was a growing professionalization of the church musician alongside the development of resources and programs to support this trend. This section ranges over a broad historical period to give a sense of the developing trend of professional musicians in church employment.

In the nineteenth century, prominent evangelistic ministries served to heighten the role of musicians in Christian ministry. Musicians like Ira Sankey became increasingly synonymous with big-name evangelists such as D.L. Moody. Sankey's ministry in song became an indispensable counterpoint to the preaching of the gospel. In this source, Sankey himself reflects on both the evangelistic power of song and the widespread nature of preacher-musician teams, to the extent that people sometimes merged two distinct people into one!

Source: Ira David Sankey, *My Life and the Story of the Gospel Hymns and of Sacred Songs and Solos* (Philadelphia: P. W. Ziegler Co., 1907), v–vii, 88.

In 1873, God was pleased to send Mr. Moody and myself to Great Britain, where a work of grace was begun that has continued until the present day. About the same time Whittle and Bliss were doing a remarkable work in the United States, Bliss becoming one of the greatest song-evangelists of that age. For the last two or three years we have had the splendid campaign of Torrey and Alexander in Australia, Great Britain and America. In their work the prominent feature has been the use of praise, their most popular hymn being "The Glory Song," which perhaps is the most generally used Gospel song of the day.

We all agree with what Dr. Pentecost has said regarding the power of sacred song: "I am profoundly sure that among the divinely ordained instrumentalities for the conversion and sanctification of the soul, God has not given a greater, besides the preaching of the Gospel, than the singing of psalms and hymns and spiritual songs. I have known a hymn to do God's work in a soul when every other instrumentality has failed. I could not enumerate the times God has rescued and saved my soul from darkness, discouragement and weariness by the singing of a hymn, generally by bringing one to my own heart and causing me to sing it to myself. It would be easy to fill many pages with interesting facts in connection with the use of hymns in the public worship of the house of God. I have seen vast audiences melted and swayed by a simple hymn when they have been unmoved by a powerful presentation of the Gospel from the pulpit."[2] . . .

At a meeting in Norfolk, as Mr. Moody was about to begin his sermon, after I had sung a number of hymns, the minister of the church stepped up and said: "I want to make a little explanation to my people; many of my members believe that Moody and Sankey are one man, but brethren and sisters, this man is Mr. Moody, and that man at the organ is Mr. Sankey; they are not one person, as you supposed."

Phil Kerr (1906–1960) was a travelling evangelist, composer, and musician who was ordained by the Assemblies of God. This source—a textbook used across a number of Bible schools at the time[3]—argues that because music is so important to the evangelistic mission of the church, the song leader carries a heavy duty. Because eternal souls hang in the balance, the church musician needs to be more than musically prepared. They must be spiritually prepared to lead spiritually empowered singing.

Source: Phil Kerr, *Music in Evangelism and Stories of Famous Christian Songs*, 3rd ed. (1939; Glendale CA: Gospel Music Publishers, 1950), 81, 88–89.

It is to be regretted that too few ministers and evangelists and Christian workers realize the potential evangelistic power of inspired and Spirit-anointed gospel music. It is as though a soldier, facing tremendous opposition,

---

2. Here, Sankey is quoting from George F. Pentecost, introduction to *Song Victories of "The Bliss and Sankey Hymns," Being a Collection of One Hundred Incidents in Regard to the Origin and Power of the Hymns Contained in Gospel Hymns and Sacred Songs* (Dover NH: D. Lothrop and Co., 1877), 11–12.

3. For more information, see Edwin Anderson, "The Passing of Phil Kerr," *Pentecostal Evangel* (Jan 8, 1961), 30.

deliberately ignored a high-powered machine-gun which was ready for his use, and chose instead to fight with less effective weapons. If it be true that music can be a powerful force in the realm of evangelism, surely every Christian worker should realize its importance and learn to employ it to the utmost advantage....

If music is powerful, and if music which has divine anointing is *doubly*-powerful, then indeed the gospel singer should realize the serious importance of his mission. He has as important a commission as the gospel preacher. Souls can be won to Christ through the singing of a sacred song just as truly as through the preaching of a sermon. With divine anointing resting upon the singer and upon the song, souls *may* be drawn to the Lord,—souls which may possibly never have another chance. And if those souls are not reached, because of a *powerless* song, when they *might* have been reached through a *powerful* song, the responsibility for their eternal doom rests upon the singer who had performed his task so lightly and carelessly!...

The gospel singer should be entirely consecrated, and should make an intensive spiritual preparation before each service as does the preacher....

Technical preparation, as needful as it is, is not sufficient. Vocalizing is not sufficient preparation. If an hour spent in vocal preparation for a certain service, the same length of time, or more, should be spent in spiritual preparation.

Despite the popularity and centrality of evangelistic preacher-musician duos, the emergence of a professional class of evangelical musicians was slow in the twentieth century. Looking back over the developments of the twentieth century, Don Hustad notes the dramatic growth of resources and conferences aimed at professional church musicians. An indirect result of this was that a variety of Protestant denominations were persuaded to invest in professional musicians. This helped to contribute towards the development of professional music leaders as a role within the church leadership.

Source: Don Hustad, *Jubilate!: Church Music in the Evangelical Tradition* (Hope Publishing, 1981), 48.

The strongest impetus for evangelicals to move to a professional ministry of music came at the end of the Second World War. Professional organizations dedicated to the improving of church music were formed and remain active in various denominational bodies; they usually publish educational materials or conduct a periodical church music conference, or both. The Fellowship of United Methodist Musicians has published *The Music Ministry* and meets annually. The Fellowship of American Baptist Musicians convenes at Green Lake, Wisconsin every summer; they also receive a newsletter which is a part of a special FABM edition of *Journal of Church Music*, published by Fortress Press, a subsidiary of the Lutheran Church in America. The Lutheran Society for Worship, Music and the Arts releases a periodical bulletin and publishes the magazine Response. *Church Music* is another Lutheran magazine, published by Concordia. Presbyterians conduct a national church music conference annually at Montreat, North Carolina; the Presbyterian Association of Musicians cooperates with the two largest Presbyterian bodies in publishing *Reformed Liturgy and Music*. The National Church Music Fellowship was organized in 1952 by leaders in Bible schools and colleges who were concerned with the church music needs of smaller conservative denominations and of churches which consider themselves to be nondenominational; they too conduct an annual convention and distribute a newsletter. All of these organizations give significant help and guidance to both full and part-time directors of church music activities. Together with the impact of the burgeoning church music curricula in Bible schools, colleges, universities and seminaries, they encourage more and more churches to move toward engaging a full-time professional minister of music.

Perhaps the most dramatic growth and development in church music during the last generation has been experienced by Southern Baptists. In 1952 their Church Music Department was organized as a part of the Sunday School Board of the Southern Baptist Convention. The department regularly publishes eight magazines: *The Music Leader, Music Makers, Young Musicians, Opus One, Opus Two, Gospel Choir, Choral Praise,* and *The Church Musician*. It also conducts annual Church Music Leadership Conferences at the denomination's assemblies at Ridgecrest, North Carolina and Glorieta, New Mexico, as well as many other specialized conferences at their headquarters in Nashville, Tennessee. The Church Music Department also assists in the development of local church music activities, working through state music secretaries. These individuals plan music institutes, workshops and festivals, and generally assist churches in obtaining musical leadership and in improving the contribution of each individual musician. . . .

Baptist seminaries in Wake Forest (N.C.), Louisville (Ky.), Fort Worth (Tex.), New Orleans (La.) and San Francisco (Calif.) are at present training some eight hundred graduate music students each year, most of whom are preparing to be ministers of music in Southern Baptist churches. At the present time, according to the records of the Church Music Department,

3500 of 33,000 Southern Baptist Churches employ a full-time Minister of Music.[4]

The trend described by Hustad was also evident among classical Pentecostal denominations. This source, a key textbook used in the Church of God (Cleveland) for its Church Training Course, emphasizes the need for Pentecostals to invest educational resources in cultivating a more rigorous and relevant music ministry. The source argues that the increasing sophistication of society, which is regularly exposed to high-quality music, necessitates the development of more trained musical professionals within the church.

Source: Delton L. Alford, *Music in the Pentecostal Church* (Cleveland: Pathway Press, 1967), 20–21.

There exists today a great need for development of methods and techniques of providing for a more spiritually significant and musically proficient program of church music.

Never before has so much good music been available to so many people than in the twentieth century. Radio broadcasts, television programs, recorded albums, and concerts by professionals and amateurs are available to almost all segments of our society and have become highly influential in developing the levels of musical taste and appreciation of this generation.

... It becomes the responsibility of the church of today to keep pace with the aforementioned developments and to provide musical experiences, music instruction, and musical expressions which will be meaningful to and appreciated by those who would attend its services.

The time has arrived for the development of a new concept of the "ministry of music" in the Pentecostal church: a ministry which serves the educational, emotional, aesthetic, and spiritual needs of a contemporary church. This concept of music ministry calls for emphasis on the utilization of educational resources to provide excellent training for all the constituents of the church, both young and old.

With the rise of contemporary worship services in the 1990s based upon attracting the unchurched to hear the gospel, the role of the worship leader grew

---

4. Additionally, Southern Baptists also started experimenting with the concept of the "music missionary" during the 1980s. Music missions became an increasing part of the seminary curriculum from 1967 onwards. See T. W. Hunt, "Music in Missions" in *Encyclopedia of Southern Baptists* (Nashville: Broadman Press, 1982), 4:2361–62.

in importance. In this context, the worship leader's role was not to lead the congregation into an encounter with God but to facilitate the smooth flow of the worship event so that the overall "message" of the service was clear. (Notice how this source can assume that his readers understand the position of a worship leader, even if it has not reached full acceptance.)

Source: Charles Arn, *How to Start a New Service: Your Church Can Reach New People* (Grand Rapids: Baker Books, 1997), 165–66.

The traditional approach to service planning is to determine the activities of the service (special music, announcements, offering, sermon, solo), then designate a person responsible for each activity. During the service, each person performs his or her responsibility, followed by the next person on the schedule, until everyone has accomplished his or her task and the service is over. The result is at best a collection of independent yet related activities. At worst it is a hodgepodge of unrelated and confusing experiences. In any case we hope God has used some part of the service to say something to someone. And we go home.

But the new paradigm demands more. Remember, the service is the message. Making sure this message is clear is the primary task of the worship leader. This person is on the platform to facilitate communication, to orchestrate continuity, and to effectively tie each element into a clear part of the overall message of the service. He or she is the conductor of the symphony.

For some pastors the idea of a worship leader (other than the pastor) is threatening. Even though there may be others who participate in the present service, at least the pastor is center stage during the most important (or at least most lengthy) part of the service—the sermon. But the idea of a person other than the pastor receiving such regular visibility in each and every service may begin to gnaw at a weak ego.

In reality, however, a worship leader actually strengthens the pastor's spiritual leadership in the eyes of the congregation. Whereas the worship leader's activities leading up to the sermon should clarify the problem, the pastor's role is to clarify the answer.

The greatly expanded role of musicians within the church did not keep pace with their theological training. Church musicians were often musicians first and pastors second. The next few sources address this concern. This first source describes the innovation of university-based courses of study to serve new cohorts of musicians preparing for leadership in the church. These programs sought to provide a more holistic formation for musicians that recognized the significant pastoral and liturgical role that musicians were starting to play. While some musicians (like the one quoted in this source) sought traditional theological education, the turn of the twenty-first century saw the introduction of worship degree programs at schools like Regent University and Liberty University.[5]

Source: Robb Redman, "Expanding Your Worship Worldview: Education and Training for Worship Leaders," *Worship Leader* (May/June 2000), 19.

Ignore the voices (including the one in your ear) that say musicians can't stick with it. . . . It's time to put the same kind of discipline into preparation for ministry that we put into our music.

It takes practice to be a good musician, and effective ministry takes preparation. Paul encouraged his protégé Timothy to prepare himself well for his ministry. "Do your best to present yourself to God as one approved, a workman who does not need to be ashamed and who correctly handles the word of truth" (2 Timothy 2:15, NIV).

. . . Formal higher education can give worship leaders a crucial edge in ministry. Kevin Navarro, worship leader at Bethany Evangelical Free Church in Littleton, Colo., has two music degrees and served for several years with the Continentals, a touring Christian music group. But Kevin thinks his education makes the difference in his ministry. "I felt I had a lot of training as a musician, as an artist, but there is a whole theological side to the church that I didn't feel equipped to deal with." So after leaving the Continentals, he enrolled in the M.Div. program at Denver Seminary. His friends asked if he planned to be a pastor, but his goal was always worship ministry. . . . "I learned that we lead out of who we are, and I grew in my thinking and understanding of who God is, and what worship is."

In this source from The Worship Pastor, *Hicks addresses contemporary worship leaders. He reminds them of the significant theological and pastoral role that church musicians play in shaping how their congregations fundamentally*

---

5. For the recent historical development of worship degree programs after 2000, see Jonathan Ottaway, "The Rise of the Worship Degree: Pedagogical Changes in the Preparation of Church Musicians," in *Essays on the History of Contemporary Praise and Worship*, ed. Lester Ruth (Pickwick Publications, 2020), 160–75.

relate to God through the actions and content of their corporate gathering. Whether they realize it or not, musicians have become pastors.

Source: Zac Hicks, *The Worship Pastor: A Call to Ministry for Worship Leaders and Teams* (Grand Rapids: Zondervan, 2016), 13–14.

Dear Worship Leader:

You have an extraordinary job with high stakes and grand opportunities. You aren't *just* a song leader. You aren't *just* a lead musician. Your set lists aren't *just* inspiring medleys of well-glued songs. You aren't merely on a stage, and those people out there aren't merely the audience. They are Christ's bride, God's beloved, gathered in from the four corners of the world that they might be reclaimed by and reaimed toward the Author and Perfector of their faith. They are disciples, followers. What you do and how you lead have a direct and formative impact on their journey of faith. Whether you know it or not, you are *pastoring* them.

Each and every week, you are helping people answer the question, How do I approach God? Every worship service consistently shapes the faith of God's people by training them on what relating to God looks like. And faith shaping is pastoral work. Ready or not, you're a pastor.

Each and every week, you put words into people's mouths that become the language they will use to relate to God the other six days of the week. We wish people were regularly reading their Bibles and consistently engaging in life-on-life community, but if we're honest, many aren't. The only way many learn how to talk to God is through the words, lyrics, and prayers of the services you lead. Those things all come together as the corporate prayers of your church that week, teaching the people how to express their private prayers. Prayer shaping is pastoral work. Ready or not, you're a pastor.

Each and every week, you shape the beliefs of the people who gather. Your songs and words don't just inspire. They teach. They help people answer their basic questions: Who is God? What is He like? Who am I? How do I look at this world? Your words and songs shape people's theology, and that kind of teaching is pastoral work. Ready or not, you're a pastor. . . .

Each and every week, you are looked up to as an example and a leader. You have a sphere of immediate influence. Because you stand in front of people and lead them in God's holy worship, you are given the status of leader. Most disciples of Christ look to mentors and leaders to lead them and help them grow. Because you are regularly up front, you are one of those people. Ready or not, you're a pastor.

If some, like Zac Hicks, are concerned that worship leaders fail to realize the pastoral vocation they have assumed, other recent commentators have expressed concern for the musical preparation of future church musicians. The following source argues that the future leaders of the church's musical life have not received adequate musical training. Instead, seminaries and colleges have focused too much time preparing musicians to lead popular evangelistic expressions.

Source: Paul S. Jones, *Singing and Making Music: Issues in Church Music Today* (Phillipsburg, NJ: P & R Publishing, 2006), 144–45.

The Baptist seminaries and independent Bible colleges are training church musicians, and have been for years, predominantly for service in churches of a congregational nature. They must be given credit for actually doing something, and the required coursework in theology/Bible is an excellent beginning. In this author's estimation, the focus on "worship techniques" in such schools (with credit-level coursework in clowning, puppetry, mime, dance, play and scene-writing, drama teams, contemporary worship ensembles, and such graduate level required courses as "Leadership in Contemporary Expressions of Corporate Worship" and "Producing and Staging Church Drama") indicates an attempt to equip musical leaders with what is "currently out there" in evangelical churches. Unfortunately, it also seems to exhibit a degree of willingness to compromise musical excellence to accommodate the relativism of the postmodern church. One wonders how much stronger the graduates of these programs could be if hours spent on such courses were instead allotted to a deeper study of great music, history, and liturgy. But all institutions feel the pressing need to find prospective students (and to graduate them "employable"), and this factor wins out over a commitment to change the musical landscape for the better.

Yielded Vessels: The Spiritual Leadership of the Worship Leader

The rise in importance of the worship musician has generated a whole body of writing and teaching on the spiritual qualities that a worship leader needs to lead the congregation in worship. In this section, we provide a sample of these sources that reveal two major impulses. The first emphasizes that worship leaders exercise an anointed ministry by being attuned to the Holy Spirit, guiding the congregation to perceive and respond to this divine activity. The second emphasizes that anointed worship leaders lead by fully abandoning themselves to the presence of God as an example of the true heart of worship that the congregation should emulate.[6] By themselves, these impulses are not necessarily contradictory. As we will see though, leaders have detected a tension between these two impulses in the leadership of the congregation's worship.

In this source, Graham Kendrick, a renowned British songwriter of the 1980s and 1990s, reflects on the importance of worship leaders developing the ability to discern what is happening spiritually during worship.[7] While this discernment is crucial for those in authority over the church, Kendrick emphasizes that worship leaders' discernment must strike a balance between exercising their leadership and empowering the congregation to fulfill its own priestly vocation.

Source: Graham Kendrick, *Worship* (Eastbourne: Kingsway, 1984), 163–66.

It is important for many reasons to be spiritually prepared on a personal level in advance of leading worship, not the least of these reasons being the need for discernment. Once again this should be a shared responsibility and not just fall upon one person. Discernment is the ability to perceive clearly what is going on, and in Christian worship this is on both a spiritual and a natural level. It is not appropriate here to go into great detail about the gift of discernment of spirits, and precisely what it is, but there is certainly a need to discern between the good, bad and indifferent contributions that

---

6. This concept has been explored in Joshua K. Busman, "Amateurism-without-Amateurishness, or Authenticity as Vanishing Act in Evangelical Worship Music," in *Ethics and Christian Musicking*, ed. Nathan Myrick and Mark Porter (Routledge, 2021), 88–104.

7. For an insider's perspective on the history of British worship music, see Les Moir, *Missing Jewel* (David C Cook, 2017). See also, Pete Ward, *Selling Worship: How What We Sing Has Changed the Church* (Paternoster, 2008). The important impact of British worship on global Contemporary Praise & Worship is documented in Monique M. Ingalls, "Transnational Connections, Musical Meaning, and the 1990s 'British Invasion' of North American Evangelical Worship Music," *The Oxford Handbook of Music and World Christianities* (Oxford University Press, 2013/2016).

people bring, and the source of their "inspiration." Such discernment is important so that the meeting can be kept from wandering aimlessly, focusing on unhelpful things or being dominated by certain personalities moving against the "flow" of the Spirit.

. . . There is a further area where discernment needs to be applied if the worship is truly going to be a corporate expression. It should be obvious that the leaders, though in positions of authority and hopefully under a special empowering of the Spirit, will not have a monopoly on being led by the Spirit. In fact there is a strong sense in which the leaders should be led through the people. The context of Paul's instruction for order in church gatherings in 1 Corinthians 14 is clearly one in which there is no lack of participation from the people. The problem there was not how to stir them up, but how to keep their enthusiasm and sheer volume of contributions under control!

Discernment is not the only prerequisite of good worship leadership. In this source, prominent Pentecostal pastor Jack Hayford argues that another marker of the anointed worship leader is the cultivation of a heart like King David.

Source: Jack Hayford, *Worship His Majesty* (Waco: Word Publishing, 1987), 118.

There is a fundamental prerequisite for everyone who would worship God or lead others to do so. David abundantly manifests that quintessential trait of a heart filled with a passion for God: "My soul thirsts for You; my flesh longs for You in a dry and thirsty land where there is no water. So I have looked for You in the sanctuary, to see Your power and Your glory."

David reveals a largeness of heart, which not only desires God's working in his own life, but that longs for His manifest glory "in the sanctuary." The deep cry of such a leader's soul for both his own needs and that of his people will never go unrewarded.

Part of the issue that churches were encountering is that churches often found it was difficult to find skillful musicians who could also function well in ministry leadership. Speaking in an interview in 1995, one of the founders of the Vineyard movement, John Wimber, expressed this recurrent issue of musicians who are well-versed in secular music but are not well-discipled as followers of Christ.

Source: "The Music in Revival" from *Let Your Glory Fall: Songs and Essays / Worship & Revival Songs & Essays / Worship & Revival Conference/Seminar Reader* (Vineyard Music Group, 1995) (reprint from *Worship Together* magazine, n.d.), 224.

Interviewer: As writers, musicians and worship leaders, then, how should we prepare for what God has in store for us?

John: The difficulty will not be so much in the writing of new and great music; the test will be the godliness of those that perform and deliver it. In that sense some of our worship community is not well prepared for revival. Many have been allowed into worship leading because of this new emphasis on contemporary groups and music, and the consequent need for their worship skills and music skills. But little has been said to them about the need for godliness, spirituality and depth of maturity in their individual and family lives.

Despite the new prominence that musicians have received as leaders of worship, a counter-theme in the literature is the necessity of worship leaders to lead invisibly. Worship leaders are to avoid drawing attention to themselves but instead are to exercise their leadership to draw attention to God.[8] As this source argues, worship leaders achieve this through providing an example of authentic and abandoned praise, but not eschewing the necessary leadership.

Source: Bob Sorge, *Exploring Worship: A Practical Guide to Praise and Worship* (Lee's Summit: Oasis House, 1987), 172.

The best way I know to become invisible is to radiate a joyful, worshipful countenance. As we lift our hands and face to the Lord with an expression of joyful expectancy, we cease being anything anyone would want to watch. Instead of looking at us, people are drawn to behold the object of our attention: the Lord.

We should avoid any quick or large movements that would draw attention to ourselves. When we are announcing songs to be sung, giving signals

---

8. In recent works of scholars of congregational music studies, there has been a broader discourse on the concept of how authenticity is performed by musicians and worship leaders, for example Marcell Silva Steuernagel, *Church Music Through the Lens of Performance* (Routledge, 2021); Nathan Myrick, "Double Authenticity: Celebrity, Consumption, and the Christian Worship Music Industry," *The Hymn*; Boston 69, no. 2 (2018): 21–27; Nathan Myrick, "Authenticity and Purity in Worship Music," *Theology* 128, no. 1 (2025): 25–32, https://doi.org/10.1177/0040571X241307355.

to the pianist, trying to get the drummer to tone down, trying to speed up the choir, directing the congregation with our arms, and singing loudly into the microphone, the obvious tendency is for everyone to be gazing with rapt attention at this one-man circus.

... We can also become less visible by being no louder on the microphone than is necessary and being no more extroverted in hand motions than is necessary to provide leadership for the singing. If the people are singing the current song easily enough, we can back away from the microphone a bit so that our voice blends in with the entire congregation, and then sing strongly into the microphone when the next verse or chorus is to be introduced.

This source from a longtime worship leader in the Vineyard Church reflects on how the worship leader is a servant of the kingdom of God. Andy Park picks up an important theological focus at the center of the teaching of John Wimber on the love of God and the divine presence. Here, the worship leader yields to the power of God as King. As they operate under that authority, the worship leader enables the power of the God to work in the congregation. Note, too, the evangelistic turn at the end of the passage; the emphasis on presence in worship is not at odds with believing that the power of God can save the lost.

Source: Andy Park, *To Know You More: Cultivating the Heart of the Worship Leader* (Downers Grove: InterVarsity Press, 2002), 67.

Worship has everything to do with the kingdom of God. Because the kingdom of God is an overarching theme for any kind of ministry, it is a key framework for the worship leader. We are subjects of the King, submitted to his rule. Every spiritual gift we employ in worship leading is a product of God's kingdom near us and in us. The worship leader invites God's kingdom to come and invite people to submit to God's benevolent reign.

If we are under God's authority, we can be vessels or ambassadors of his authority. As we minister under his kingship, all kinds of things happen. His glory appears to people; hearts are pierced with a tangible sense of the father's love; unbelievers sense the divine presence, they realize that this is real, and they want to be part of it.

In this source, a Pentecostal pastor and worship leader reflects on the necessity of spiritual anointing upon worship leaders. Phifer distinguishes between a musician who merely leads the congregation's singing and one who can release the sovereign action of the Holy Spirit. The author weaves together many themes we have encountered already in other sources.

Source: Stephen F. Phifer, *Worship That Pleases God* (Trafford Publishing, 2005), 288–89.

A worship leader is a man or woman who is called of God to lead in worship. If we want the power of God to flow in our worship, the leader must be a person GOD has selected. The anointing is as essential to this ministry as it is to any other ministry. Those whom God calls, He enables. Without this enablement, the worship time will be mired in imitation and fleshly effort. Many congregations are waiting, week after week, for song leaders to become worship leaders or yield the position to a worship leader. . . . Musical skill and understanding are essential. Music must be handled properly or it will inhibit the flow of God's Spirit. A skillful musical mind can release the powers of music to support the expression of God's people. On the other hand, unskillful handling of music can spoil the sacrifice of praise of the whole church, the Holy-Royal Priesthood.

The author of this source argues that the internal spiritual qualities of the worship leader is the most critical factor. Riddle envisions true worship leadership as a dynamic interaction with the Holy Spirit wherein the leader facilitates and extends the Holy Spirit's ministry. It is this kind of leadership that will enable God to fulfill his good and sovereign purposes in worship.

Source: Jeremy Riddle, *The Reset: Returning to the Heart of Worship and a Life of Undivided Devotion* (Anaheim: Wholehearted Publishing, 2020), 57.

Without question, the greatest need we have in this hour is for men and women who are full of the Holy Spirit. We do not lack gifted singers, communicators, songwriters, song leaders, or massive corporate songs. They abound more than ever. What we desperately lack is the mighty presence and power of the Spirit flowing through yielded vessels. The Holy Spirit *makes all the difference.* I'm convinced that even the most unskilled and unqualified person, *if they are yielded to the Holy Spirit,* can accomplish far more than an army of people possessing all the natural gifting and charisma in the world.

We are in desperate need of true *worship leaders*. The difference between a song leader and a worship leader, *is the Holy Spirit*. Almost anyone can play four chords and lead people in a singable chorus. But true worship leading is a Spirit empowered activity. It is by learning to lead and sing in the Spirit, with the Spirit, and by the Spirit. . . . It is the touch of the Spirit on a song and on a leader that causes hearts to open and releases the worship and fragrance God's heart is longing for.

Responding to the kind of arguments made by leaders like Riddle and Sorge, this Vineyard worship leader argues instead that worship leaders need to envision their role as a bus driver. Because musical worship is a journey that leads the congregation into the presence of God, worship leaders are responsible for making sure that the vehicle of music helps the congregation to reach its destination. For this author, that means the worship leader must be attentive to the congregation and the band.

Source: Brent Helming, *Hot Tips for Worship Leaders* (Vineyard Music, 2000), 27–28.

There is a debate within worship leading circles as to the best way to lead. In one camp are those who believe that the best way to lead is for the worship leader himself to enter into a personal time of worship (modeling) and hope that the congregation follows. Those on the other side of the debate argue for leadership first and modeling (personal worship) second. This is my perspective. Let me explain by using an analogy of the worship leader as a tour guide/bus driver.

As a tour guide your job is to make sure that everyone knows what is happening around them (Bridges of Understanding). You want them to know that they are on the right bus and that they are headed to the right destination. If these things are not known their trip could be a disaster or at least a huge disappointment. As the bus driver you want to make sure that the bus (the worship team) is in good working order and that nothing mechanically will disrupt the journey.

So it is with leading worship. We are tour guides in the sense that we are taking the congregation from point A (disconnected from God's presence) to point B (the presence of God). Therefore we want to bring as many people along with us as possible by making sure they are able to participate in worship. Worship leaders are also like the bus driver in that they constantly need to be checking the bus (the band) to make sure that everything is functioning properly and won't break down in the middle of the trip. Although this analogy is limited it does bring home an important point. Worship leaders must not engage in a personal time of worship (modeling) at the cost of effectively leading.

As musicians and leaders have become increasingly aware of the global diversity of Christian worship, some voices have called for a changing model of worship leadership. The author of this source argues that if the church's worship is to become more representative and collaborative, churches will need to rethink the model of a singular worship leader. Giving too much attention and focus to one leader results in worship that includes some at the exclusion of others. She suggests that the church adopt a new, shared model of leadership.

Source: Sandra Maria Van Opstal, *The Next Worship: Glorifying God in a Diverse World* (Downers Grove: InterVarsity Press, 2015), 78–80.

Worship leaders are treated like rock stars! They hold their guitar or microphone and become the center of our attention. We follow them in flocks. We pay $50 to $100 to hear them in concert. We spend thousands to travel to conferences where they are featured. We spend even more acquiring their songs so that we can consume them at our leisure. Particularly in a culture that is perpetuating the rock-star worship leader, why would we share our leadership? And how do we do it? Very few of us have seen it done, especially by the American-worship idols who have captured our attention and dollars. We don't expect it, we can't envision it and no one has taught us how to share. The very position that is supposed to help people enter into the presence of the self-sacrificing God ends up fostering ego battles. Ironically, a priestly role actually lends itself to creating idols. . . .

We will not host well without collaborating with people from other communities. Unless we have a community of diverse leaders who can speak into the situation and co-create spaces, we will repeatedly go to our favorite foods, music, decorations and event-planning processes. Thus, people of different ethnic, cultural, class and generational backgrounds will not feel fed. Leading worship in relevant, dynamic ways for the future of a diverse church depends on our ability to share leadership. It begins with an environment of mutual learning and collaboration in which worship-team participants can add value and perspective from their diverse traditions.

This approach is distinctive in that it is not primarily about collecting songs and components from different traditions and assigning people from those traditions to lead (tokenism), but allowing the traditions of team members to shape the overall community and worship experience.

Discussion Questions

- What are the benefits and challenges of the increasing professionalization of worship leadership that has been explored in this chapter?
- Consider the double responsibility that worship leaders have as musical leaders and spiritual leaders. What does that responsibility mean for how worship leaders need to prepare to lead congregational singing on a Sunday?
- In leading worship, should worship leaders prioritize responsivity to the needs of the congregation or their own spiritual engagement as their primary act of leadership? Do these priorities compete with one another?
- Does musical leadership impact the spiritual experience of the worshiper within the service? Who is responsible when worshipers do not find worship to be meaningful, accessible, or enjoyable?
- Some of the sources in the chapter have described the tension between the visibility that worship leaders enjoy and the humility that worship leaders need to embody in their leadership. How should worship leaders navigate that tension practically in their ministry? Do you recognize this tension in the ways in which the Christian music industry treats its artists?

CHAPTER 6
EXCELLENCE: DOING WORSHIP MUSIC WELL

Throughout the history of the church, aesthetics in worship has long been used to display the nature of who God is and who the church is. Some Christians built grand churches with ornate architecture and elaborate (and expensive!) artistic details to illustrate the power, majesty, and worth of God. Others built sparse buildings with white-washed walls and bare wooden pews to celebrate the church as a community gathered around the preaching and hearing of the Word. In this way, aesthetic choices about worship convey theological ideas.[1] However, aesthetic choices are never purely theological. These choices are often just as revealing about the historical, cultural, and societal waters that the church swims in.

Throughout this book, we have constantly witnessed the intersection of theological and socio-cultural impulses in shaping Contemporary Praise & Worship. For instance, chapter 1 explored how churches increasingly embraced a common theological position on the use of popular music in worship. Their understanding of what constituted popular music was also shaped by cultural and historical influences. When Pentecostals were concerned about the apparent Satanic roots of rock music entering the church, they were still reflecting on worship at the intersection of theology and culture. Similar observations might be made about the power of musical worship, the leadership of worship,

---

1. As an example of this idea in practice, see Robbie B. H. Goh, "Hillsong and 'Megachurch' Practice: Semiotics, Spatial Logic, and the Embodiment of Contemporary Evangelical Protestantism," *Material Religion* 4, no. 3 (2008): 284–304.

and the organization of worship. Cultural contexts always shape the horizons of the theological imagination and filter through into the worship of the church.[2]

More than any other chapter in this book though, the topic that this chapter explores—the performative quality of Contemporary Praise & Worship music—is especially influenced by socio-cultural expectations. For many leaders and pastors quoted in this chapter, the pursuit of excellence in worship was primarily a concern for the church to keep pace with cultural standards. Twentieth- and twenty-first-century leaders and congregants alike had cultural expectations about the quality of music, performance, and sound that were rooted in their time and place. These Christians have believed that if church leaders were to offer something that would be attractive and engaging to these attendees, they had to be diligent about the excellence of their worship. As we will uncover in this chapter, while this concern for excellence was broader than music, it has been especially felt in that arena.

Focusing on excellence allows us to talk about a topic that has been little discussed so far in the book: technology. Today, a pervasive use of audio/visual technologies marks the most visible drivers of mainstream Contemporary Praise & Worship music through amplification, lighting, and video.[3] These cultural leaders have also engaged with emerging forms of technology to amplify the church's reach through tools such as social media and AI. As part of a broader commitment to performing worship at a level that would be culturally acceptable and desirable,

---

2. For a study of how meaning is made in worship, including through theological and cultural narratives, see Steven Félix-Jäger, *How to Worship for All Its Worth: A Guide for Pastors, Worship Leaders, and Students* (Zondervan Academic, 2025).

3. The recently published issue of *Yale Journal of Music and Religion* reflects on the topic of timbre and the multiple ways that contemporary worship practices engage music technologies. See for example Dylan Crosson, "A Sunlit Ambience: How Reverb Pedals Influence the Contemporary Worship Music Imagination," *Yale Journal of Music & Religion* 11, no. 1 (2025); Joshua Busman and Nathan Myrick, "From the Heaviest, Dirtiest Depths to the Washy Ambient Clouds: Guitar Timbre in/as Schismogenesis in North American Christianity," *Yale Journal of Music & Religion* 11, no. 1 (2025).

churches have found it necessary to adopt technology that would keep pace with society.[4]

As with our previous chapters, while Pentecostal worship has looked similar to their broader evangelical context, their reflection on excellence in worship comes from a slightly different angle. Put briefly, Pentecostal teachings have emphasized that musical worship should be excellent because God is worthy of the very best effort that we can bring as the church ministers unto the Lord. Because worship also invites worshipers into a deep and intimate encounter with the divine, excellence is also important so that no barrier is placed in the way of the congregation experiencing God's presence.

Minimizing the "Cringe Factor": The Broader Evangelical Emphasis on Excellence in the Twentieth Century

As we explored in chapter 1, evangelicals in the early twentieth century were earnestly reflecting on how they might attract people to hear the Christian gospel. One answer that evangelicals increasingly settled on was the adoption of what Charles Finney called New Measures—using new language, technology, styles, etc.—to win an audience for the church's message. Here, we explore another emphasis that became equally prominent throughout the twentieth century. Churches increasingly reflected upon how the quality of their services made outsiders (and congregants!) more or less likely to attend. This formed the broader context within which evangelicals began to reflect on how this push for excellence should implicate the musical practice of the church's corporate life.

In this source from early in the twentieth century, the author notes a number of factors that churches ought to attend to in order to attract visitors. The undergirding concern is that visitors to the church should feel comfortable within

---

4. A recent edited collection addresses multiple technological concerns as it relates to music in worship. See Anna E. Nekola and Tom Wagner, eds., *Congregational Music-Making and Community in a Mediated Age* (Routledge, 2016).

the church and should not be distracted from their engagement with the gospel message. Accordingly, Elliott advises churches and pastors to attend to those things that a visitor to their church would most likely notice.

Source: Ernest Eugene Elliott, *How to Fill the Pews* (Cincinnati: Standard Pub. Co., 1917), 79–80.

Many a church is known as "The Friendly Church" because it pays attention to the stranger within its gates. The following suggestions are worthy of more than passing attention. . . .

HOW TO MAKE THE SERVICES ATTRACTIVE.

CLEANLINESS. Nothing is more beautiful than cleanliness. Begin the campaign by a house-cleaning party. Have the ladies and a few men designate a day; come with your lunches and mops and brooms, and make the house all beautiful within. Make needed repairs; use paint and varnish, and it will richly repay you, in the attractiveness of the house. We should insist that the janitor keep the church clean.

BEAUTY. After the building is cleaned, it can and should be made beautiful—stove polish, carpet, rugs, flowers and plants all used with good taste—and the house will be made attractive in beauty.

VENTILATION. Many a sermon has been weakened in power by bad ventilation. If you have a man of sense, put him in charge of the ventilation; do not leave it to the janitor.

USHERS. Have you a head usher, who is on hand twenty minutes before the hour of service, and who never leaves his place near the door until all the congregation is seated? He is the Reception Committee, to greet every stranger and turn him over quietly to an usher, who will seat him near the front and place a hymn-book in his hands. Welcome strangers graciously, but not offensively.

THE SERVICE. Let the service be well planned, and each one know his part in it before the hour of beginning. Make the service beautiful by its orderliness and its reverence. Let all things be done in decency and in order.

Nero once said: "I wish all Roman people had but one neck, that I might cut off all their heads by one blow." If all our sins against public worship had but one neck, that one neck would be irreverence in God's house. If we can destroy that, all the rest of the beauty of holiness will be added unto us. Let us be reverent.

Let every member feel that you are in your own home, and greet a stranger just as you would greet him if he came into your parlor. You make the advances; you greet the stranger cordially; you try to make him feel at home. So do in the church.

If you do these things, you will give to the church the beauty of cleanliness, the beauty of flowers, the beauty of orderliness, the beauty of reverence, the beauty of worship, and the beauty of hospitality to strangers.

Twenty-five years later, youth-centered evangelistic programs carried forward a similar concern to maximize the hospitality of their programming. Excellence was necessary, both to attract listeners and to get local churches to participate in the programming. In the source below, music is listed prominently among the things that Johnson and Cook deemed necessary for their evangelistic ministry to excel in. This demonstrates a growing realization that young people were becoming both increasingly attuned to and discerning about high-quality experiences. At this point in time though, music was just one component of many that needed to be done well. Notice, too, the mention of radio in this source.[5] The recognition that youth media needs to embrace new forms of media points forward to the ways in which technological adoption would become a critical part of evangelistic hospitality.

Source: Torrey Maynard Johnson and Robert Cook, *Reaching Youth for Christ* (Chicago: Moody Press, 1944), 36–37.

It is a mistake to try to sell the idea to the community until you have something to sell. Organizations and individuals will co-operate more readily if they can see behind your plans and promotion some solid thinking and the presence of a competent staff to head up the work.

You need, for instance, good music. The old cliche, "special music," no longer holds an appeal for today's young people. They still thrill to good gospel melodies, and messages, but they want the best.

Oddly, radio has spoiled things for the careless gospel musician; for your young folk can hear, if they wish, worldly music, perfectly produced, any hour of the day or night. It is not that they appreciate the gospel less,

---

5. See also the discussion of the growth of Christian radio in Don Cusic, *The Sound of Light: A History of Gospel and Christian Music* (Hal Leonard, 2002). See also Michael Stamm, "Broadcasting Mainline Protestantism: The Chicago Sunday Evening Club and the Evolution of Audience Expectations from Radio to Television," *Religion and American Culture: A Journal of Interpretation* 22, no. 2 (2012): 233–64.

but that they have found out what good production is, and, brother, they'll hold you to it. Dare to offer them something shoddy, and they'll shun your meeting.

So, look for God's choice of musicians for your program. You need a pianist (or organist) with enough background to accompany well, and enough imagination to improvise upon familiar gospel themes. Nobody temperamental, please! You need a competent song leader who knows God. Bad song leading, or even good song leading with the flesh in it, can kill your meeting. For all your soloists and musical groups, emphasize high quality and spiritual sincerity. And always rehearse, rehearse, rehearse! If someone wants to put on his number without rehearsal, tell him to take it elsewhere—you don't want it. Set this standard at the very start, and it will save you untold embarrassment later.

You'll need some one who knows publicity. Many good ideas die for lack of proper promotion. "Chicagoland Youth for Christ" was launched at the beginning of summer what most Christians call the slack season and in the face of such odds as that, good publicity helped a lot.

Now, find a place where the meeting can be held. It ought to be a neutral spot, one that will appeal alike to saints and sinners, with equal attraction for members of various denominations. Some "Youth for Christ" movements are housed in large church auditoriums. This is good, but many feel that a large secular hall . . . is better. Suit yourself, and ask God for His direct guidance in the matter. If God laid the work on your heart, He will tell you where to hold the meeting.

This word about size: Humanly speaking, you should select an auditorium that is just a little smaller than the crowd you anticipate. The world would class this as smart showmanship. Spiritually speaking, you ought to pray thoroughly enough to secure God's guidance, for He alone knows the size of the crowd He will send you. What if "Chicagoland Youth for Christ" had been launched in an auditorium seating only five hundred?

Some one asks: "What about radio? Must we have a broadcast?" The answer to that one would be this: In a youth program, dare we neglect the one thing which . . . more nearly typifies the spirit of young people than anything else? . . . Isn't radio a part of every youngster's environment today? Furthermore, doesn't the world present its best via radio? Then how can you conceive of a Christian youth program that does not include some broadcast in which the young people themselves can take part?

Near the end of the twentieth century, the rise of the Church Growth movement intensified the emphasis on excellence in the church's corporate life. In this source, George Barna, the founder of the market research firm The Barna Group, argues that because Americans are discerning consumers, churches need to tailor their programs to that expectation. Indeed, Barna claims that poor quality programs are actually worse than not having a program at all!

Source: George Barna, *Marketing the Church: What They Never Taught You About Church Growth* (Colorado Springs: Navpress, 1988), 26, 112–13.

First, the church is a business. It is involved in the business of ministry. As such, the local church must be run with the same wisdom and savvy that characterizes any for-profit business. As in the business world, every church must be managed with purpose and efficiency, moving towards its goals and objectives. Our goal as a church, like any secular business, is to turn a profit. For us, however, profit means saving souls and nurturing believers. . . .

Again, it is critical to recognize that simply having a program is of no intrinsic value. The American public is a discerning lot. We have come to expect quality in every product and service we encounter. Those that lack quality will be discarded because we believe we deserve the best, and because there are so many available options that we will eventually locate the best. If your church cannot provide an excellent program—whether it is a children's program, a men's program, the church service, or any other endeavor—you would do the Body of Christ a service by not offering the program at all.

Following up on Barna's claims above, James Emery White claims that a lack of excellence in the church's corporate life undercuts the very believability of the gospel. If churches believe that their message is crucial to a listening world, then they must attend carefully to how their message is communicated.

Source: James Emery White, *Opening the Front Door: Worship and Church Growth* (Nashville: Convention Press, 1992), 55–56.

One of the first marks of growing churches that is instantly perceived is a commitment to excellence, an attitude that strives for quality and rejects mediocrity. As George Barna's research has revealed, the battle cry of growing, healthy churches is "Do it right, or don't do it at all."

Think of the impact it must have on a nonchurched person to come to church and see poor quality, inattention to detail, inadequately rehearsed music which is poorly performed, and then hear that the message we proclaim is the most important one in the world! In their minds, what we say does not go along with what they observe. . . .

A lack of quality is thus a subtle form of hypocrisy. And as a result, Christianity just doesn't add up in the thinking of a non-churched person as something to be seriously considered.

At the time of writing the following encouragement, Lee Strobel was a teaching pastor at Willow Creek Community Church in South Barrington, Illinois. Willow Creek in the 1980s and 1990s was one of the most significant megachurches influencing thousands of other congregations.[6] One of the key emphases at Willow Creek was the development of "seeker services," in which the entire service was oriented toward the type of unchurched suburbanite ("unchurched Harry and Mary") that Willow Creek was targeting in its evangelistic mission. According to Strobel, one of the values that such folks brought to their assessment of Christian worship was a desire for excellence. Accordingly, churches that settled for mediocrity risked off-putting the people they were trying to reach.

Source: Lee Strobel, *Inside the Mind of Unchurched Harry & Mary: How to Reach Friends and Family Who Avoid God and the Church* (Grand Rapids: Zondervan, 1993), 189–90.

The cringe factor is a major reason why many church members turn a deaf ear when pastors plead for them to invite Unchurched Harry and Mary to a service or event. You see, they don't want to subject themselves or anyone else to the anxiety and embarrassment that are generated when a program is poorly produced.

Unfortunately, while the secular world is pursuing excellence in business and industry, many ministries are mired in mediocrity, and that's a major stumbling block to reaching the unchurched. In sum, "good enough" just isn't good enough in trying to reach seekers.

After all, it's biblical for God's people to honor God with the best that

---

6. For liturgical theological assessments of Willow Creek's service orders, see Melanie C. Ross, "The Evolution of the 'Frontier Ordo': Anton Baumstark Visits Willow Creek," *Worship* 93, no. 2 (2019): 139–57; Lester Ruth, "Lex Agendi, Lex Credendi: Toward an Understanding of Seeker Services as a New Kind of Liturgy," *Worship* 70, no. 5 (1996): 386–405.

they have. Under the Old Testament's sacrificial system, it was unblemished lambs that were supposed to be offered to him. (See Malachi 1:14.)

It's important to emphasize that the pursuit of excellence doesn't mean neurotic perfectionism. Yet it does mean that the building, grounds, sanctuary, music, drama, media, and message are the best that can be accomplished given the church's level of resources and talents.

I've been at churches where paint was peeling from the walls, sound systems were plagued by distortion, lighting was so dim I could barely see the face of the speaker, musicians read their lyrics instead of having them memorized, and the message sounded as if it were ad-libbed.

Church members seemed oblivious to their surroundings because that's how church has always been done. But if they could see the service through the eyes of an unchurched person who spends his weekdays pursuing excellence in his career, they'd experience the cringe factor for themselves.

Nancy Beach was another key minister at Willow Creek Community Church. Starting in 1984, she led the congregation's worship arts team for twenty years before transitioning onto the leadership team. In her position, Beach played a key role in planning and conducting this congregation's seeker and worship services as well as instilling the values by which they were offered. As part of her wider argument here about the necessity of a devotion to excellence, Beach reflects on some of the reasons which she has encountered for why churches settle for mediocrity.

Source: Nancy Beach, *An Hour on Sunday: Creating Moments of Transformation and Wonder* (Grand Rapids: Zondervan, 2004), 144–45.

No phrase uttered by Christian leaders stirs my wrath more than this one: "It's only church." The unstated assumptions are that what happens in the hour on Sunday isn't important enough to warrant passionate energy and effort, that neither the attenders nor God expect all that much of us, and that we should all just chill out. . . .

Fear is often the underlying reason for mediocrity. Fear of failure immobilizes countless artists and teachers. We fear disappointing the pastor, the team, or the congregation. Most of all, we are afraid of failing ourselves. . . . Some fear that pursuing excellence puts an excessive emphasis on production values. None of us want words and phrases like slick, outrageously, expensive, over-the-top, or massively complicated to describe the hour on Sunday. We are also afraid that focusing on excellence might result in neurotic, unhealthy team behaviors and an unbalanced emphasis on human effort over the Holy Spirit's more important work. We don't want to be accused of competing with other churches, trying to woo attenders with a "better show," or keep from losing them to a church with a bigger choir or flashier technology.

Most of all, we desperately want to avoid caving into the world's obsession with superstars, ratings, and the latest, greatest techniques. Church should be distinguished from all that insanity, we reason. And so we slide toward mediocrity, because we are afraid and don't know what to do with all these understandable concerns.

Others live in the extreme of mediocrity not because they are afraid but, truth be told, because they simply don't want to work all that hard. We can even spiritualize our lack of quality by saying God will do his mighty work no matter what, and we don't want to take any earthly credit!

Music Carries the Service: Pursuing Excellence in Congregational Song

Music received a special emphasis within the broader attention on excellence in church programming for the sake of communicating the gospel. For many evangelicals, excellence in music was especially important because it represented a significant percentage of what actually happens when the church meets together. Accordingly, if the worship service was going to exude excellence, the music also needed to be excellent.

Reflecting on recent evangelistic ministries, this article from a magazine produced by Seventh-day Adventists reflected on the importance of music for drawing in an audience. Unlike many other contemporaneous accounts that were beginning to reflect on the importance of popular music, this author argues that style of music is unimportant. Instead, for music to be effective, it must be done with excellence.

Source: J. Harker, "Music of the Message: Music in Present-Day Evangelism," *The Ministry* 12, no. 9 (September 1939): 13.

Not only is good music a means of impressing the heart with spiritual truth, and a valuable asset in the work of educating the mind in spiritual things, but it is also good advertising, if properly managed. Whether it be the trained cathedral choir, the Salvation Army band, or the modern pentecostal meeting, the people will go where there is inspirational singing. Good singing is good advertising. On the other hand, poor singing is bad advertising. If the people attending a series of meetings are sent away each night with an appealing melody ringing in their ears, the chances are they will sing that melody all the week, and come back again without any further inducement.

As we move later into the twentieth century, the concern for the worship service to connect with non-Christians necessitated fresh reflection on the performance of music. For this author, if churches want to save souls, worship music needed to be both excellent by being spirited, enthusiastic, and accessible. (Although the word "contemporary" does not get used in this quote, there are strong resonances here of the ideas we saw in chapters 1 and 2). It is only this kind of excellent performance that will allow music to connect with listeners' hearts.

Source: John R. Bisagno, *How to Build an Evangelistic Church* (Nashville: Broadman Press, 1971), 71–72.

Long-haired music, funeral dirge anthems, and stiff-collared song leaders will kill the church faster than anything in the world. Let's set the record straight for a minute. There are no great, vibrant, soul-winning churches reaching great numbers of people, baptizing hundreds of converts, reaching the masses that have stiff music, seven-fold amens, and a steady diet of classical anthems. None. That's not a few. That's none, none, none.

Let's get the record straight on something else. We talk about a worship service on Sunday morning when what we mean is a funeral service. Worship is not necessarily synonymous with excitement and emotionalism. I am not saying that it is certainly not synonymous with quietness either, and most of us think it is. . . . You say you have a worship service on Sunday morning simply because you are quiet? They are quiet at the funeral parlor too! But, it is not because they worship, it is because they are dead! Where the spirit of the Lord is, there is liberty, warmth, life, enthusiasm, and joy. The song leader had better put some enthusiasm and life into the singing and present spiritual music that people can understand and that is as concerned with the message as with the notes. I could cite uncounted examples across the Southern Baptist Convention of what I am saying. The music should be done well. The minister of music should strive for perfection, but it is not music for music's sake which we seek. Rather, it is music for Jesus' sake, music for power's sake, and music for heart's sake.

In a book about ensuring your congregation was dynamic, best-selling author Kennon Callahan mentions in passing—and without reference or citation—that a sizable portion of a typical worship service was musical. By extension, a church needs to be very attentive to the quality of the music in order to be an "effective church." After publication of his book in 1983, Callahan's percentage figure was soon circulating widely in similar literature as a worship-related given.[7]

> **Source:** Kennon L. Callahan, *Twelve Keys to an Effective Church: Strategic Planning for Mission* (San Francisco: Harper & Row, 1983), 22–28.

Music constitutes 40 percent of the service of worship. On those Sundays when my own preaching is off, I count on the music to carry the service. Music is extraordinarily important in the course of the worship service, and a solid music program is vital to achieve corporate, dynamic worship. . . .

The third ingredient [in a strong music program] is the quality and depth of the music itself. The work of the pianist, the organist, the choir director, and the choir itself should be of high quality. It is important that the music be played and sung competently and that the people who sing it be committed Christians. Their commitment as Christians will not compensate for a lack of competence. Indeed, it is precisely their commitment that fuels their desire to be one of the best choirs to the glory of God in the community that surrounds the church.

The numbers-based approach of the Church Growth movement of the 1980s–90s had multiple suggestions to make about worship and worship music as it advocated for a more contemporary form of worship. In the following passage, a Baptist Church Growth expert uses survey data to argue that having good music is essential for growing any church numerically. The use of such statistical data gives an appearance of a scientific basis for pushing for musical excellence.

---

7. See, for instance, Herb Miller, *How to Build a Magnetic Church* (Nashville: Abingdon Press, 1987), 53; William M. Easum, *The Church Growth Handbook* (Nashville: Abingdon Press, 1990), 47; James Emery White, *Opening the Front Door: Worship and Church Growth* (Nashville: Convention Press, 1992), 82.

Source: C. Kirk Hadaway, *Church Growth Principles: Separating Fact from Fiction* (Nashville: Broadman Press, 1991), 67–68.

A full 90 percent of large, growing churches rate their music program as excellent or good, as compared to 78 percent of plateaued churches and 53 percent of declining churches. Among smaller churches, 65 percent of growing congregations rate their music program as excellent or good, as compared to 37 percent of plateaued churches and 35 percent of declining churches. Obviously, a strong relationship exists for large and small congregations.

Music makes a difference to the growth of a church; so pastors, worship leaders, choir directors or ministers of music should take planning music very seriously. Too many churches have piano players who are too old to hit all the notes; too many churches have choirs which have not practiced, cannot carry a tune, or have not been trained to sing in harmony; and too many churches sing and play a single type of music which may fit a large segment of the congregation, but which does not interest unchurched residents in the community.

While these earlier sources affirmed that music must be excellent, the topic of what that excellence looks like is harder to define. This source attempts to address that. For Morgenthaler, the markers of musical excellence center on managing a balance between musical sophistication (both in its complexity and variety) and congregational participation.

Source: Sally Morgenthaler, *Worship Evangelism: Inviting Unbelievers into the Presence of God* (Grand Rapids, MI: Zondervan, 1995), 152.

Build a worship team that emphasizes vocal dynamism as well as instrumental excellence. Go all out to achieve a unified pop vocal ensemble sound. Use three- and four-part vocal arrangements of praise choruses, not just unisons.

Add variety by featuring a worship team ensemble or soloist on verses with everyone joining in on choruses. This enables use of songs with more content and musical complexity.

Add energy with a few instrumental breaks (interludes). These must be excellent. Do them only if your band is top-notch.

Set music in keys that ensure a comfortable singing range in each congregational song, modulations included.

... Use congregational hymns that are easy to sing. Let your worship team sing those that feature unpredictable meters, wide pitch range, and difficult melodic intervals (i.e. "Wake Awake, for Night Is Flying" by Philipp Nicolai).

Fuse hymns to praise choruses that feature similar themes.

Pull out all the stops when doing hymns; stress excellence even more when repackaging the traditional.

This source, from a youth ministry leader at Saddleback Church (Rick Warren's church), writes about the necessity of excellence in youth services (which he calls "crowd programs"). At Saddleback, they would use a combination of performance songs and congregational songs as part of their youth services. For Fields, the most important question he is asking about music is what will be effective in evangelizing non-Christian youths. He argues that it would be better to exclude music entirely if it cannot be performed excellently.

Source: Doug Fields, *Purpose-Driven Youth Ministry: 9 Essential Foundations for Healthy Growth* (Grand Rapids, MI: Zondervan, 1998), 130–32.

Our band is good! Although it didn't start that way, it has become as good as any student band I have ever heard. One reason for this excellence is that our church makes music a priority, and the students are taught at an early age that they can use their musical skills to build up the church. We have learned the importance of having a "farm system" of backup talent so that we don't have strong years followed by weak ones.

The two opening numbers [of youth services] are usually songs from the hottest new Christian artists. These are intended to be performance songs rather than sing-alongs. When the band begins playing, it's the cue for everyone to find a seat. . . .

Our second set of songs is usually praise songs. . . . We have found that good music and authentic worship by Christians is a witness to un-churched students. Non-Christians usually don't sing, but they do watch others and listen to the words. If the band is good and the words make sense, they are not turned off by the singing. They have already been impressed with the musical ability of the student band, and now they are hearing the gospel sung, and spiritual seeds from music are being planted.

I don't encourage youth workers to use singing at their crowd programs if they don't have quality music. Prior to Saddleback Church I never used singing during our crowd program. We didn't have good musicians, and only a few "front row" students did all of the singing. It was embarrassing for an unchurched student. Praise singing is definitely not needed to start a crowd program.

For this author from the Vineyard Church, musical excellence involves trying to replicate the sound of a recording artist. Because poor playing is a disservice to the church's worship, he suggests musicians need to develop their skill intentionally. Better performance is connected to better worship experiences.

Source: Dan Wilt, *How to Lead Worship Without Being a Rock Star: An 8 Week Study* (Wild Pear Creative, 2013), 53.

Here are just a few foundations, learned from the school of hard knocks, that enable us to lead effective sets. After looking at these, we'll get very practical on how to actually execute the set in detail.

Play The Songs With The Tightness Of One Who Is Recording

This is a tough one for today's worship leaders to grasp. Let's not mince words—*forget sloppy playing*—it just doesn't work and distracts people from engaging with the song. A poorly connected set, musically, can't be blamed on the Holy Spirit and us just "flowing."

Granted, raw music, unrefined and spontaneous, can still breed beautiful worship experiences. However, that is the exception and not the rule. When we try to make it the rule, it may just reveal that we are too lazy to get good at what we do. How's that for honesty?

Without intentional development many worship leaders play like they did when they were younger, and were slamming out tunes in a garage band. Without taking care that every strum is full and exact, and every picking pattern solid and clean, worship leaders begin to just strum and pick away without thought to the tightness of their shared performance. We may think it's cool, but it's not. It's just distracting.

Performance is not a bad word if the heart is engaged with God and the people.

As musical excellence became increasingly critical, churches realized that it was sometimes necessary to hire musicians rather than relying on volunteers. In this source, Charles Arn makes the case that churches can achieve the best musical sound if they hire professional musicians for their services. Unlike volunteers, hired musicians are both financially incentivized to produce the best quality musical sound and can give a greater consistency of excellence from week to week.

Source: Charles Arn, *How to Start a New Service: Your Church Can Reach New People* (Grand Rapids: Baker Books, 1997), 169–70.

My recommendation is that your music talent be paid. Since the music is the most important part of the service, you should want the best talent possible on your platform. Most larger congregations would have little difficulty finding members willing to donate their time in a musical position, so why not save money and go with volunteers? Here's why I believe you are better off paying your musicians:

- *You have more control.* You tell paid musicians what you want. You ask volunteers what you'd like. People who are paid take orders much more easily.

- *You have more accountability.* You control the time of paid musicians. Volunteers control the time of volunteers. It's not an option for a paid employee to miss a rehearsal and go to the beach.

- *The quality is better.* Paid musicians, as a rule, are more concerned with producing a quality product. Volunteer musicians tend to have lower standards of excellence and demand less of themselves. If the quality of your paid musicians is not up to your standards, you can demand better or dismiss them. Try that with volunteers!

- *Everyone has more tolerance.* A constant leadership challenge in working with volunteers is keeping them happy. And volunteers know (as do you) that if they become unhappy, they can walk. One of the benefits of paid musicians is their greater tolerance of discontentment.

In this prominent book on church planting in the twenty-first century, Tim Keller makes a theological and practical case for the church's artistic excellence—especially in music—in the church's evangelistic vocation. For Keller, artistic excellence exists among a spate of other important markers (such as using everyday language, explaining the service, addressing non-believers, celebrating the church's mission, and proclaiming the gospel clearly in word and action) that evangelistically oriented churches need to adopt. These markers fundamentally make worship comprehensible and inclusive to outsiders.

Source: Timothy Keller, *Center Church: Doing Balanced, Gospel-Centered Ministry in Your City* (Grand Rapids: Zondervan, 2012), 305.

The power of good art draws people to behold it. It enters the soul through the imagination and begins to appeal to the reason. Art makes ideas plausible. The quality of our music, your speech, and even the visual aesthetics in worship will have a marked impact on its evangelistic power, particularly in cultural centers. In many churches, the quality of the music is mediocre or poor, but it does not disturb the faithful. Why? Their faith makes the words of the hymn or the song meaningful, despite its lack of artistic expression; what's more, they usually have a personal relationship with the music presenter. But any outsider who comes in as someone unconvinced of the truth and having no relationship to the presenter will likely be bored or irritated by the expression. In other words, excellent aesthetics *includes* outsiders, while mediocre aesthetics *excludes*. The low level of artistic quality in many churches guarantees that only insiders will continue to come. For the non-Christian, the attraction of good art will play a major role in drawing them in.

A Sound Investment: The Importance of Technology and Media for Church Excellence

Accompanying the effort to enhance the quality of the church's musical offering, there was an accompanying embrace of new audio and visual technology. The rationale for this adoption was largely the same: since worship services were seen as a means of reaching the unchurched with the gospel, and because contemporary audiences have cultural expectations shaped by high-quality media, churches needed to incorporate the latest technology to communicate effectively with modern listeners. Additionally, in the same way that music came to serve a dual function—both as an attraction in itself and as a medium for conveying a message—so too did technology. The sources in this section walk a middle ground between desiring to impress audiences with their technological sophistication while striving for their technology to function so seamlessly that it fades into the background, allowing the pure gospel message to shine through unhindered.

In this book focused on how the church's ministry can be made attractional to the boomer generation, the author makes an early case for the importance of adopting new technology. Murren argues that good quality technology is one of the most fundamental aspects of hospitality. Conversely, a failure to invest in good quality sound equipment will be received as offensive by potential churchgoers.

> **Source:** Doug Murren, *The Baby Boomerang: Catching Baby Boomers as They Return to Church* (Ventura, CA: Regal Books, 1990), 204–5.

Churches, as a whole, overlook the fact that the concerts we boomers generally attend and the music we listen to are directed and orchestrated by those who spend millions to obtain a high quality of sound. So when it comes to sound quality, boomers are very sophisticated. And we are no less demanding when it comes to the quality of musicianship. . . . So just by improving their sound system or their instrumentation, churches can vastly increase their potential for reaching boomers. Yet one of the mistakes made repeatedly by churches is trying to make do with inferior sound systems that are equipped with little more than treble and bass knobs. . . . So at seminars I like to tell pastors, "It's okay to have hard chairs, but please have good sound. Go without carpeting if you have to, but do have good music. You don't need bulletins, but you do need to buy the best instruments you can afford. Good sound and production excellence will attract a large number of potential boomer members to your church in any city. Unchurched baby boomers are actually offended and turned off when the quality of the sound system and musicianship are substandard. So if your church will put good money into these systems, you will increase tenfold the interest of boomers in your messages."

As a sign of the prominence of technological adoption occurring, the popular periodical Worship Leader *devoted an entire edition in 2000 to the topic. The next few sources come from that edition. In this article, the author argues that successful churches need to actively audit the quality of other presentations in their community so that they can keep pace. Church productions can certainly be above this level, but they should never be below.*

Source: Wayne Graham, "Production Values for Staging Church Dramas," *Worship Leader* (Summer 2000), 8.

We are constantly bombarded by images with high standards of production quality and excellence. People know quality. People will always recognize excellence. In achieving excellence in church presentations, the attention of the audience can be gained, creating a platform to tell the wonderful message of Christ's love. But how can this be achieved or make the change to a higher standard?

The first step needed in raising the bar of production values in your presentations is to be aware of the quality of other presentations in your community. Assess what level of production is generally being done in your area, and then aim about this level. Purpose not to do anything below this level.

The higher your production values are above this general level, the more platform you will have to tell the good news. Having a solid idea of the production values you would like to attain is the easy part; implementing them is always harder.

With the growing complexity of church technology and its deployment in worship, a new professional position started to become necessary in larger churches: the media director. This author makes the argument that if churches want to deploy technology well in their worship (i.e., in ways that are seamless and conducive to the church's message being well received) they could no longer rely on well-trained volunteers. Instead, just as secular and evangelistic events hired technology experts, churches also needed to fund similar positions.

Source: Donald C. Cicchetti, "Is It Time for a Media Pastor: Combining Technology and Ministry," *Worship Leader* (Summer 2000), 20–21.

When we look at modern worship styles, it is no understatement to say that they are very heavily involved with and influenced by technology. As those involved in the area of enhancing church worship through the explosion of hi-tech innovation, our goal should always be to make technology (sound, video, computer display and lighting) as transparent to the person in the pew as possible. . . .

By transparency, I mean that wonderful condition where all the equipment disappears—you forget it is there—and the content flies right through the medium, without you even being aware that there is a medium. The best live concerts, meetings, evangelistic series, and other events accomplish this, but never by accident. It is accomplished through the dedication, skills, and hard work of professional sound, video, lighting and computer people. . . .

It is my belief that any larger church with plans to utilize a modern style of worship, (drama, praise bands, video/computer projection, special concerts, etc.) should have a full-time director or pastor of media technologies who is part of the pastoral staff and included in the planning of all events. . . .

The seeker that walks into our churches today, as well as our members we see every week, is more technologically sophisticated than ever before. Good intentions are not enough by themselves. Good planning and good production are also required because those people will judge our commitment to what we believe by the services we present to them. The right media pastor can contribute these presentations in a very powerful way.

Writing in 2010, this successful church-planter writes about a different position that the adoption of new media and technology has necessitated—the position of a producer. In this source, the author details the complexity of managing all of the elements that need to flow seamlessly for the worship experience to go flawlessly.

Source: Olu Brown, *Zero to 80: Innovative Ideas for Planting and Accelerating Church Growth* (Atlanta: Impact Press, 2010), 168–69.

Worship is a live experience: a dynamic, ever-flowing, ever-changing experience. To ensure a seamless and efficient flow, we've employed several practices from the radio and television world. Specifically, we have a "tech sheet" and a "producer" for each experience.

The tech sheet gives the background detail of the various worship components along with the time, leader notes and other information that might come in handy when preparing for or troubleshooting live worship.

The producer arrives no later than 8:30 Sunday morning or even earlier when something exceptionally complex is happening. Our worship experiences are at 10:00 a.m. and 12:00 noon. The producer comes with the tech sheet in hand (printout of the flow of the day, our checklist) and immediately starts setting up props where they are needed, and making sure the stage is in good shape. As the musicians warm up, the producer facilitates getting a quality sound check. Finally, the producer reviews the tech sheet with all worship leaders to ensure everyone has a clear understanding of their role in the worship experience for the day. The producer highlights anything special they need to do (e.g., hand off the microphone, exit the stage in a different direction, etc.) The producer makes sure the lighting is set up appropriately and asks if there are any questions about cues or transitions. The producer knows what the entire experience should be and is there to help facilitate the plan. When we recruit producers, we look for people who are cool and calm under pressure; people who have a heart for worship, and who are able to multi-task all the details that go into our worship experiences.

One common concern that is often raised about Contemporary Praise & Worship is whether churches use media and technology in manipulative ways. This source responds to these concerns by arguing that the goal of helping people to receive your message through the use of technology is, at worst, neutral.

Source: Donnie Haulk, *God's Laws of Communication: Exploring the Physiology and Technology of Worship* (AE Global Media, 2011), 98, 103.

It has taken hundreds of years, but here's the simple truth that most church leaders today have finally come to embrace: God made us in a very specific way to be impacted by our environment; he gave us two ears, two eyes, a nose and mouth, a body that resonates and feels both sound and light. Perhaps even more important, there are emotional responses that occur during worship that are connected to endorphins released in the brain during worship. These endorphins that make us "feel good" are influenced by stimulus provided by various technological media used during worship.

Even in an era where once-technophobic preachers are now self-proclaimed computer geeks, you'd be surprised at how many of them are still wary of investing in state-of-the-art sound, video and lighting equipment. "We don't need all that stuff—it just manipulates congregations!" they say. "It's deceptive, a tool of the devil."

In the wrong hands, I suppose any tool can be dangerous. But I've always viewed technology that improves communications between pastor and his or her flock as positive. After all, what's manipulative about creating an atmosphere in which hundreds to thousands of people are fully engaged in your message, whether it's as soft as a sigh or loud as a shout? Isn't the goal of anyone on stage to capture the attention of their audience? In my world, creating an environment that achieves this is not manipulation—it's simply good design.

While some (like Haulk, above) argued that there was nothing inherently dangerous or suspect in using technology to work upon the senses of the worshiper, other prominent voices have argued the opposite. One helpful example is found in the below source from one of the most popular worship textbooks of the last two decades. Here, Bob Kauflin argues that powerful experiences in worship are ambiguous and, by themselves, do not indicate whether a worship service has been faithful. Accordingly, overinvesting in technology can ultimately be a distraction away from the fundamental task of the worship service to extol the greatness of God.

Source: Bob Kauflin, *Worship Matters: Leading Others to Encounter the Greatness of God* (Wheaton: Crossway Books, 2008), 59.

We can also get sidetracked by importing a "concert mentality" into our Sunday meetings. We put together "worship sets," singing the latest worship hits, and overwhelm people with special effects. Technology becomes crucial and governing rather than secondary and serving. We can certainly learn from concert settings. They show us how sounds, lights, images, and music can be used for emotional impact or to focus attention. Concerts are intended to be intense, emotional, and multisensory. But on Sunday mornings we're not trying to emotionally stimulate people or provide a moving experience regardless of the source. I once heard a woman describe how Bono and U2 taught her more about worship than any Sunday morning worship leader. That's an alarming statement. Our goal as worship leaders is unlike that of any concert and is far more significant. We're seeking to impress upon people the greatness of the Savior whose glory transcends our surroundings and technology.

Technological advances have not only changed the nature of the church's sound but also the look of its worship too. Accordingly, churches have started to increasingly reflect on how the visual aspects of worship also contribute to the wider whole of the service. This author makes an important distinction between the technology itself and the use to which it is deployed. Just as music is a neutral medium that can be used for worship, media technology is also a neutral medium that can be used to draw people into the presence of God.[8]

---

8. See also, Marcia McFee, *Think Like a Filmmaker: Sensory-Rich Worship Design for Unforgettable Messages* (Truckee, CA: Trokay Press, 2016),

Source: Stephen Proctor, Foreword to *The Worship Media Handbook* (Church Motion Graphics, 2014).

"Visual Worship" is a phrase that many in the creative community are using to describe a layer of worship that engages people in visual ways. It involves seeing God's glory and creativity displayed around us, inspiring us to worship Him with our eyes and imagination, as well as responding to God's revelation in visually creative ways. This might take place in personal, more intimate settings, or it may be in the context of community where a "visual worship leader" is present.

As it is with any layer of biblical worship, visual worship has to do with our heart, mind and soul. Visual worship is NOT technology, images on a screen, creative projection, lighting, art or any form of production. These are mere tools. They are mediums through which we can visually worship, just as music is a medium for singing our worship. They might be the result and evidence of people who worship visually, but not always. The gear and creative result in and of itself is NOT visual worship.

Worthy of Our Best: Praise and Worship Approaches to Excellence

As in previous chapters, the evangelical concern for evangelistic pragmatism is not the only theological framework that has sat behind the concern for excellence in worship. Pentecostals emerging out of the Praise and Worship movement have, instead, emphasized that worship is to be excellent in order to reflect the excellence of God. Musical offerings in worship should, accordingly, be a worthy sacrifice of praise.

Prominent worship artist of the 1990s Ron Kenoly makes the argument here that Christians should reflect God's creativity in the beauty of their worship. For Kenoly this means that if the worship leader or musician is not yet skillful in their craft, they need to grow and mature.

Source: Ron Kenoly and Dick Bernal, *Lifting Him Up* (Orlando, FL: Creation House, 1995), 63–64.

I believe that worship is a matter of the heart, and you can have the best band, the best dancers, the best banners, but if there is no heart-involvement you have nothing more than a show. On the other hand the Bible does not say anything against pageantry. God is an artist! If you want to see real pageantry just look at how beautiful and detailed this world is.

I want to be careful in saying this, because I know God will, and does, bless any genuine effort of worship, anywhere from one person playing guitar by themselves to a full-blown orchestra and choir. The issue raises when we use this as an excuse for not growing or maturing. . . . At whatever stage we are at we need to give God our best in order to mature and move on to the next step.

For this Pentecostal author, musical excellence stems, in part, from the priority of evangelism ("the harvest"). And yet, musical excellence is not about attracting outsiders primarily but is about testifying to the glory of the Lord sonically. This author envisions musical excellence as forming a joyful and creative context that can grow and flourish unto the blessing of the world.

Source: Steve Phifer, "Music in Worship: Our Heritage of His Power and Presence," *Advance* (January 1991), 8.

Isaiah prophesied that God's kingdom will become a place of eternal excellence (Isaiah 60:15). The harvest demands this excellence. The church must become a place of encouragement, training, creativity, and joy. God's people want to honor Him with their gifts, and they want leadership to show them the way.

Musicians must set an example by continually learning new skills. Choral people can learn about orchestra, and instrumental people learn about choir. Music readers can learn to improvise and by-ear players learn to read music.

The "highways and mountains" of Isaiah 40 challenge us all. We each have valleys of skill that need to be built up, and mountains of attitudes that need to come down. . . . The glory of the Lord will be revealed when He finds a people willing to build such a road. "It's good enough for church music," will not bring in the harvest.

As we build God's kingdom, excellence will be accompanied by the joy Jesus promised, the joy of the branch in the vine, and the joy of productivity. A pastoral atmosphere encourages the flow of creativity from the vine through His branches. Our joy is to carefully tend the branches and ensures their full fruition. This joy and excellence of God's people will touch the world.

For this author, musical excellence is not just its own priority. Excellence also implicitly reveals the spiritual qualities of the musician or the worship leader. Musicians who prioritize musical excellence are likely to be those who also have the capability to lead God's people in true worship.

Source: Chris Dupré, "Tabernacle of David" in *The Lost Art of Pure Worship*, ed. James W. Goll and Chris DuPré (Destiny Image Publishers, 2012), 73.

David put others into their God-ordained places of ministry and leadership. (See, for example, First Chronicles 15:16-24.) As he did so, David released them to be true leaders by giving them the authority to recruit and appoint others to places of leadership. . . . Though I always try to look mainly at the person's heart, I also look for a level of ability and excellence in musicians. Sloppy musicianship is often a red flag for a sloppy lifestyle. David understood this; we see him putting Kenaniah in charge of all the singing because he was skillful at it (see I Chron. 15:22). The account doesn't say he was the most skillful, but we do see that David was moving in wisdom when he put a very skilled man in charge because he must have carried that wonderful combination of heart and skill.

For the author represented in this source, bringing musical praise of low quality is an affront to God. Because God is a mighty king, he demands the very best that can be offered. Indeed, the author suggests that the church risks coming under the wrath of God because it has not been diligent in its artistic expression. The church is called to lead the way in all cultural spheres of life to demonstrate the power of God.

Source: Zach Neese, *How to Worship a King: Prepare Your Heart. Prepare Your World. Prepare The Way* (Charisma Media, 2015), 44–45.

God says He will not accept a lame offering. Malachi 1:8 says that God considers it evil to bring Him less than our best. He goes so far as to curse people who have it in their power to present an offering fit for the King but bring Him less than their best. . . .
    I have a responsibility to the people of God to make sure that our offerings of music are excellent offerings—the best we can bring. It may not

be the best in the world, but He is not asking for that. He is asking for the best we can bring. And He is worthy of it because He is the greatest King in all the world.... The last line of Malachi 1:4 should not be neglected [They will be called the Wicked Land, a people always under the wrath of God]. You see, for the last fifty years the church has been mocked by the secular world because of the quality of its offerings. As leaders of the church, we must repent before the Lord for offering art, music, books, plays, and movies of laughable quality....

The church should be making the best music in the world, because music is not the realm of Lucifer; it is the realm of God....

If we will stop offering God "special music" and offer Him "worship"—the absolute best we have—we can win the attention of the world. If Christians led the way in every field of human endeavor (which is our destiny), the world would know that our God is a powerful King to be feared among the nations.

Pentecostals were not the only Christians though to reflect on excellence in music as a reflection of the praise that the church offers to God. This source, a long-standing textbook in Southern Baptist seminaries that has been continuously revised and expanded in the forty years since its first publication, argues that excellence in music is critical because the God of Christian confession is worthy of it.

Source: Franklin Segler, *Christian Worship: Its Theology and Practice* (Nashville: Broadman Press, 1967), 107.

God deserves only the best music in worship. It is imperative that the leadership of the church seek the highest possible standards for church music, even in the smaller churches. All music selected for worship should contribute to a particular purpose for which the congregation is assembled—namely, to turn hearts and lives toward God.

The level of appreciation for good music can be raised in any congregation. They can be trained to understand the primary purpose of church music. Their knowledge concerning hymnology can be increased. A congregation should not be willing to settle for its present level of knowledge and appreciation of church music. Attitudes should be disciplined in reaching for higher standards.

Performance Versus Presence: Worship Practitioners Express Caution about Excellence

This chapter concludes by considering a few authors and leaders who have raised concerns about the emphasis on excellence in musical worship. While each of these sources explain distinct worries about the way in which excellence can deform worship or the worshiper, they are all fundamentally undergirded by the concern that the real divine-human encounter of Christian worship is being compromised.

Influential worship leader Matt Redman argues here that the emphasis on excellence can end up foregrounding the worship leader or the musician and distracting from the real task of worship—encountering God.

Source: Matt Redman, *The Unquenchable Worshipper: Coming Back to the Heart of Worship* (Ventura: Regal, 2001), 88–89.

One trend in worship that increasingly worries me is the whole performance thing. It's been creeping up for years. Somehow we've come to a place where we'll even call worship events a gig or a concert; the danger is that words like those throw us right off the scent of what worship really is. Too many times I've found myself in a meeting where I'm longing to engage with God while struggling to get past the impressive yet ultimately distracting show going on up front. Some may argue that performance can be worship, and that's true. In one way, everything can be worship if there's a good heart behind it. But performance is not necessarily a good way of leading worship. A worship leader needs as much as possible to be the unnoticed worshipper, simply encouraging the worship of God by setting an example for others to follow. To draw attention to ourselves in moments meant for a holy beholding is a pretty unbiblical approach. In fact, it's probably even a dangerous one.

In this training manual produced by Vineyard Music, Helming writes about the tendency of musicians to try and recreate the same sound as music recordings as part of their commitment to excellence. He discourages this in favor of producing a sound that is authentic to both the sound of the musicians and the spirituality of the leaders.

Source: Brent Helming, *Hot Tips for Worship Leaders* (Vineyard Music, 2000), 49–50.

One of the most common areas of frustration that I've heard voiced from other worship leaders is in trying to make their worship team play a song exactly like it is on the CD. They want their team to use the same sounds, the same guitar riffs, and the same background vocal harmonies in hopes of capturing that special quality of worship the CD that inspired them to do the song in the first place. Some have even told me that for them it's an issue of excellence. They want to pursue excellence in worship so they try to sound like the CD. This may seem somewhat noble but in reality it's an impossibility—save for a handful of worship teams who employ professional musicians. . . .

I believe in pursuing excellence within the context of reality. Otherwise the pursuit is not a good thing but rather it becomes an acting out of a twisted brand of works mentality. The "context of reality" is made clear by the make-up of your team. What is the quality level of your players? What are the strengths? What are the weaknesses? What instruments do you have available with which to arrange the song? These are the questions that bring the "reality of excellence" into focus.

. . . Another reason I give my team the freedom to not sound like the CD is that I want the worship we play to be authentic and from the heart. Not that authenticity does not happen when songs are played exactly like the CD, but I want my musicians to feel like they have a sense of ownership in the worship they lead. By allowing my guitar player to play his own riffs, instead of copying the guitarist on the album, he is able to give a part of himself to the music.

In this source, Kurtis Parks tries to navigate a path between two extremes—on the one hand emphasizing excellence to the loss of spontaneity in worship and, on the other, emphasizing the spontaneous work of the Spirit to the detriment of quality.[9]

---

9. For one example of how scholars have studied the balance between spontaneity and structure in worship music, see Shannan K. Baker, "A Typology of Ad-Libbing: Performing Authenticity in Contemporary Worship," *Religions* 14, no. 3 (2023): 3, https://doi.org/10.3390/rel14030337.

Source: Kurtis Parks, *Sound Check: How Worship Teams Can Pursue Authenticity, Excellence, and Purpose* (Colorado Springs: David C. Cook, 2016), 129–30, 134.

In the realm of worship, there has always been the discussion about performance-driven worship versus Spirit-led worship. We've probably all been in that service (or may even led worship in that service) where it feels like the freeform jazz odyssey at the end of *Spinal Tap*. . . . I've also been on the other side, leading worship at a televised event, where the producer gave me a death stare if I went 3.5 seconds over the allotted time we were given for "Our God." Don't you dare sing that bridge again! . . . When it comes to performance and presence (of God), I don't think the two are mutually exclusive aspects of worship. . . . There are some nuggets an authentic leader can take from each background. Too often we overlook the need for excellence in an environment that has a high focus on the movement of the Holy Spirit. On the flip side, there are many churches that end up putting God in a box by never allowing the Holy Spirit to have His way, which might sometimes mean veering from the production run sheet every now and then. . . .

The skill of leading worship is not about how impressively we play, but about how we can play less and give space for the Lord to move in worship. It goes without saying that we should always seek to play skillfully, as David did, and give our very best out of deep gratitude to Jesus, who gave everything that we might live resurrected and grace-filled lives. He held nothing back from us, so how could we hold anything back from Him? Genuine worship leaders know that you don't pursue excellence in music just to sound like a well-oiled machine. You do it because the God of the universe, and King above all, deserves nothing less.

Discussion Questions

- What different theological reasons have Christians held for pursuing excellence in worship? Which of those reasons do you find the most compelling?

- How do you respond to the argument that high-quality production is a form of cultural hospitality to those who might visit your church? Are there other modes of hospitality that we should prioritize?

- What does it mean for worship leaders (and worshipers) to offer God their best in worship? What does that commitment look like in practice, in preparation, in leadership?

- Some of the sources in this chapter have been concerned about the concept of worship as a performance. What dangers are present in thinking about worship this way? Are we able to navigate these dangers while still holding a commitment to excellence? Are there ways to practice worship that are not performative?

- Think about a recent worship service you attended or led. What theological values were communicated by the way in which the physical worship space (including in its use of technology) was designed, equipped, and laid out? Do you think those were the theological values that the church intended to communicate?

- How do cultural expectations shape what "excellence" looks like in worship? Do churches have an evangelistic responsibility to adapt to these expectations?

CONCLUSION
HISTORY AS FORMATION FOR WORSHIP RENEWAL

In *Why Study the Past: The Quest for the Historical Church*, the former Archbishop of Canterbury, Rowan Williams, argued that the fundamental good that historical writing achieves is to help its readers (and writers) grapple with "the strangeness of the past" so that we can *construct a sense of our identity in the present*.[1] Williams continues that for this kind of identity formation to happen, historians and students need to avoid two temptations: the first is to engage with a version of the past "that is just the present in fancy dress"; the second is to write off the past as ignorant, other, or unknowable.[2] Both temptations shortcut the formation process that history can provide. Both are tantamount to refusing to leave the safety of our familiar, contemporary bubble. It is only as we hear a cacophony of historical voices—some of which are familiar and others of which are strange to us—that we start to become aware of those things which we have taken for granted or assumed to be true. In this process, we develop a more mature, fully realized understanding of who we are.

We might say something similar about the value of the history of Contemporary Praise & Worship that we have narrated in this book. We have written this book with the aim that this history will help you as readers to construct a fuller sense of your identity as worshipers and as leaders. Among the multiplicity of voices in the book, you doubtless will have found some that resonate with your own experience. Others though

---

1. Rowan Williams, *Why Study the Past: The Quest for the Historical Church* (London: Darton, Longman and Todd, 2005), 23–24.
2. Williams, *Why Study the Past*, 24.

may have seemed confounding, irrelevant, or just plain wrong. Whatever your reactions may have been, our hope is that, by hearing these different voices, you will have gained a new awareness of the beliefs that you implicitly hold about worship, the values that you have internalized, and the formations that have shaped you.

On one level, this kind of identity formation work may strike you as frustrating. As worshipers, our first question is often about how the church *should* worship. The variety of voices that we have heard rarely offer such a harmonious answer. Indeed, they can make the task of thinking prescriptively about worship so much harder. History, after all, makes us increasingly aware of a great cloud of witnesses who do not all seem to sing from the same hymnbook! However, if we can set aside our prescriptive questions for a moment to engage with history, we are able to take those questions up again with a more careful, reflective, and wise view about how the church can worship more faithfully. Only after we understand where we have come from can we start to turn a more discerning eye toward where we are going.

There are many important decisions on the horizon that will require us to carry out thoughtful reflection about our values and practices as the church. We have written this book at a time when the technology of AI is starting to become increasingly sophisticated and ubiquitous. Many of you are likely already familiar with how AI is disrupting education, business, or entertainment. AI promises to disrupt Christian worship as well. Churches are already experimenting with AI-generated videos; pastors are relying on AI to help them craft sermons; new AI technologies are already starting to impact the performance of live music. If we, as leaders, are going to be wise about the place of AI in worship, it will help us to understand the implicit values that have *already* shaped us. Considering the questions we have explored in this book, such as how the church should borrow cultural forms in its worship (chapters 1–2) or what standards of excellence we apply to our worship (chapter 6), will help us to locate ourselves in this ongoing conversation.

An additional example is found in how Christian worship should respond to the recent waves of scandals—sexual, financial, and legal—that have rocked the Christian worship industry. It is becoming increasingly apparent that the industry contains structural issues and theological problems. Accordingly, a critical need of the moment is for churches and leaders to reflect on the ways in which this industry exercises an outsized influence on the musical styles and choices of local congregations. Grappling with the beliefs that we hold about music's evangelistic or formational power (chapter 3) or confronting how our theologies of worship risk creating unaccountable artist-leaders (chapter 5) may well help to guide our reflections in these areas.

Speaking to the pressing issues that we are encountering as worshipers and leaders (not to mention the new issues that will arise in the future) will take more than a quick proof-texted Bible verse. We need to engage in discernment, shaped by honest, historically informed reflection upon who we are as individual worshipers and who we are becoming as worshiping communities. History does not provide quick answers in this task. It does, however, provide us with a robust foundation for reflection, a better sense of perspective, an ability to ask difficult questions, and a sense of humility as we recognize that our efforts to worship faithfully never take place in a vacuum but always within the wider historical community of the church.

APPENDIX A
CHRONOLOGICAL LIST OF SOURCES

The sources used throughout the book have been organized into a chronological list here. When sources have been published multiple times, we have included the source according to its earliest publication date.

Charles G. Finney, *Lectures on Revivals of Religion* (New York: Leavitt, Lord & Co., 1835), 167–68.

George F. Pentecost, introduction to *Song Victories of "The Bliss and Sankey Hymns," Being a Collection of One Hundred Incidents in Regard to the Origin and Power of the Hymns Contained in "Gospel Hymns and Sacred Songs"* (Dover, NH: D. Lothrop and Co., 1877), 11–12.

Catherine Mumford Booth, *Papers on Practical Religion* (London: Partridge, 1879), 140–41.

Ira David Sankey, *My Life and the Story of the Gospel Hymns and of Sacred Songs and Solos* (Philadelphia: P. W. Ziegler Co., 1907), v–vii, 88.

Christian Fichthorne Reisner, *Church Publicity; the Modern Way to Compel Them to Come In* (New York, Cincinnati: The Methodist Book Concern, 1913), 18–19.

"Vigilance and Strength: Now Is the Time for Vigorous Actions and Close Fellowship and Harmony." *Church of God Evangel* 8, 5 (February 1917). Edited by A. J. Tomlinson, 1.

Ernest Eugene Elliott, *How to Fill the Pews* (Cincinnati: Standard Pub. Co., 1917), 79–80.

Music Committee of the Sunday School Publishing Board, *Gospel Pearls* (Nashville: Sunday School Publishing Board [of the] National Baptist Convention, U.S.A., 1921), preface (no page number).

Full page advertisement in *The Kansas City Star*, Saturday, April 3, 1926, 5.

R. H. Morrison, "The Foursquare Conservatory of Music," *Foursquare Crusader* (February 6, 1929), 12.

H. Augustine Smith, *The New Hymnal for American Youth* (New York and London: The Century Company, 1930).

J. Harker, "Music of the Message: Music in Present-Day Evangelism," *The Ministry* 12, 9 (September 1939): 13.

Phil Kerr, *Music in Evangelism and Stories of Famous Christian Songs*, 3rd ed. (1939; Glendale, CA: Gospel Music Publishers, 1950), 81, 88–89.

Percy B. Crawford, *Pinebrook Praises* (Wheaton: Van Kampen Press, 1943), foreword.

Torrey Maynard Johnson and Robert Cook, *Reaching Youth for Christ* (Chicago: Moody Press, 1944), 33–34; 36–37.

George H. Warnock, *The Feast of Tabernacles* (Springfield, MO: Bill Britton, 1951), 91.

A.W. Tozer, *Born After Midnight* (Harrisburg, PA: Christian Publications, 1959), 37–39.

Reg Layzell, *The Pastor's Pen: Early Revival Writings of Pastor Reg Layzell*, comp. B. Maureen Gaglardi (Vancouver: Glad Tidings Temple, 1965; edited by Marion Peterson and privately published, 1979), 159, 163.

Mahalia Jackson and Evan Mcleod Wylie, *Movin' On Up* (New York: Hawthorn Books, 1966), 32–33; 62–63.

Liner notes to *Mass for Young Americans*, by Ray Repp. FEL Publications, 1966, LP.

Delton L. Alford, *Music in the Pentecostal Church* (Cleveland: Pathway Press, 1967), 20–21.

Franklin Segler, *Christian Worship: Its Theology and Practice* (Nashville: Broadman Press, 1967), 107.

Floyd E. Werle, "Church-O-Theque," *Music Ministry* 9, 6 (February 1968): 3, 5–7.

James F. White, "Worship in the Age of Marshall McLuhan" in *Christian Worship in North America: A Retrospective: 1955–1995* (Collegeville: The Liturgical Press, 1997), 135–41. Originally published as "Worship in an Age of Immediacy," *The Christian Century* 75 (February 21, 1968): 227–30.

Myron B. Bloy, Jr., ed., *Multi-Media Worship: A Model and Nine Viewpoints* (New York: The Seabury Press, 1969), 7–8, replicating the account from the October 25, 1968 edition of the student newspaper, *The Michigan Daily*.

Graham Truscott, *The Power of His Presence: The Restoration of the Tabernacle of David* (San Diego: Restoration Temple, 1969), 215–18.

Richard K. Avery, "The Church Is Alive and Singing," *Presbyterian Life* (October 15, 1971), 9–10.

John R. Bisagno, *How to Build an Evangelistic Church* (Nashville: Broadman Press, 1971), 71–72.

James L. Christensen, *Contemporary Worship Services: A Sourcebook* (Old Tappan, NJ: Fleming H. Revell, 1971), 11–12.

John Killinger, *Leave It to the Spirit: Commitment and Freedom in the New Liturgy* (New York: Harper & Row, 1971), xiii, xviii, 7.

James F. White, *New Forms of Worship* (Nashville: Abingdon Press, 1971), 33–34.

Country and Western Hymnal, comp. Fred Bock (Grand Rapids: Singspiration Music of the Zondervan Corporation, 1972).

Ronald M. Enroth, Edward E. Ericson, Jr., and C. Breckinridge Peters, *The Jesus People; Old-Time Religion in the Age of Aquarius* (Grand Rapids: Baker, 1972), 86–87.

Chuck Smith and Hugh Steven, *The Reproducers: New Life for Thousands* (Glendale, CA, G/L Regal Books, 1972; Philadelphia: Calvary Chapel of Philadelphia, 2011), 79–80.

Judson Cornwall, *Let Us Praise* (Plainfield, NJ: Logos International, 1973), 24–26.

Charles E. Pierson, "Right and Wrong Ways of Introducing Contemporary Music," *The Church Musician* (September 1973), 19–22.

John Gillies, "What's So Sacred About Music," *The Church Musician* (May 1974), 50–51.

Mack Moore, "Current Trends in Youth Musicals," *The Church Musician* (July 1974), 54.

Robert H. Schuller, *Your Church Has Real Possibilities!* (Glendale: Regal Books, 1974), 39.

David K. Blomgren, *Song of the Lord* (Portland, OR: Bible Press, 1978), 3, 43.

Reg Layzell, *Unto Perfection: The Truth about the Present Restoration Revival* (Mountlake Terrace, WA: King's Temple, 1979), 13–14.

E. Charlotte Baker, *On Eagles Wings: A Book on Praise and Worship* (1979; Shippensburg, PA: Destiny Image, 1990), 6–7, 92, 93–94.

[Barry Griffing], "Catechism Corner," *Music Notes* 2, 4 (1980): 4 (emphasis original).

Donald McGavran and George G. Hunter III, *Church Growth: Strategies That Work* (Nashville: Abingdon Press, 1980), 107–8.

Don Hustad, *Jubilate!: Church Music in the Evangelical Tradition* (Hope Publishing, 1981), 48.

Mike and Vivien Hibbert, *Music Ministry* (Christchurch, New Zealand: Self-Published, 1982), 43, 72–73.

John Wimber, "Zip to 3,000 in 5 Years," *Christian Life* 44, 6 (October 1982): 22.

Kennon L. Callahan, *Twelve Keys to an Effective Church: Strategic Planning for Mission* (San Francisco: Harper & Row, 1983), 22–28.

Judson Cornwall, *Let Us Worship* (So. Plainfield, NJ: Bridge Publishing, 1983), 154–57.

Jack W. Hayford, *The Church on the Way: Learning to Live in the Promise of Biblical Congregational Life* (Old Tappan, NJ: Chosen Books by Fleming Revell Co., 1983), 102–3.

Jimmy Owens and Carol Owens, *Words and Music: A Guide to Writing, Selecting, and Just Enjoying Christian Songs* (Waco, TX: Word Music, 1984), 29, 114–15.

Graham Kendrick, *Learning to Worship as a Way of Life* (Minneapolis: Bethany House Publishers, 1984), 144–51.

Graham Kendrick, *Worship* (Eastbourne: Kingsway, 1984), 163–66.

Joannah Glaeser, "The Use of Chord Progressions in Spontaneous Worship," *Symposium 85: 8th Annual International Symposium* (August 1985).

David Wilkerson, *Set the Trumpet to Thy Mouth* (Lindale, TX: World Challenge, 1985), 86–87.

David K. Blomgren, *Restoring God's Glory: The Present Day Rise of David's Tabernacle* (Regina, Saskatchewan: Maranatha Christian Centre, 1985), 30–32.

Tom Brooks, "Spontaneity in Worship," *Worship Times* (Summer 1986), 4.

Jack Hayford, *Worship His Majesty* (Waco: Word Publishing, 1987), 118.

Bob Mason, "I Inhabit Your Praises," *Psalmist* 2, 3 (April/May 1987): 20.

Bob Sorge, *Exploring Worship: A Practical Guide to Praise and Worship* (Lee's Summit: Oasis House, 1987), 172.

Jimmy Swaggart and Robert Paul Lamb, *Religious Rock 'n' Roll: A Wolf in Sheep's Clothing* (Baton Rouge: Jimmy Swaggart Ministries, 1987), 45–47.

George Barna, *Marketing the Church: What They Never Taught You About Church Growth* (Colorado Springs: Navpress, 1988), 26, 112–13.

"The Praise Band," *Worship Times* (July/August 1989), 2.

John Wimber, "Worship: Intimacy with God," *Worship Conference* (Mercy Publishing, 1989).

Doug Murren, *The Baby Boomerang: Catching Baby Boomers as They Return to Church* (Ventura, CA: Regal Books, 1990), 204–5.

Terry Raburn, "A Powerful Tool: Use It for God and the Gospel," *Advance* 26, 10 (October 1990): 9.

C. Kirk Hadaway, *Church Growth Principles: Separating Fact from Fiction* (Nashville: Broadman Press, 1991), 67–68.

Charles Green, "The Pathway of Praise," in *Spirit-Filled Life Bible*, ed. Jack W. Hayford (Nashville: Thomas Nelson, 1991), xxix, 770.

Steve Phifer, "Music in Worship: Our Heritage of His Power and Presence," *Advance* (January 1991), 8.

James Emery White, *Opening the Front Door: Worship and Church Growth* (Nashville: Convention Press, 1992), 55–56.

Lee Strobel, *Inside the Mind of Unchurched Harry & Mary: How to Reach Friends and Family Who Avoid God and the Church* (Grand Rapids: Zondervan, 1993), 180–81, 189–90.

Rick Warren, "New Churches for a New Generation: Church Planting to Reach Baby Boomers: A Case Study: The Saddleback Valley Community Church" (D.Min. thesis, Fuller Theological Seminary, 1993), 37–38, 280, 283, 285–86.

Carlyle Fielding Stewart, *African American Church Growth: 12 Principles of Prophetic Ministry* (Nashville: Abingdon Press, 1994), 59.

"The Pastor Wears Tennis Shoes," *Circuit Rider* 18, 10 (December 1994/January 1995): 14.

"The Music in Revival" from *Let Your Glory Fall: Songs and Essays / Worship & Revival Songs & Essays / Worship & Revival Conference/Seminar Reader* (Vineyard Music Group, 1995) (reprint from *Worship Together* magazine, n.d.), 224.

David S. Luecke, *The Other Story of Lutherans at Worship: Reclaiming Our Heritage of Diversity* (Tempe, AZ: Fellowship Ministries, 1995), 11, 98–100.

Sally Morgenthaler, *Worship Evangelism: Inviting Unbelievers into the Presence of God* (Grand Rapids, MI: Zondervan, 1995), 152, 157.

Cathy Townley and Mike Graham, *Come Celebrate! A Guide for Planning Contemporary Worship* (Nashville: Abingdon Press, 1995), 28–29.

Rick Warren, *The Purpose Driven Church: Growth Without Compromising Your Message & Mission* (Grand Rapids: Zondervan, 1995), 255–56.

Ron Kenoly and Dick Bernal, *Lifting Him Up* (Orlando, FL: Creation House, 1995), 23–26, 63–64.

Charles Arn, *How to Start a New Service: Your Church Can Reach New People* (Grand Rapids: Baker Books, 1997), 165–66, 167–68, 169–70.

Joseph L. Garlington, *Worship: The Pattern of Things in Heaven* (Shippensburg: Destiny Image Publishers, 1997), 19–20, 26–28.

Donald E. Miller, *Reinventing American Protestantism: Christianity in the New Millennium* (Berkeley: University of California Press, 1997), 83–85.

Mark W.G. Stibbe, *From Orphans to Heirs: Celebrating Our Spiritual Adoption* (Oxford: Bible Reading Fellowship, 1999), 84–85.

Rodney A. Teal, *Reflections on Praise & Worship from a Biblical Perspective* (privately published, 1999), 19–21.

Donald C. Cicchetti, "Is It Time for a Media Pastor: Combining Technology and Ministry," *Worship Leader* (Summer 2000), 20–21.

Wayne Graham, "Production Values for Staging Church Dramas," *Worship Leader* (Summer 2000), 8.

Jack W. Hayford, *Explaining Worship* (Tonbridge, England: Sovereign World Ltd, 2000), 37–38.

Myles Munroe, *The Purpose and Power of Praise & Worship* (Shippensburg, PA: Destiny Image Publishers, 2000), 120–26.

Robb Redman, "Expanding Your Worship Worldview: Education and Training for Worship Leaders," *Worship Leader* (May/June 2000), 19.

Brent Helming, *Hot Tips for Worship Leaders* (Vineyard Music, 2000), 27–28, 49–50.

Matt Redman, *The Unquenchable Worshipper: Coming Back to the Heart of Worship* (Ventura: Regal, 2001), 88–89.

Darlene Zschech, *Extravagant Worship* (Minneapolis: Bethany House, 2001), 172–73.

Andy Park, *To Know You More: Cultivating the Heart of the Worship Leader* (Downers Grove: InterVarsity Press, 2002), 67.

Paul Baloche, Jimmy & Carol Owens, *God Songs: How to Write and Select Songs for Worship* (Lindale, TX: Leadworship.com, 2004), 43–44.

Nancy Beach, *An Hour on Sunday: Creating Moments of Transformation and Wonder* (Grand Rapids: Zondervan, 2004), 144–45.

Dan Kimball, *Emerging Worship: Creating New Worship Gatherings for Emerging Generations* (Grand Rapids: Zondervan, 2004), 83–84.

Stephen F. Phifer, *Worship That Pleases God* (Trafford Publishing, 2005), 288–89.

Charles E. Fromm, "Textual Communities and New Song in the Multimedia Age: The Routinization of Charisma in the Jesus Movement" (PhD diss., Fuller Theological Seminary, 2006), 176, fn. 7.

Paul S. Jones, *Singing and Making Music: Issues in Church Music Today* (Phillipsburg, NJ: P & R Publishing, 2006), 144–45.

Bob Kauflin, *Worship Matters: Leading Others to Encounter the Greatness of God* (Wheaton: Crossway Books, 2008), 59.

Paul Baloche, "Revealing the Divine," *Worship Leader* 18, no.1 (January/February 2009), 10.

Kim Miller, *Redesigning Worship: Creating Powerful God Experiences* (Nashville: Abingdon Press, 2009), 74.

Constance M. Cherry, *The Worship Architect: A Blueprint for Designing Culturally Relevant and Biblically Faithful Services* (Grand Rapids: Baker Academic, 2010), 193–96.

Joe Horness, "Contemporary Music-Driven Worship," in *Exploring the Worship Spectrum: 6 Views*, ed. Paul A. Basden (Grand Rapids: Zondervan, 2010), 103–4.

Olu Brown, *Zero to 80: Innovative Ideas for Planting and Accelerating Church Growth* (Atlanta: Impact Press, 2010), 168–69.

Donnie Haulk, *God's Laws of Communication: Exploring the Physiology and Technology of Worship* (AE Global Media, 2011), 98, 103.

Timothy Keller, *Center Church: Doing Balanced, Gospel-Centered Ministry in Your City* (Grand Rapids: Zondervan, 2012), 305.

Chris Dupré, "Tabernacle of David" in *The Lost Art of Pure Worship*, ed. James W. Goll and Chris DuPré (Destiny Image Publishers, 2012), 73.

Dan Wilt, *How to Lead Worship Without Being a Rock Star: An 8 Week Study* (Wild Pear Creative, 2013), 32–33, 53.

Rodney Williams, Sr. (Prophet), *The Key of David: Davidic Patterns and Blueprints for Worship Leaders* (Zion Muzik, 2014), 30–31.

Stephen Proctor, Foreword to *The Worship Media Handbook* (Church Motion Graphics, 2014).

Sandra Maria Van Opstal, *The Next Worship: Glorifying God in a Diverse World* (Downers Grove: InterVarsity Press, 2015), 78–80.

Zach Neese, *How to Worship a King: Prepare Your Heart. Prepare Your World. Prepare The Way* (Charisma Media, 2015), 44–45.

Brian T. Russell, *The Complete Contemporary Worship Handbook: How to Build and Sustain Meaningful Worship in Modern Denominational Churches* (Austin: Langmarc Publishing, 2016), 37–38.

Kurtis Parks, *Sound Check: How Worship Teams Can Pursue Authenticity, Excellence, and Purpose* (Colorado Springs: David C. Cook, 2016), 129–30, 134.

Zac Hicks, *The Worship Pastor: A Call to Ministry for Worship Leaders and Teams* (Grand Rapids: Zondervan, 2016), 13–14.

Chris Oyakhilome, *Rhapsody of Realities: A Topical Compendium*, vol. 5 (Lagos, Nigeria: LoveWorld Publishing, 2018), 98.

Stacey B. Jones, *(i)Pastor Hip-Hop: Bridging the Gap Between Hip-Hop and the Christian Faith Community* (One Communications LLC, 2020), 12–13.

Jeremy Riddle, *The Reset: Returning to the Heart of Worship and a Life of Undivided Devotion* (Anaheim: Wholehearted Publishing, 2020), 57.

Undated Sources

James Beall, *The Ministry of Worship and Praise* (Detroit: Bethesda Missionary Temple, n.d.), 18–19.

Mike Herron, "The Song of the Lord" (unpublished teaching materials, n.d.)

Paige Blair, "What Is a U2 Eucharist (or U2charist)?" at http://s3.amazonaws.com/dfc_attachments/public/documents/414/What_is_a_U2charist.pdf (accessed 11 June 2024).

www.ingramcontent.com/pod-product-compliance
Lightning Source LLC
Chambersburg PA
CBHW011749220426
43669CB00022B/2959